Application Integration
By Linking Semantically Related Objects
Shared Across Applications

By

Parames Ghosh

A thesis
Submitted for the degree of
Doctor of Philosophy

University of Technology, Sydney
June, 2001

CERTIFICATE OF AUTHORSHIP / ORIGINALITY

I certify that this thesis has not previously been submitted for a degree nor has it been submitted as part of requirements for a degree except as fully acknowledged within the text.

I also certify that the thesis has been written by me. Any help that I have received in my research work and the preparation of the thesis itself has been acknowledged. In addition, I certify that all information sources and literature used are indicated in the thesis.

Signature of Candidate

_____

ACKNOWLEDGMENTS

Special thanks must be extended to several people who have provided information and conceptual framework used in this study.

In particular, I would like to express my regards and sincere thanks to my project supervisor Dr. George Feuerlicht, who has provided me guidance and encouragement all along. A few events in my personal life delayed the work on this thesis. Once I had a serious accident on the road - which forced me in the hospital for about 14 weeks, and restricted my movements for sometime thereafter. George cared to send reading materials to me, when I was going through rehabilitation in the hospital. Also, industrial recessions and major restructuring in the I.T. industries, in the current business environments, forced me to spend more than normal hours on my full-time job; this drained lot of my energy and enthusiasm, which was needed for these part-time research activities. My wife Mamata and daughter Payal provided me support and encouragement during the difficult days at the hospital and made me ready for the arduous life that followed.

My sincere thanks are extended to my employers, who have provided me the opportunities to take up this study as a part of my Ph.D. programme and my colleagues who have allowed me access to information needed for data modelling and specifying the requirements of the integration architecture. I acknowledge the encouragement received from Dr. Ian Montgomery, Dr. W Zwaenepoel, John Cady and Jean Robb during my study of Object-Oriented Database, Distributed Operating Systems, Object-Oriented Programming, and Database Management.

Lastly, I convey my sincere regards to University Of Technology and its various staff for providing access to latest information on relevant research activities, building up my knowledge base, and developing my analytical abilities without which this study would not have been possible.

Parames Ghosh
June, 1999

PREFACE

Back in 1991, when I was working for my Masters degree in Computing Sciences, my background in Management of Business Administration (MBA with University Of Technology, Sydney) was still shaping the ideas about how I can contribute to the multi-faceted problem of application integration. The main idea behind this thesis is one common management principle that eighty percent of the results can be achieved by concentrating on twenty percent of the things we are involved with. We need not concentrate on the applications in their entirety, when we want to integrate them; rather we may concentrate only those parts of the applications that matter in the integrated system - which is the information that each application likes to share with other applications. This idea, in its preliminary form, was first published, in 1991, in form of the project work for my Masters degree in Computing Sciences. This, in turn, led my principal supervisor, George Feuerlicht, to invite me to work further on this topic for the PhD thesis.

It is a favourable coincidence for me that, at the same period I was exposed to the new ideas of distributed operating systems and object oriented paradigms. The techniques of the distributed operating system showed the ways to achieve the distribution transparency, where a distributed application appears as if not distributed. Object oriented paradigms prompted me to hide the implementation of the eighty-percent of the data items, that are private to the application, and no other application need know about those data items and their implementation. This thesis mainly says that we need to consider only the data items that are shared across applications; however we need to consider a bit more than what is actually shared. If a piece of information is shared, we need to know how this information is accessed - that is where the information belongs, i.e. the key or identifier of the information. Again the information, which is passed on, may be related to other data items - i.e. there could be some integrity constraints involving those items which appear to be shared with other applications. These integrity constraints force us to look at other data items too, when we access information from one database with intent of updating the information. If some of the public data items are updated, then some of the private data items must be updated to honour the integrity constraints and thus to maintain the consistency. This thesis, therefore, defines the shared data items as those data items which are visibly exchanged plus the data items that indicate where they belong, plus any other data item that are involved in constraints with them.

When the shared objects from the component applications are identified, they need to be integrated together into an integrating application. In order to model these shared objects into the data model of the integrating application, we need to find out how the shared object of one application is related to a shared object of another application. This relationship between shared objects can be semantic equivalence and semantic relationship. It has been explored in this thesis how the semantic relationship can be used in linking these objects across applications.

However, since I started working on the idea of integrating application systems by concentrating only on the broad definition of shared data items, we have seen a few epoch-making ideas in information technology. One of these is CORBA or Common Object Request Broker Architecture, the other one is World Wide Web defined over the Internet. One may find some similarities between the idea of Object Request Broker and my idea of an integrating application using objects representing shared data items from every participating application. But the main difference in the two architectures is that CORBA specifies how interface definitions are written, while this thesis identifies which data items are to be selected and how they are selected so that interface definitions can be written about them. Similarly, WWW or World Wide Web shows how we can link threads of information, but if we want to set up links between threads of information that will help us assess the integrated view of the related application, we need to identify the data items which need be linked together. If we follow the ideas of what need be put together to integrate various application systems, we may even use these facilities including JAVA to send objects across platforms. In this thesis, we have recommended that the integrating application would be object-oriented. However, if we have the integrating application on world-wide-web, XML could be used in this integrating application to mediate between heterogeneous databases of the component applications. However, though XML will help implement the integrating Web application, we would still need to identify the objects of the component applications, and these objects will be involved in the mediation by the integrating Web application.

A few events in my personal life too delayed the work on this thesis. I had a serious accident on the road in November 1992 - which forced me in the hospital for about 14 weeks, and restricted my movements for sometime thereafter. Also, industrial recessions and major restructuring in the I.T. industries, in the current business environments, added stress and anxiety in my full-time job; the work often encroached the personal time, leaving little time and energy for the part-time research activities. However, the main ideas of the thesis are still useful; the new technological developments would rather help these ideas, because they still show where to concentrate our efforts to get the maximum benefits.

Research on integration of decentralised information systems was initiated in mid 1970s and has since evolved rapidly. These research findings can be classified on the scale of their operations, as follows:

- integrating two application systems of an organisation, by comparing and matching their schemas,
- setting up an architecture, where all constituent applications build interfaces using one canonical data model and data manipulation language - so that they appear homogeneous,
- setting up an infrastructure, using CORBA or similar standards, where a participating application needs to comply with the rules for traders or object-request-brokers.

Though we look forward to the days when systems can be assembled by using off-the-shelf objects with well-defined interfaces, applications built under the infrastructure, prevailing now, need lot of efforts to ensure compliance to the infrastructure standards like CORBA. Semantics of the data items still need be understood to achieve compliance with the infrastructure standards, we still need to reconcile the differences in data structures of the same information represented differently on different application systems. Until all participating applications use objects that have standard meaning and standard interfaces, we cannot take advantage of the infrastructure standards like CORBA. The most fundamental problem of schema integration still remains that facts can be modelled in many different ways. The same real world can be represented by different modelling structures; depending on how the designer views a phenomenon, it can be modelled as an object, an attribute or as a set of attributes.

We like to solve this multifaceted problem of application integration, by concentrating on only the information shared across application systems, while the information, that concerns individual application systems only, need not be considered.

The Following table provides a brief outline of the structure and contents of this thesis.

CHAPTER	DESCRIPTION
1. Introduction	In this chapter, we have introduced the problem of application integration, addressed in this thesis. This is followed by discussion on how this problem is dealt in this thesis, and the original contribution of the thesis.

In this chapter, we have identified the problem of this thesis as the problem of data integration for integrating applications. In this thesis, we have proposed to solve the multifaceted problem of integrating application systems, by concentrating on only the information that matters, i.e. the information shared across applications. We have expanded the definition of shared objects/data items by including those items required for accessing one or more shared objects, and those items which are involved in constraints with one or more shared objects. For the items on the list of shared objects, semantic relationships between objects from different applications have been considered for modelling them into the schema of the integrating application.

2. Preliminaries and Definitions	The primary objective of this chapter is to provide definitions of the terms to be used in this thesis – so that we have consistent understanding about the terms like application, objects, semantic equivalence etc.

The broad area addressed in this thesis is the integration of application systems, with main emphasis on semantic similarities between objects across application systems. By the term 'application' we mean a set of data items and functions packaged together as an unit to be delivered by IT departments to the user. An application views a real world object in terms of its schema or the set of attributes relevant to the application; therefore the internal object of the application or the application object will show only these attributes. Another application may be interested in a different set of attributes of the same class of real world objects; hence its application object will show a different set of attributes.

3. Reconnaissance	In this chapter, we have analysed how the semantics of real world objects are modelled into application objects. Also, we have discussed various issues of application integration, leading to the structure of and contents of various chapters in the thesis.

Semantics of real world objects are modelled into application objects; the problem of this thesis is identified as the problem of linking semantically related objects across applications in order to integrate them. Customer Relationship Management system has been chosen to exemplify the difficulties of the problem. History of isolated applications is considered, followed by appreciation of the need to make them inter-operate with one another. We have checked that the application development processes, using different tools and environments, cause technological, syntactic and semantic differences that lead to different abstraction of the same facts. We have checked that the participating applications may inter-operate with one another directly or indirectly. It is observed that the problem of integrating application schemas still persists, in spite of technological advancement facilitating connectivity. A solution to this problem is perceived - to identify semantically related objects in the export schemas of the applications, to assert the relationship among them, and to construct an object-oriented application with these semantically related objects.

4. Review Of Work Done To Integrate Applications	This chapter reviews various research activities on integration of isolated applications - where the main aim is to relate the semantically similar objects in the participating applications so that they can inter-operate, and work together as an integrated system.

The problem of application integration is investigated at various scales of operations, as follows:

- comparing and matching the schemas of two applications of an organisation, in order to get them integrated,

- setting up an architecture, where many applications can be translated into one canonical data model and data manipulation language - so that they appear homogeneous

- setting up an infrastructure, using CORBA or similar standards, where the participating application can be fitted by complying with the rules for object-request-brokers.

This chapter discusses research activities for organisational integration, and infrastructural integration, and then reviews current research activities.

In the sections for *Organisational Integration*, we have reviewed a few selected architectures, a reference model for object-oriented distributed systems, and a reference architecture for schema integration proposed by Sheth and Larson.

In the sections for *Infrastructural Integration*, we have reviewed Common Object Request

Broker Architecture (CORBA), Open Distributed Processing (ODP), and synergies in various developments of ORBs and ODBMSs.

In the sections for *Current Research Activities*, we have reviewed the papers on using new technologies and concepts for application integration.

5. Inter-Application Conflicts & Correspondences	This chapter classifies the conflicting definitions in different applications as schema conflicts and data conflicts. We also discuss cases, where the same information is expressed as metadata in one application, while as data in another. Other objectives of the chapter are to discuss the role of context in integration, correspondence assertions to link semantically related objects, and existing conflicts in component databases

In spite of schema and data conflicts, two applications may represent the same or related real world objects. Asserting correspondence between application objects that represent same real world objects provides a way to link these applications.

We have identified the conflicts that need be resolved to achieve integration of application.

6. Ways To Resolve Conflicts In Disparate Application Systems	This chapter discusses two ways of integrating applications - (1) applying a number of schema transformations, so that similarities are increased to facilitate the process of schema integration, (2) identifying correspondence between conceptual schemas of the component applications, so they can be linked without transformation.

This chapter formalises the process of schema integration: (1) schema transformation to increase similarity between conceptual schemas, (2) schema comparison to identify correspondences and achieve compatibility, and integration based on correspondence assertions.

This chapter has shown that it is feasible to show inter-schema correspondences without requiring a preliminary step to translate all existing schemas into their equivalent schemas based on some common model. Thus, applications can be integrated without any transformation allowing them to continue their existing features.

7. The Proposed	In this chapter, we propose to simplify this integration

Architecture	process by identifying a subset of data items of each involved application, so that the integration of the entire applications can be achieved by integrating only the selected subsets of the applications. The selected subset from each application includes only those objects, which are accessible by other applications.

In this chapter, we have proposed an architecture considering only the *Shared Data Items*. An object can be built on top of each component application considering only the *Shared Data Items* . These objects will participate in a homogeneous application.

Main ideas that contribute to the proposed architecture are (1) Export Schema instead of the entire schema, (2) Correspondence Assertions between elements of the Export Schemas, (3) Encapsulation to hide the details of the schema not appearing in the Export Schemas, (4) Canonical data model of the integrating application.

We have also provided a definition of the *Shared Data Items*:

- Data items exchanged across application boundaries,
- Data items which are keys or identifiers for accessing items exchanged,
- Data items involved in constraints with other items.

This chapter also discusses the major components of the proposed architecture. We have reviewed the proposed architecture using the reference architectures. The other approaches of application integration are also compared with the proposed architecture.

8. Implementing Integration Of Applications	This chapter describes the steps for implementing the proposed architecture are: - documenting export and import schemas of participating applications, - deciding on if some more data items to be included in the export schemas to ensure data integrity - design and construction of object-oriented application systems using data items from export and import schemas, - building up interfaces between the integrating application and the underlying applications.

This chapter shows what needs be done to implement the proposed architecture in one organisation. It checks the possibilities of replication of data items in the integrating application. Implementation of the proposed architecture of integration is, to a great extent, transparent to the users of the pre-integration applications. This means that the service levels of these applications before and after the implementation would be almost the same. One gain is the extra window in each application to view some data items from other applications. The other major gain is the consistency of the sharable information achieved through the controlling objects, inter-operating in an application system. For the sharable data items, all aspects of integrity, security, concurrency control and recovery are brought under the control of one central application. This ensures the consistent view of the same data item from different applications.

9. **Evaluation Of The Proposed Solution & Conclusion**   This chapter evaluates how our proposed solution meets the target set in the introduction of this thesis. It also identifies the areas of further research to make this solution more effective and recommends action plans for I.T. communities and users of I.T. products.

This chapter checks that the architecture proposed in this thesis for application integration by modelling shared data only is as good as the schema integration by modelling all the data items of the participating applications. Since the existing applications will continue, the services provided by them will be maintained while additional services will be provided from the shared objects of other involved applications. Inclusion of any extra object, which are not shared by the applications, would not provide any extra information that can be used by other applications in the federation.

This chapter recommends how the proposed architecture can help us get the best of both worlds - continue reaping benefits from existing information resources without any major investments on reverse engineering, assimilate at the same time the benefits of emerging technologies. We would also suggest the roles of general information users to make the best use of the architecture. The strategy for users of information technology products would be (a) to get the hardware and software that best serve the business functions, (b) not to maintain the skills for specialised hardware and software, which should be maintained by their suppliers, (c) to build interfaces between individual applications and the integrating application, (d) to modify the integrating application, if required, to meet changing business needs.

10. **Further Work**   In this chapter, we shall check how the implementation of this architecture can be improved and show the areas, where

further research will facilitate interoperation of applications. Both the vendors of information technology facilities and the users of those facilities can take advantage of this architecture involving only the export schemas of the applications.

As the proposed architecture shows ways to establish semantic links between applications using different technologies and methodologies, the manufacturers need not strive for resolving their differences. For manufacturers of hardware and software facilities, the strategy should be to find the most effective and economical ways to carry out the business functions, irrespective of varieties in technologies, as long as the interfaces can be maintained with a standard set of object-oriented applications.

This chapter is only an extension to show how vendors of software and hardware should focus on providing best possible ways to provide a service, while keeping an option to interface an object-oriented application, so that the application can be integrated with other applications. This will help to achieve optimum services from an application, while getting it integrated with other applications.

11. Index	Index has been built for selected words and definitions, to facilitate access to those definitions.
12. Glossary	Some of the less common terms used in the thesis have been explained in the glossary.
13. Bibliography	The bibliography provides a consolidated list of references used in this thesis, while the references used in any individual chapter have been shown as footnotes attached to the deliberations.

TABLE OF CONTENTS

LIST OF ILLUSTRATIONS AND TABLES

LIST OF ILLUSTRATIONS AND TABLES (CONTD.)

LIST OF APPENDICES

ABSTRACT

Application integration, addressed in this thesis, is no longer an organisational issue, but a global problem. Organisational boundaries are often redefined with mergers/acquisitions. Customers require services that cannot be provided by a single organisation. Applications from one organisation often need to interact with applications of other organisations; they need to package services that are supplied by other organisations. Organisations can no longer work in isolation.

Increase in the need for interoperability of applications has been matched by the increase in the speed and quality of communication. Organisations are now highly interconnected and have access to many information sources, but they still have problems in identifying what data from other organisations are relevant or meaningful to them. In this thesis, we have shown how to link relevant data across applications and model their relationships in the integrating application.

A computer application represents real world objects that are relevant to it; again from these objects it selects only the relevant attributes. The same real world object may be modelled in many applications, but different sets of attributes are represented in those applications, because data models support different constructs, designers have different perceptions, or the contexts of the application explain unspecified details. When the real world object represented by one application object is same as the real world object represented by another application object, these application objects are semantically equivalent. When the real world counterparts are related, the application objects are semantically related. We have proposed to link semantically related objects of two or more applications in spite of their schematic differences, and model these objects for an integrating application in terms of the semantic relationships of their real world counterparts.

We have further simplified this approach to integrate decentralised application systems by identifying a subset of data items of each involved application. These subsets represent the shared information across the applications. Thus, the integration can be achieved by integrating only the selected subsets of the applications. The traditional approaches are to integrate applications by considering all data items of involved applications; these attempt to understand the semantics of all objects in the distributed complex and hence cannot be easily implemented. In this proposed approach, the subsets of the involved applications are expressed as export objects, which contain the shared information of each involved application for the integrated application. After semantic relationships of the export objects across applications are established, an object-oriented application can integrate the semantically related objects across applications and help the applications inter-operate with one another. Identification of semantic links between the involved export objects facilitates setting up their relationships in the data/object models. The proposed architecture will help us get the best of both worlds – continue using existing applications, at the same time add new technologies for the competitive edge.

1. INTRODUCTION

1.1 Introduction

Even a decade ago, integration of applications used to be carried out mainly to integrate applications of the same organisation. In today's business world, it is no longer restricted to one enterprise. Growth in mergers, acquisitions and cooperation among organisations has increased the need of integrating applications across organisations. More recently, E-business has increased the interactions among organisations via Internet. They can no longer work in isolation. Inter-organisation integration is now as necessary as intra-organisation integration for the applications.

Increase in the need for interoperability of applications has been matched by the increase in the speed and quality of communication. Thanks to technological advances, we have now achieved adequate speed of communication and ease of connecting systems across sites. Organisations are now highly interconnected and have access to many information sources, but they still have problems in identifying what data from other organisations are relevant or meaningful to them. In spite of the increasing need for application integration and the increasing speed of communication between organisations, we need to identify what application objects are relevant and need be linked together, and how these links can be modelled, so that the integrated application would appear like one application.

In this chapter, the motivation for application integration is considered first. Then we identify the problems that will be addressed in this thesis to facilitate application integration. Original contributions of this thesis to resolve this problem are then discussed.

1.2 Motivations

The need for interoperability among applications is increasing fast in today's business world. Organisation boundaries are being redefined with mergers/acquisitions. Mergers and acquisitions are very frequent in today's business, and these often require applications from different organisations to be integrated into one set of applications.

Distance is no barrier now thanks to WWW & Internet. When connected via Internet, there is hardly any difference between the next-door neighbour and a person at the other end of the world. But we need to establish that each of the communicating parties describes the same thing with the same name; the same real world objects represented in different applications are treated in the same way.

Recently, e-business has changed the ways of transacting business. Electronic Data Interchange (EDI) was started a few years ago, which has now been taken over by electronic data exchange over the Internet. More and more businesses are considering Internet as one of the major channels for communicating with customers, suppliers and traders.

Customers often ask for services that span more than one organisation. Customers require services that cannot be provided by one organisation alone. Organisations now need to liaise with other service providers to tailor a service that a customer requires. Banks now may offer tailor-made services to suit individual customers. Customers can decide what services need be packaged in the product for them - which may include a choice of merchants where a credit card can be presented, choice of investments for excess funds available in an account, and so on. But this means Bank's applications need be integrated with those of other service-providers.

Enterprises can no longer survive in isolation. They cannot survive unless they provide the services that their customers want. If they work in isolation, they cannot provide the services. Enterprise Application Integration now is must for many businesses. Enterprises need to integrate their applications for mere survival.

The need to integrate applications has increased with the increase in capabilities to access other applications. In mid seventies, applications within the same organisation only were considered for integration; now the integration of applications is being implemented across organisations to increase the efficiency of inter-organisation functions. An individual organisation may now choose not to maintain the information which are available from other organisations, but to access information from various involved organisations and integrate them into applications to suit its own particular needs. The more information is accessed across organisation, the more is the need to understand the meaning of the information from the other organisation in the context of the accessing organisation. An organisation needs to find out which object from another organisation provides information, which are related to those available in an object of its own.

While the need of application integration has largely increased, and the speed of communication across the world has been enhanced, one basic problem of application integration still remains to be solved. Each application still represents the same real world objects differently, and makes different real world objects appear like the same. This is because, the application designers may perceive the same real world object differently, or the technological constraints make the designers abstract the same facts in different ways.

The context of each application makes up for the differences in the abstractions made by the designers.

The main motivation behind this thesis is the need to identify the relevant objects from different applications, when they represent the same or related real world objects, and to find ways to link these objects across applications.

1.3 The Problem Addressed in This Thesis

The broad area addressed in this thesis is the problem of integrating applications. One major goal of application integration is to create the illusion that the component applications are not disparate, but they provide services as components of one application. This goal can be achieved mainly in two different ways:

(1) To have only one application replacing all the individual applications meant to be integrated. This means no illusion; this application needs to provide all the services, which were provided by individual applications.

(2) To allow the individual applications to provide their own services, in a consistent and harmonious way, so that together the applications perform as if they are all components of one application.

If we follow the method (1), i.e., one application is implemented to replace the set of applications targeted for integration, then its schema needs to include all objects or data items of all individual applications in the set. All proposals for one global schema for data integration, irrespective of the methodology used, require substantial human intervention to integrate local/individual schemata.

If we follow the method (2), we need to modify each application, so that it can exchange information with every other involved application. This exchange of information, again, may be implemented either by direct interfaces between each pair of applications or by indirect communication via an intermediating application. If we interface each application directly with every other individual application, number of interfaces grows rapidly with the number of applications, because the number of interfaces is the number of possible combinations of selecting two applications from the total number of applications to be integrated. On the other hand, if we have one intermediary application interfacing with each of the involved application, the number of interfaces can be reduced to the number of applications. However, this intermediary application needs to have information about all items, each application is prepared to exchange with other applications, and specifications of those items for receiving applications. This means, the intermediary application needs to have information about a subset of each individual application schema. But we have a problem here to find out exactly what objects need be selected from the individual application schema so that these can be put together to design the schema of the intermediary application. We also have a problem to specify the relationships between these selected objects, so that they can be modelled into the schema of the intermediary application. These are the two problems, that will be addressed in this thesis: (1) what objects from individual applications need be selected into the schema of the integrating intermediary application, (2) modelling of these objects from individual applications, so that they can be adequately linked in the integrating application.

We may note here that, there are two major aspects of application integration. One, we need to set up connectivity between the applications by using appropriate hardware software combination, so that one application can access the values of an object maintained by the other application, and vice-versa. The other aspect, is the schema of the applications. The integrator needs to know, which object of one application needs be connected to another object of a different application.

'With high interconnectivity and access to many information sources, the primary issue in the future will not be how to efficiently process the data that is known to be relevant, but which data is relevant.'[1] This thesis has focussed on data or schema aspects of the applications.

Schema integration, too, is a well-researched topic. We shall see in the review of research work in application integration, that generally attempts have been made to integrate all objects of one component application, with all objects of other component applications. Thus, integration of large applications has become too difficult to achieve, because it involves modelling of all objects of all the component applications. Whatever methodologies may be used, the implementation of one global schema is too complex and requires a substantial human intervention to integrate the local/individual schemas. Therefore, we need to find out what objects from individual schemas must necessarily be included in the schema of the intermediary integrating application, so that they are sufficient for the application integration.

---

[1] Sheth, A.P. and Kashyap V., (1992), So Far (Schematically) yet So Near (Semantically), *Proceedings of the IFIP DS-5 Semantics of Interoperable Database Systems, Lorne, Victoria, Australia,* Vol 1, p 278

Applications are often developed in isolation, with a limited focus and a limited domain, and consequently definitions of data maintained by these applications could be conflicting. In other words, the application schemas, that contain the definition of data maintained by the applications, may define the same real world objects differently. Also, they may so define the different real world objects that they appear the same. This means that conflicts could be introduced among the schemas of those applications, the same facts of the real world could be implemented differently, depending on the perspective of the designer. The designers model the real world facts so that they can be represented on computerised systems. But the contexts of each system, and the background knowledge available to the designers make the representation of the real world different in each application. In this thesis, we shall also address the problem of linking the objects from individual applications, in the integrating application, in spite of their differences in schema specifications.

In summary, the main problems addressed in this thesis are:

(1) What objects from individual applications need necessarily be selected into the schema of the integrating intermediary application to provide the same quality of application integration, as achieved by selecting all objects from individual applications.

(2) Modelling of these objects from individual applications, so that they can be adequately linked in the integrating application, in spite of their differences in schema specifications.

1.3.1   A Practical Example Of The Problem

A practical example can be found in the problem of integrating a bank's applications to provide customer relationship management [CRM]. In the past, a human bank manager used to provide this service to customers. He used to understand the semantics of the information available about the customer in various bank applications and his personal notes. He could link the related information together to get a clear view of the circumstances the customer is in and provide advice on using bank products. The emphasis is now on in automating this task by semantic linking of bank's applications, running on heterogeneous platforms.

The bank manager, referred above, was required to maintain up-to-date information about the customer by studying the bank ledgers, and by discussing with the customer about his/her portfolio of investments. The bank manager kept himself aware of the major events of customer's life, so that he could advise about investments that meet the customer's needs. He could advise about insurance policies at the time when he has started his working career, about loans when he needs a car, and then about finance for the house and so on. The bank manager needed hours to gather information and hours to discuss with the customer. The design goal of Customer Relationship Management [CRM] systems is to provide the same level of service on a large scale, so that a telephone banking staff in the call-centre, spending only a minute or two, matches the services, once provided by bank managers. However, without a CRM system, the telephone banking staff needs to identify what informations from various bank applications are semantically related to the customer's needs. He/she then accesses the relevant information from relevant applications, often on heterogeneous platforms. The designer of the integrating CRM system needs to understand the semantics of all applications to find out how the schemas of the individual applications can be integrated.

A customer may have a number of accounts with the bank for a number of loan and investment products. These products could be maintained by isolated applications, possibly on heterogeneous platforms. A customer may use a number of front-ends like ATM, POS, Internet Banking etc to operate on these accounts. Also the bank staff may administer the customer accounts for setting up limits and fee structures, by using administrative terminals. Depending on the query of the customer, CRM needs to provide the means to review the customer's information in various applications and transactions at various front-ends. CRM should also help to check related administrative transactions affecting customer limits etc., and to find out how the pattern of deposits and withdrawals changes with the major events in the customer's life. CRM needs to be designed to help the telephone banking staff to review the statistical scores of the customer maintained by the behavioural scoring application, and the free-form notes maintained about the customer. Thus CRM would enable the telephone-banking staff to add values to the bank's services provided to the customer, and elicit more business. However, if not equipped with CRM, the telephone banking staff needs to understand the semantic links between applications, so that he/she gets the relevant information about the customer from various applications. He/she needs to have a fair idea about how the data is structured in each of the involved application, and how the relevant data can be accessed from each application, possibly by using the unique identification of the client. When the account details are accessed in the involved application, he/she would be able to view the balance of the account as on a date and also the history of transactions that changes the balance. He/she should be able to trace the same customer in the application that maintains behavioural scores of the customer, and get the pattern of the transactions and demography of the customer. If not equipped with a CRM system to integrate the related applications, the telephone banking staff need to identify the semantic links, which could be the unique customer number linked to the account number of a loan or savings account and the behavioural scoring details.

In this example, a bank customer may have one or more accounts with the bank in the following categories:

Loans: Home Loan, Investment Loan, Personal Loan, Credit Cards - Visa/ MasterCard/ BankCard

Savings: Term deposits, Bonds, Savings

Mixed: Cheque, Direct Deposit.

The transactions can be traced to ATMs, cheques, deposit and withdrawal slips transacted over the counter, there could be Internet and BPAY activities as well.

From all related applications, the telephone banking staff needs to find out the following information about the bank customer:

- the balance in the cheque account,
- monthly credits to the balance,
- monthly debits to the balance,
- the balance in the loan account,
- monthly repayments,
- other similar aspects of the accounts maintained by the customers, and
- assets and collaterals maintained as the security for the loan account.

If all these applications could be merged into one central application, the task of customer relationship management becomes much simpler. The telephone banking staff could have checked one application to find all relevant information about the customer. Computer Telephony Integration [CTI], being available on most call centre phones, the telephone banking staff could have gone straight into this central application using the smart contact details gathered from the telephone. However, integration of all these applications into one application is a very big and complex task. It is difficult, if not impossible, to maintain such a big application, because products need to be modified to suit competition, regulatory requirements and customers' expectation. We can easily see the plight of the telephone banking staff, when all these applications are isolated. He needs to check each of these application to find out which accounts in each application relate to the same customer, and how the pieces of information from individual application need be put together to get the total picture of the customer. We can also see that the designer of the integrating CRM application has a very big task of understanding the semantics of the component applications. Later in this thesis, we shall check how we could solve this problem using our proposed architecture, and help the designers in building customer relationship management application.

1.4 How This Thesis Addresses The Problem of Application Integration

First, in Chapter 2, we have provided definitions of the terms to be used in this thesis – so that we have consistent understanding about the terms like application, objects, semantic equivalence etc. For example, by the term 'application' we mean a set of data items and functions packaged together as an unit to be delivered by IT departments to the user.

Next, in Chapter 3, we have made a reconnaissance of various issues of application integration. Our literature survey confirms that the occurrence of isolated applications continues to be a major issue for the organisations, and the need of application integration will be even more in the future considering mergers/acquisitions and access to many information sources. We have also checked that the problem of application integration persists, in spite of extensive research and technological breakthroughs.

Next, in Chapter 4, we have reviewed the literature of work done so far for integrating applications. These research findings can be classified on the scale of operations ie (1) integrating two application systems of an organisation, by comparing and matching their schemas, (2) setting up an architecture, where all constituent applications build interfaces using one canonical data model and data manipulation language and (3) setting up an infrastructure, using standards like CORBA, where any participating application needs comply with the rules for traders or object-request-brokers.

Next, in Chapter 5, we identified the problem of schema and data integration between component applications. Intensional differences appear when the same piece of reality is modelled in different ways, either because the data models support equivalent constructs, or because designers have different perceptions of the reality. Extensional differences are caused by differences in domains, update cycles etc. For example two different city offices of the same international organisation may maintain data about the local population using the same schema structure, but follow different timings for updating the information. The data maintained at two city offices are same intensionally, but different extensionally.

Next, in Chapter 6, we have identified two main ways of achieving schema interoperation among the component systems:

(1) By transforming the schemas of the existing systems to increase their similarities and then by merging the transformed schemas,

(2) By identifying the correspondence among the related elements of the schemas involved and adding constructs to specify these inter-schema correspondences, while the original schemas are allowed to continue as before.

In Chapter 7 of this thesis, we have proposed to solve the multifaceted problem of integrating application systems, by concentrating on only the information that matters, ie the information shared across applications, while the information, that concerns an individual application only, need not be considered for modelling into the integrating application. Three main ideas that provided inspiration to this thesis are (1) Export Schema, which is a fraction of the entire schema, (2) Correspondence Assertions between elements of the Export Schemas, (3) Object Modelling to hide the details of the schema not appearing in the Export Schemas.

(1) The idea of *Export Schema* has been developed from the concept of federated database architecture.[2] Our definition of shared data items has been expanded to include the data-items that identify the information exchanged and serves as the identifiers or keys to those information, and also the data items involved in constraints with the data items actually exchanged. This means, in the example of our banking problem, we need not model the entire schemas of ATM applications or Home Loan applications. We need to maintain information about the data items that matter – for example the transaction amount, debit/credit code, Bank and account identification etc from ATM application, and the account identification, the account balance and history of repayments for the Home Loan application.

(2) The techniques of *Model-Independent Assertions* for correspondence of the shared data items of the participating application systems have been developed from the work

---

[2] Heimbigner D., & McLeod D.(1985), A Federated Architecture For Information Management, *ACM Transactions on Office Information Systems*

carried out by Spaccapietra, Parent and Dupont.[3] But, in this thesis, this technique has been applied only to the shared data items, instead of working through the entire schemas of participating applications. Also the correspondence assertions are incorporated in the object-oriented model in terms of generalisation and specialisation of classes. For example, we need to have correspondence asserted between the account identification from the ATM transaction and the account identification of the Home Loan application.

(3) The concept of a central application intermediating between applications has been discussed in section 2.2 in this chapter. The central application has been proposed, in this thesis, to be designed to consist of *Objects* on top of each application; the export schemas of the component applications will be modelled together in the central object-oriented application.

In the example of banking application, when we build an object on top of the ATM application, we can hide the complex details of the ATM software, all we need to know is which accounts of which bank are involved, the type of transaction and the amount. These are the items, which will be in the export schema and modelled as an object.

Object-Oriented data models can qualify as canonical data models for their operational equivalence, by guaranteeing the same response to the same query. The attributes of information hiding enable an object to integrate the individual applications by sending a message and getting a reply, without any need to know how the reply is implemented.

A central application can be designed to consist of objects on top of each application. Each of these objects needs to know only the public parts of the database/files maintained in the underlying application. The central application will model interactions, ie messages and replies between objects. Thus a central O-O application will integrate all these isolated applications which are on heterogeneous databases. Each of the participating applications, need to communicate with this central application only, there is no need for any cross talk between any pair of participating applications.

This solution provides the following advantages:

• Implementation differences among underlying applications/databases are simply bypassed, as objects need not care how the methods are implemented in other objects.

---

[3] Spaccapietra S., and Parent C.(1993), View Integration : A Step Forward In Solving Structural Conflicts, *IEEE Transactions on Data and Knowledge Engineering*
Spaccapietra S., and Parent C., Dupont Y.(1992), Model-Independent Assertions for Integration of Heterogeneous Schemas, *Very Large Databases Journal*, Vol.1, No.1

- Semantics of relationships between various data-items in the databases are much better captured in the object-oriented data model, at all levels of granularity.

- Since the objects are designed only on the sharable or the export attributes of the individual application bases, no expensive data-modelling is required in understanding the entire semantics of individual applications

The steps for implementing the proposed architecture are dealt in Chapter 8 as: (1) documenting export and import schemas of participating applications, (2) deciding on what data items need be included in the export schemas of the applications, (3) design and construction of object-oriented application systems using data items from the export and import schemas, (4) building up interfaces between the integrating application and the underlying applications.

In Chapter 9, we have checked how the proposed architecture would fit in a typical environment and achieve its objectives. This chapter also recommends (a) to get the hardware and software that best serve the business functions, (b) not to maintain the skills for specialised hardware and software, which should be maintained by their suppliers, (c) to build interfaces between individual applications and the integrating application, (d) modify the integrating application, if required, to meet changing business needs. This chapter also recommends that the strategy for manufacturers of hardware, software, and middleware, should be to find the most effective ways to carry out the business functions, in spite of varieties in technologies, ensuring that the interfaces can be maintained with a set of object-oriented applications. In the chapter 10, we have identified further work for enhancing the proposed architecture to take advantage of the new technological developments.

1.5 The Original Contribution of This Thesis

The original contribution of this thesis is in our approach to solve the problem of application integration. Various aspects of our approach, as explained below, make our approach unique, when they are considered together.

We have considered that our solution will include one or more intermediary applications to exchange information among the individual applications. We do not recommend combining all individual applications into a single application, because the design and implementation of one global schema is complex and requires substantial human intervention. Also, we have proposed that each application should not be directly interfaced with every other individual application. Because, in that case, the number of interfaces is the number of possible combinations of selecting two applications from the total number of applications, and hence the number of interfaces is close to the square of number of applications, when a large number of applications are integrated.

We have viewed an application as of a set of objects, which represent a set of real world objects relevant to the processes carried out in the application. Therefore the problem of application integration appears to us as the problem of integrating sets of objects from different applications. While most legacy applications have been designed as sets of business processes, we have considered the real world objects represented in those applications.

We have considered the semantics of objects in an application, in terms of types of its attributes and values, and the functions provided by the objects. Each of these objects represents a real world object, which is simulated in the application. Each object conveys a set of meanings to the application. For example, a person may mean a height, a weight, a volume of space required for its occupation. The object 'bank customer', in our practical example of customer relationship management, means a number of attributes the bank staff needs to check. For example, these attributes could be the balance in the cheque account, monthly credits, monthly debits, the balance in the loan account, monthly repayments, assets, collaterals etc.

A different application consists of a different set of objects, which are relevant to the processes carried out in the second application. Two applications may include objects, which are the models of the same or related real world objects. Integration of these two applications consists in linking of the same or related objects of these two applications.

Again, an application object does not fully describe its real world counterpart. An application is not interested in all attributes of a real world object, it abstracts only those attributes, which are relevant to the application. Our original contribution is in highlighting the fact that the same real world object may look different to different applications, because they abstract different sets of attributes from the same real world object. In the eyes of the beholder, two different real world objects may appear the same - an application is the beholder that chooses the attributes, it likes to see. If an application views two different real world objects for the attributes of their common super-class, these objects will appear to be of the same class to the application.

When a real world object is represented in two different applications using different sets of attributes, we need a way to establish that the two application objects are equivalent, because they represent the same real world object. This can be done by identifying the attributes, which are represented in both applications. In terms of these common attributes, we can establish that the same class of real world objects are represented in two applications, when the same domain of values are applicable to these common attributes. When two application objects represent the same class of real world objects, they are intensionally equivalent. They can be considered extensionally equivalent, when we can establish that the same instance of the class of real world objects has been abstracted in two applications; this can be done by matching the attributes that uniquely identify an instance of a real world object.

We have considered that the full set of objects from each application is not necessary for application integration. We have recommended that a subset of objects from each application should be enough to be considered for integration, because only this subset of objects is relevant to other applications.

We have gone through the process of selecting a sub-schema i.e. a subset of objects from each individual applications, and modelling these sub-schemas together into the schema of the intermediary integrating application. The relevant sub-schema includes the objects, which one application needs to share with other applications. The objects, which are accessed by other applications, need to be included in the subset, plus we need those objects, which are unique identifiers of the accessed objects, plus we need those objects, which are involved in constraints with the accessed objects.

Since, we recommend the use of the shared objects only for application integration, we do not need to integrate all objects of all applications. This means, all the application objects will not be linked together into one big application. An application, consisting of the shared objects only, will intermediate with the component applications.

We have shown the ways of preparing the data model for the integrating application using sub-schemas from individual applications. Semantic relationships between the objects selected from different application can be expressed in terms of equivalence, disjoint, intersection, and inclusion. When we design an application that links all shared objects together, they can be modelled on the basis of their semantic relationships.

Some of the objects from the sub-schema of one individual application are often same as or semantically related to objects maintained in the sub-schema of other isolated applications. When they are semantically same they represent the same class of real world objects; when they are semantically different they represent different classes of real world objects. When they are semantically related they represent different classes of real world objects, which are related in some way. Based on these relationships, these objects are modelled into the object-oriented schema of the integrating application.

Identification of semantic links between the elements of involved export schemas has facilitated setting up their relationships in the data/object models. We have considered that the applications view the objects in terms of selected attributes. Based on the domain of values of these selected attributes of the objects of different schemas, they can be considered as semantically equivalent, or semantically related. This equivalence or relationship can be modelled in the integrating application.

Unlike in the centrally integrated applications, functionalities of the original applications are maintained as before integration. This is because the proposed solution allows the applications to continue their original functions.

In summary, the original contributions of this thesis are as follows:

1. We have proposed that our solution will include one or more intermediary applications to exchange information among the individual applications.

2. We have proposed the way of viewing each individual application as a set of objects, irrespective of the original configuration of the application.

3. We have proposed a method of identifying the objects that need to be in the schema of the intermediary application. The principal contribution of our methods are:

    • We have considered that the schema of the intermediary application(s) need to include at least all the objects, which individual applications need to share with other applications to keep them informed about these objects.

    • We have added to this list, (i) the objects, which are involved in constraints with objects selected for the intermediary application(s), and (ii) the objects, which are required to access the objects selected for intermediary application(s).

    • We have expanded this list till no other objects need to be added for these two reasons.

4. We have proposed the method of modelling the schema of the intermediary application. We proposed to assert the semantic relationships among the shared objects from

different applications in terms of equivalence, disjointness, intersection, and inclusion. Based on these relationships, these objects are modelled into the object-oriented schema of the integrating application. We have considered that semantic relationship can exist between objects at different levels of granularity; this means that an object of one application may be related to a lower level object or an attribute of another application.

5.   We have proposed an object-oriented application to be constructed based on the object-oriented schema of the intermediary application. Optionally, we could have other forms of intermediary applications. For example, the intermediary application can be designed to be an Internet based application with XML links to individual applications.

1.6 Conclusion

In this chapter, we have first looked at the motivations for application integration. As organisational boundaries are often getting redefined because of mergers and acquisitions, we often have to integrate applications, which originated from two different organisations. With the growth of E-business, applications of one organisation now need to cooperate with those of other organisations.

The need for integration has also been matched by the technological advancement to keep organisations connected to Internet and each other. But there is a problem of establishing semantic links between applications, we still need to identify which data of one application is relevant to another application. We have identified the problem of this thesis as the problem of identifying which objects from each involved application need be put together in the integrating application, and how the semantic links between the selected objects will be modelled in the integrating application.

We have also previewed in this chapter the original contribution of this thesis in concentrating on only the information that matters, i.e. the information shared across applications. For the items on the list of shared objects, semantic relationships between objects from different applications have been considered for modelling them into the schema of the integrating application.

In the next chapter, a reconnaissance of various issues of application integration will be made to design the structure of the thesis.

2. PRELIMINARIES AND DEFINITIONS

2.1   Introduction

The broad area addressed in this thesis is the integration of application systems, with main emphasis on semantic similarities and relationship between objects across application systems. The primary objective of this chapter is to provide definitions of the terms to be used in this thesis – so that we have consistent understanding about the terms like application, objects, semantic equivalence etc.

2.2   Applications

By the term 'application' we mean a set of data items and a group of functions packaged together as an unit to be delivered by IT departments to the user. "It is meaningful to group together a set of business processes and automate them in a single application for delivery to the user."[4] Some common examples of applications are Payroll, Inventory Management, Bills Payable, Bills Receivable etc.

We may note here that the term 'application' has been used differently by a few other authors, but in this thesis we have used the definition of the preceding paragraph. Dietz J[5] has equated business process workflow to I.T. applications. Muhlberger R and Orlowska M[6] have defined an application 'as a set of transactions, not all of which need to commit, nor even be executed for the application to run successfully. A transaction is taken to be a set of operations, all of which must complete successfully for a transaction to be able to commit, else a complete rollback must be performed.' In our definition for an application, we include the objects that perform operations, and objects on which the operation is performed, while the operations are considered as methods or features of those objects in the application. Both code and data are required to support the operations in an application.

As per Andrade J.M., et al, an application consists of the software and permanent resources (databases, files, etc.) used to automate a business function. An application that runs on multiple computers is a distributed application. New functionality is added to extend applications, by adding new software and possibly new resources. In order that the boundaries of an application be understood, it is often useful to define the application

[4] Tozer J.,(1993), 'Beyond 'rapid' applications', *Insight IBM, January 1993*
[5] Dietz J.,(1994), 'Business Modelling for Business Redesign',*Proceedings of the 27th Hawaii International Conference on system Sciences*, IEEE Computer Science Press, 1994
[6] Muhlberger R. M. and Orlowska M.E.,(1996), 'A Business Process Driven Multidatabase Integration Methodology', *Database Reengineering and Interoperability*, ISBN030645288, pp 283-295

through some configuration system. Typically this identifies the code, data objects, and computer resources that comprise the application[7].

The code and data to support the applications may be maintained in various ways. The code can be maintained in forms of programs that are maintained separately from the data, or the code and data can be kept together in form of objects. The definition of objects will be provided in this chapter.

Applications maintain their data in some sort of data repositories, which could be files or databases. When the data is maintained in files, a file contains records ie logical groups of data items. The data can also be maintained in forms of databases – relational, network or any other type; data together with code can also be maintained in forms of object-oriented databases. When a number of applications are integrated into one application, their data repositories are also integrated.

2.3   Objects and Data Items

An application maintains repositories of data items to represent the real world objects, which constitute the part of the real world an application represents. An application also maintains repositories of methods that can be applied on these data items. While earlier generations of applications maintained data and code separately, the newer generations of applications encapsulate data and methods pertaining to a real world object in form of an application object, or simply as an object. The application software does not directly deal with the real world objects, but with their appropriate computer representations, which may also be called objects. One may call the real world objects as external objects, and their computer representations as internal objects[8] or application objects. In this thesis, by the term object we mean the application object, which is the class of external objects as modelled in the application. These objects may be modelled at any level of representation viz. attribute level or entity level. When an object is modelled without the methods for its behaviour, it can be referred simply as a data item.

2.4   Instances

While a class of real world objects is termed as an object for an application, each individual real world object is termed to be an instance of that class. While a class of real world objects can be termed as the object 'cricketer', Alan Border is one instance of the object 'cricketer'. Similarly, while the savings account is an object, a specific account of the

---

[7] Andrade J.M. et al, (1996), The TUXEDO System: Software for Constructing and Managing Distributed Business Applications, Addison Wesley Publishing Company, Massachusetts, p 53

[8] Meyer B. (1988), *Object-Oriented Software Construction*, U.K., Prentice Hall International Ltd., pp 67-68.

class of savings account is an instance. An instance of the real world object is also represented as an instance of the application object in the concerned application.

2.5   *Attributes*

A real world object is described to an application by the values of selected features of the object. These selected features are the attributes of the object. An attribute could be a static value of one of the feature, for example the date of birth of a person; it could also be a method by which an object responds to an event. The attribute of an object is also considered to be an object at a lower level.

2.6   *Schema*

The schema is a collection of attributes by which an object is described to an application. The same real world object may be described differently i.e. in terms of different sets of attributes, to different applications, and hence the same real world object can have different schemas for different applications.

2.7   *Semantic Equivalence and Relationships*

As per Oxford Dictionary, 'semantic' means 'of meaning(s) in language'. In this section, we shall define semantic equivalence between two different objects, and then between two instances of the same object. Instances of two different objects are not considered for equivalence, even if they may have the same value.

2.7.1   *Semantic Equivalence and Relationships Between Objects*

If a data item or object of one application conveys the same meaning as another object of the same or a different application, then the first one is semantically equivalent to the second one. As we have seen in the previous section, an application views a real world object in terms of its schema or the set of objects and attributes relevant to the application; therefore the internal object of the application or the application object will show only these attributes. Another application may be interested in a different set of attributes of the same class of real world objects, hence its application object will show a different set of attributes. If the application object of the first application models the same class of real world objects, as modelled by the application object of the second application, then these two application objects are semantically equivalent. The set of attributes, which are common to both application objects, will satisfy the ranges for the same class in each of these application objects. In other words, these two application objects are semantically equivalent in terms of the common attributes, appearing in schemas of both applications. Our definition of Semantic Equivalence matches closely with that of Sheth and Kashyap – "Two objects are defined to be semantically equivalent when they represent the same real world entity or concept."[9]

2.7.2   *Semantic Equivalence and Relationships Between Instances*

Semantic equivalence may also be considered at the level of instances. Semantic equivalence at the instance level means that the same real world object instance has been represented as an instance of the first application object, and also as an instance of the second application object. In this case values of all the common attributes in both applications will be identical.

Semantic equivalence is one form of the semantic relationship. We may consider various forms of semantic relationship as follows:

• Suppose that, for any instance of the first application object, there exists an instance of the second application object, and common attributes of these two instances are identical. Suppose further that there exists no instance in either application, for which there is no corresponding instance in the other application, then these two application objects are semantically equivalent.

If the first application object is of class X_1 and the second application object is of class X_2, we will express their semantic equivalence, in this thesis, as: $X_1 \equiv X_2$.

• If for any instance of the first application object, there exists no instance of the second application object, so that common attributes of these two instances are identical, then these two application objects are semantically disjoint.

If the first application object is of class X_1 and the second application object is of class X_2, we will express their semantic disjointness, in this thesis, as: $X_1 \cap X_2 = \emptyset$.

• Suppose that, for some instances of the first application object, there exists an instance of the second application object, and common attributes of these two instances are

---

[9] Sheth, A.P. and Kashyap V., (1992), So Far (Schematically) yet So Near (Semantically), *Proceedings of the*

identical. Suppose further that for other instances of the first application object, there exists no instance of the second application object, such that common attributes of these two instances are identical. Suppose further that similarly for other instances of the second application object, there exists no instance of the first application object, then these two application objects have an intersection of some common semantically equivalent subset.

If the first application object is of class X_1 and the second application object is of class X_2, we will express their semantic intersection, in this thesis, as: $X_1 \cap X_2 \neq 0$.

- Suppose that, for some instances of the first application object, there exists an instance of the second application object, so that common attributes of these two instances are identical, while for other instances of the first application object, there exists no such instance of the second application object. Suppose further that, for no instances of the second application object, there exists an instance of the first application object, such that common attributes of these two instances are not identical. This means that there is no instance of the second application object, which does not find a corresponding instance of the first application object, then the second application object is a subset of the first application object.

If the first application object is of class X_1 and the second application object is of class X_2, we will express their semantic inclusion, in this thesis, as: $X_1 \supseteq X_2$.

2.8   *Canonical Data Models*

Different applications may follow different models to suit their respective database management systems. An application that maintains its data in a relational database, will use relational data model for defining its schemas, while an application that maintains its data in an object-oriented database, will use object data model for defining its schemas. In order to compare the schemas specified in two different data models, we need to specify the schemas using the same data model. However, the data model which will be used for translating the schemas specified in different data models, need to be rich enough to translate every feature described in the source data model language. The data model, which can be used for translating the schemas specified in any data model, without sacrificing any feature, described using the original data model, is called the canonical data model. An object-oriented data model has all relevant features, which make it capable of translating any model into it. But the same arguments cannot be made for relational data models. Hence an object-oriented data model can be considered as the canonical data model, but the same comments are not applicable for relational data models.

2.9 Architectures

As per Oxford Dictionary, architecture means art or science of building, or style of building and construction. In this thesis, we use the term architecture as a style of building integrated applications from isolated applications. When we shall consider different architectures of integrating applications, we shall review what parts of applications are linked or cemented together in each style of architecture. We shall also show, in our proposed architecture, how we identify the parts of the applications that need be linked for integrating application and how we link these parts together.

3. RECONNAISSANCE

3.1 *Introduction*

In the last chapter, the main objective of this thesis has been set to explore the economical yet effective ways of integrating applications by identifying the objects that are shared across applications and modelling these objects together based on semantic similarities and relationships between them. In this chapter, a reconnaissance of various issues of application integration will be made to find out what integration of applications means in the real world terms, and why the problem of application integration persists in spite of past attempts and technological advances. Analysis of various issues will lead us to design the roadmap for this thesis.

Though applications are getting more and more capable of accessing information from various involved organisations, a substantial part of the information maintained by an application is often for its private use only, it is not shared with other applications, and hence not required for integrating the applications. This thesis attempts to link the objects, which are related meaningfully across the applications. Object modelling with only the shared objects of the involved applications will allow encapsulation to hide private objects of those applications, yet all objects relevant for application integration will be modelled on the basis of their semantic relationship.

This chapter is organised as follows: first, we have analysed how real world semantics are represented by modelling real world objects into application objects; next we have presented an overview of application integration on the basis of semantic equivalence of the application objects. The problem, this thesis addresses, is explained in the next section as the problem of identifying and linking semantically related objects across applications to achieve their integration. History of isolated applications is considered next, which is followed by appreciation of the need to make them inter-operate with one another. We have checked that the application development processes, using different tools and environments, cause technological, syntactic and semantic differences that lead to different abstraction of the same facts. Next, we have checked that the participating applications may interface with one another directly or indirectly, and reviewed the complexity and results achieved in each option. It is observed that the problem of integrating application schemas still persists, in spite of technological advancement facilitating connectivity. A solution to this problem is proposed - to identify and assert the relationship among semantically related objects in the export schemas[10] of the applications, and to construct an object-oriented application with these semantically related objects.

3.2   *Real World Semantics Of The Application Objects*

Semantics is defined by Wood[11] as the meaning and the use of data. By the term real world semantics, we mean the meaning and use of the real world counterpart of the application object. In Chapter-1, we have defined the semantic equivalence and relationships between objects. In this section, we shall use this definition to identify semantic relationships among objects of two different applications.

Each application system represents some real world objects in terms of some selected attributes of these objects. Only the attributes, which are relevant to the application, are selected and modelled in the applications. Another application may represent the same real world objects, but may be interested in different sets of attributes of the same object. When we integrate these two applications, ie when we make them inter-operate with one another, we need a mechanism to state that the two applications have portrayed the same real world objects, but described different sets of attributes of those objects. However, the set of attributes which are represented in both application systems for the same real world object instance, will have identical values in each application. For example the date of birth of a real world person like Alan Border will be the same in the applications maintained by Commonwealth Bank or National Australia Bank. The attributes of the real world object that are represented in the application specify the schema or the intension of object from the perspective of the application, while the values of these attributes specify the extension or the instance of the real object. If we restrict the intension of the real world object to the common attributes represented in both systems then both the intension and the extension of the real world object will be identical in both application systems.

In another case, two inter-operating applications may represent two different real world objects, whether or not they are represented in terms of similar sets of attributes. We need to state that the objects of the two application systems represent different real world objects. We may check if there is any common attribute in the two objects; if there is none, then the two objects are intensionally different. If there are some common attributes, there

---

[10] An export schema represents a subset a schema of an application that is available to other interoperating applications. Only the objects from the export schema can be accessed by other applications. The objects in the other part of the application schema are only for private use of the application

[11] Wood J.(1985), What's in a link?, *Readings in Knowlwdge Representation,* Morgan Kaufmann

are some intensional similarites, but from the differences in values of the attributes, we can assert that the applications are referring to different real world object instances.

In other cases, the set of real world objects represented by one application may be a subset of the real world objects represented by the other application, or the sets of real world objects represented by the applications could be overlapping.

When we need to integrate two or more applications we need a mechanism to specify whether the real world objects represented by one application is same as, different from, a subset of, or an overlapping set of real world objects represented by the other application. We could set up an integrating application that will model the objects from various applications in terms of the semantic relationships of these objects.

Again, we need not consider those real world objects that are represented by only one application, and no other application needs to know about them. Therefore, we need to consider only the objects in the export schema of each application.

3.3 Application Integration Considering Semantic Equivalence

The main task of integrating a number of applications is identifying the semantically equivalent objects in these applications. If these applications are merged into one application, each set of equivalent objects can be merged into one object and some of the redundant objects, in each set of equivalent objects, can be eliminated. However, if the applications containing equivalent objects are allowed to inter-operate as autonomous applications, the equivalent objects will appear in the schemas of each of these applications.

If an application can forego one of its own objects, and substitute it with another from a different application, then the replacing object is equivalent to the replaced object so far as the application is concerned. This means that no difference is perceived in the attributes and functions of the application when the instances of the substituting object are accessed. This leads us to introduce another definition for Semantic Equivalence, to be used in this thesis. If an object can be substituted by another object from the perspective of an application[12], then these objects are semantically equivalent.

When considering whether or not two objects of two different applications are semantically equivalent from the perspective of one user application, the user application is concerned only with the values of the selected attributes of instances of those objects. If those selected attributes of the corresponding instances of two objects are of the same values, then the application can use the corresponding instances of either of these two objects, and always get the same results in using these object instances; and hence these two objects are semantically equivalent from the perspective of the application.

Semantic equivalence, defined in the above lines, is relative to the application; what is semantically equivalent to one application could be different to another application. This is because, the first user/application may use a set of attributes which are the same in the corresponding instances of the two objects, while the second user/application may consider a different set of attributes which are different in their corresponding instances.

If an application is concerned with certain attributes of an object, and the values of those attributes can change over time, then we need to ascertain whether the values of attributes of the corresponding instances of the two objects are *always* same or *only on a certain special occasion.* If the corresponding instances of the two objects have the same attribute values not only at a point of time, but at any time, then these two objects are semantically equivalent, at any time, to the user or the application. This means it does not matter which one of the two objects is accessed and when it is accessed. In other words, the semantic equivalence of two different objects from the perspective of one user application means these two objects represent the same real world object for this application, in terms of the same list of attributes. Since the instances of these two objects will represent the instances of the same real world object, data values of these attributes of the corresponding instances of these two objects will match, and will be in the same domain of data values. If the data values of the instances of these two objects are updated at the same time to reflect the changed values of these attributes of the real world counterpart, then all instances of one object will always have the same values for the same attributes as held by the corresponding instances of the second object.

Even when the two objects are not semantically equivalent, they could be semantically related; this happens when the corresponding attributes of the two objects are not of the same value, but their values bear other relationships like inclusion, intersection, disjoint instead of equivalence. When the two objects are not semantically equivalent, the exact attribute values of one object cannot be deciphered from those of the other object, but the range of possible values can be predicted.

---

[12] A user is expected to launch an application to use an application object. The perspective of a user can be considered to be that of an application.

Most computerised application systems have been developed as isolated application systems, they have been designed to function as independent systems even though some of their objects are semantically equivalent or related to the objects maintained by other application systems. When we evaluate the attributes of these similar objects from the perspective of one user application, attributes from an object of one application system could be identical to the attributes of another object of a different application system. Therefore, to the concerned user application, these two objects of different application systems are semantically equivalent. These two objects are maintained in the respective application systems in such a way that their attributes always draw the same values from the same domains. When one user application considers these two objects to be equivalent, only certain attributes of these two objects may be relevant. To the concerned user application systems those attributes mean the entirety of the objects, and two objects are considered to be equivalent in terms of only these corresponding attributes.

The application integration needs to link the semantically related objects of two applications in spite of mainly three classes[13] of differences between these objects: *(i) technological, (ii) syntactic* and *(iii) semantic.* Later, in this chapter, we shall discuss these three types of differences and how they can be resolved. While some of the integration architectures have attempted to resolve only technological and syntactic differences, some other architectures, that tried to resolve the semantic differences, have attempted to understand the semantics of all information items of the entire distributed complex and hence have proved too difficult to implement. We need to find ways to resolve the conflicts caused by different representation of semantically similar objects, without going through the semantic reconciliation of all information items that are maintained by the participating application systems. In the next section, we have identified the problem of linking the semantically related objects in spite of differences in their representation in respective applications.

3.4 *Linking Semantically Related Objects From Different Applications*

Some of the objects from one isolated application are often same as or semantically related to objects maintained by other isolated application systems. When they are semantically same they represent the same class of real world objects. When they are semantically different they represent different classes of real world objects. When they are

---

[13] There could be other ways of classifying differences among objects, depending on the criteria of classification. Unlike us, some authors may not include both intensional and extensional differences in semantic differences.

semantically related they represent different classes of real world objects, which are related in some way.

The isolated development of applications will most likely continue, same facts will continue to get represented differently in the applications. The problem of integrating isolated applications is how to link these semantically related objects in spite of differences in their representation in respective applications, so that these applications can inter-operate on one another, and function as an integrated system.

3.4.1 History Of Isolated Applications

In most cases, especially in the past, when computer applications have been developed, there has not been enough anticipation for how they might integrate with other systems in the future. An organisation may have several such isolated application systems, developed at different times, using different technologies - hardware, software, operating systems and database management systems (DBMS). Even some new applications using latest technologies, eg. Computer Aided Design (CAD)/Image Processing, are likely to be developed as isolated, as the focus remains on harnessing technology for new functionalities, not on what information it would later share with the rest of the world. Because of the differences in technology and associated differences in methodologies of representing the real world objects, the same objects continue to get represented differently.

History of developing isolated applications will therefore be repeated; if some standards have been introduced and enforced in all application environments, then it would be possible to identify semantic similarities and differences in terms of those standards. However, introduction of new standards is hardly expected to encompass the entire environment of information systems, which are not only diverse but also changing rapidly. An intimate knowledge of each application environment is a pre-requisite for development of adequate standards. In the face of rapid technological changes, it is difficult to maintain such intimate knowledge.

An enterprise may have many applications, which are on different DBMSs and even file systems. Each of these DBMSs and file systems may have an underlying data model used to define data structures and constraints. Different data models may provide different structural primitives and may support different constraints; also different languages may be used to manipulate data represented in different data models. Differences in the system aspects of the DBMSs, for example, transaction management, concurrency control and recovery, operating systems and communication network, may cause the same real world objects to be represented differently in the applications. Even when all technological and syntactic heterogeneities are resolved, there could be semantic heterogeneity or a disagreement about the meaning, interpretation of intended use of the same data. For meaningful inter-operation between the application systems, however, the semantic conflicts between the participating application schemas must be resolved - each participating application system should clearly identify the real world objects it represents, so that the application objects could be related in terms of relationships between their real world counterparts.

3.4.2   The Need To Integrate Applications

History of developing isolated applications will continue, the real world objects will continue to be abstracted differently in different applications. Though developed as independent and isolated, application systems may be required to interact with one another at a later stage. In some cases, new application systems are added to work together with existing applications - some of which are legacy applications approaching obsolescence. Integration of these related applications are required in order to facilitate sharing of information, when a business process or application may need to gather information from more than one application, as one application may not provide all required information. Integration is required also to maintain a consistent view of all semantically related information that appears in more than one application system, but is portrayed differently in each. Integration of application systems increases relationships, efficiency and adaptability not only within one organisation, it has the potential to increase the efficiency of inter-organisation functions.

In earlier days, the integration of applications was confined within the boundary of one organisation; now capabilities are available to access other applications across the organisational boundaries and the integration of applications are being implemented across organisations to increase the efficiency of inter-organisation functions.

As more and more information is available from other organisations, small business organisations may not maintain the information which can be accessed from other organisations, but they will need to integrate the information, accessed from other organisations, into applications to suit their own particular needs.

3.4.3 Standard Interfaces of Different Applications

Applications are often developed in isolation, with a limited focus and a limited domain, and consequently definitions of data maintained by these applications could be conflicting. In other words, the application schemas, that contain the definition of data maintained by the applications, may define the same real world objects differently and may so define the different real world objects that they appear the same. This means that conflicts could be introduced among the schemas of those applications, the same facts of the real world could be implemented differently, depending on the perspective of the designer. The designers model the real world facts so that they can be represented on computerised systems. But the contexts of each system, and the background knowledge available to the designers make the representation of the real world different in each application.

The design is also influenced by the technology employed; hardware, operating systems, database management systems, middleware, and programming languages; each of these technologies could be in different versions or generations depending on the time of implementation, and may restrict or influence the design in various ways. While the technology induces the technological differences and often forces the use of different languages to cause syntactic differences ie differences in syntax/languages, sometimes the same language could be used to convey different meaning, and thus to cause differences in interpretations or semantic differences. When these individual systems inter-operate or exchanges information with one another, each need to understand how the information is interpreted by the participating system.

If a variety of hardware/software platforms are used in the applications to be integrated, formats and protocols need to be negotiated between each pair of platforms. Suppose, there are 20 applications, each uses a different language; if each wants to communicate directly to every other application, we require 20 x 19 / 2 ie 190 interpretations, but if each application translates to/from one standard language, we require only 20 interpretations. Using this concept, in order to have fewer translations/interpretations between applications, each application needs to convert its outgoing messages to one standard format and its incoming messages from the standard format to its own format. Technological compatibility can be achieved in most cases by setting up a reliable communication mechanism between each application and the intermediary application that uses the standard format.

The main hurdle for interoperation between two systems is reconciliation of these differences, syntactic and semantic. With the advances in technology, compatibility has been established between different syntaxes; also by following the specifications of the open systems standards, each participant sends messages in a standard language syntax, and receives messages by translating from the same standard syntax to its own syntax. Syntactic differences can be resolved by use of standard translation from one language to another; but for resolving semantic differences, the receiving system needs to understand the messages in terms of the context and the conceptual schema of the sending system. One way to solve this problem is to model the conceptual schema of the sending system in terms of the schema of the receiving system, another way could be to integrate the conceptual schemas of all participating systems into one schema. However, in either approach, the entire conceptual schema of a system needs be modelled. After the semantic differences are resolved, that is, when we know how the real world counterparts of the application objects are related, the syntax of various attributes of the application objects can be defined by using a standard interface definition language[14]. While only a part of the entire schema of each application is visible to other systems, the mammoth and complex task of modelling the entire schema needs be carried out before the application objects can be defined in the infrastructure, say, in the form of interface and implementation repositories.

3.4.4   Three Classes of Differences

We have already discussed that the main problem of application integration is that the same piece of reality may be modelled in different ways in different application, and the process of schema integration has the objective of linking the semantically related objects in spite of differences in their representation. In this section, we have investigated these three types of differences in representation:

- technological differences ie *differences in the hardware and the system software*

- syntactic differences ie *differences in the syntax or the language*

- semantic differences ie *differences in usage of the same language.*

The technological differences among the applications to be integrated are, for example, differences in hardware, system software - such as operating systems,

---

[14] Interfaces can be defined by using IDL (Interface Definition Language) for OMG's CORBA or Microsoft's DCOM (Distributed COM).
   [Object Management Group & X-Open (1991), *The Common Object Request Broker: Architecture & Specification*, OMG Document Number 91.12.1, Revision 1.1]

communication systems, DBMSs, communication protocols, data representation like ASCII or EBCDIC formats, number of bits and boundary alignments in words/bytes etc. Solutions are now available to resolve technological heterogeneities, standard formats and protocols have been established between different hardware and software platforms. Several commercial distributed DBMSs (Data Base Management Systems) can now run in heterogeneous hardware and system software environments. As solutions exist for resolving technological differences, we shall not discuss these differences any more in this thesis.

Syntactic differences are differences in syntaxes or languages used in various systems. For example, there could be impedance mismatch[15] between declarative and procedural languages - some systems may use procedural language like COBOL, while another system may use non-procedural language like SQL, even SQL used in different databases could have different requirements for syntax. However, by enforcing compliance to some standard protocols and standard APIs [e.g. Open Database Connectivity (ODBC)], each participating application can send messages in a standard syntax, and receive messages by translating from a standard syntax to its own syntax.

Semantic differences include differences in terms of representing the same data-item with different names, having different data-items with the same name, expressing different configurations in terms of relationships with other data-items. Unlike technological and syntactic differences, semantic differences cannot be resolved by use of standard syntax and protocols. The export context ie the meaning of the data provided by a data source may be different from the import context or the requirements of the data receiver[16]. The receiving system often cannot understand the messages without any information on how the information in the message is related to other information maintained by the sending system, and how all related information are organised in the sending system. or in other words the receiving system needs understand the meaning of a part of the conceptual schema of sending system. Neither standard protocols nor the open distributed processing standards can help reconcile the semantic differences, because the same standard syntaxes can be used to represent different interpretations[17]. While integrating applications, we may find exactly

---

[15] Impedance mismatch means differences in number of records accessed at a time, COBOL accesses one record at a time, while SQL selects a set of records.
[16] Siegel M. and Madnick S.E.(1991), Context Interchange: Sharing the Meaning of Data, *ACM SIGMOD Record*, Vol.20, No.4, pp 77-78.
[17] 'The *syntax* of a programming language describes the correct form in which programs may be written while the *semantics* denotes the meaning that may be attached to the various syntactic constructs.'
    Wilson L.B., and Clark R.G.(1988), *Comparative Programming Languages*. U.K.; Addison-Wesley Publishing Company, pp 11-13

the same syntactic constructs in two applications, but they may not always represent the same fact. Similarly, we may find different syntactic constructs in two applications, when they represent the same fact.

The syntactic structure of a conceptual schema indicates the way the application objects are related to each other. This structure indicates how the objects are grouped together and identifies their relationships. However, the final meaning associated with the structure is not so easily realised, without the knowledge about the context of each conceptual schema and general background knowledge about the world.

One example of semantic difference in intension is the data item SALARY used in various systems, for example when this item is used for Packaged Salary, it includes all fringe benefits, and otherwise fringe benefits are excluded. If we examine the context of the person earning this SALARY, it would be clear how the earnings and deductions need be computed. Similarly, the term Fare Price used by different travel agents may or may not include airport tax and hence cannot be compared against each other. The stock price at a stock exchange may be expressed in a particular currency and at a specified status of the stock price, e.g. the latest closing price or the latest nominal price. Again, if we check the context of the involved share exchange, these differences can be explained. On the other hand, the data items CUSTOMER and CLIENT could be synonyms, though appear to be different data items.

Even when there is no semantic difference in intension, there could be differences in the extension. The database involving two applications can be specified with the identical schemas, but the real world objects represented in these schemas could be different. For example one application could maintain the information about the population of Melbourne in Australia, while another application may maintain the information about the population of New York in USA; the data maintained in the database for the year 1988 may not be same as the data maintained in the database for the year 1998. Again, the particulars of the same real world person - say Alan Border, could be represented in different schemas for different banks. The details of Alan Border, maintained in various bank schemas, would be extensionally similar, in spite of differences in intensions.

Syntactic compatibility can be achieved by matching the syntaxes of the messages exchanged (say by matching QUEL and SQL or different versions of SQL for CODASYL models and relational models, by reconciling mismatches in syntaxes - types, formats, units, and granularity between each pair of systems). For syntactic compatibility, we also need a canonical data model that can be used to translate to/from any other data model. Semantic compatibility can be achieved only after syntactic compatibility is established to make all the participating systems appear homogeneous. However, to resolve semantic differences application-level knowledge about the context of using the objects in various applications is required.

3.4.5 The Inter-operations Amongst Applications

When syntactic differences are resolved, we may consider that all the applications and the underlying data stores are in homogeneous environments. Then, the inter-operations among the applications can be planned in one of the following ways:

(a) interfaces between each pair of applications,

(b) one integrating application replacing all isolated ones,

(c) one new central application acting as intermediary between any two applications.

We may check these three options in context of the sample banking problem, discussed earlier in the previous chapter. In (a), update anomalies and inconsistencies are controlled between each pair of applications/databases, ie each participant in a pair has the responsibility of checking that the information integrity is maintained before and after the updates and also the responsibility of propagating updates to all other involved databases. If the updates be propagated at different times, the information will be inconsistent in the total complex; this means - the objects would be maintained in the respective application systems in such a way that they would not always provide the same responses to the same query. An application object, which is extensionally equivalent at one point of time to its counterpart in the other application, would not remain semantically equivalent at all times.

In (b), data-items represented in individual applications are modelled into one single application, so there is no need for propagating updates to all other involved applications. But the design of a single integrating system is a mammoth task, because the semantics of each individual application has to be modelled into it. Even if such a complex application could be constructed, the users of individual applications will miss their original applications, because the substituting application is likely to change the mode of working of individual applications.

In (c), the identities of individual applications are maintained, while each application gets, via the intermediary application, an extra window through which it can view public parts of other applications. This central intermediary application needs to ensure consistency between all isolated applications, and it needs to understand each of the underlying applications.

Considering the possibilities of inconsistencies and difficulties in propagating updates to all involved applications in (a), and the complexity of the integrating model in (b), we find the approach (c) as the practicable and reliable solution. However, the central application needs to have both syntactic and semantic compatibility with each of the individual applications.

We have already discussed in the chapter of introduction that, this intermediary application needs to have information about all items, each application is prepared to exchange with other applications, and specifications of those items for receiving applications.

The main problems identified for this thesis are:

1) What objects from individual applications need necessarily be selected into the schema of the integrating intermediary application to provide sufficient application integration,

2) Modelling of these objects from individual applications, so that they can be adequately linked in the integrating application, in spite of their differences in design specifications.

3.5   *Past Attempts To Solve Schema Conflicts*

Most of the architectures, so far proposed for integrating applications, required an understanding of the semantics of the entire application. This not only increases the complexity of the global model in geometric proportion, but also adds Titanic dimensions to the project, involving multiple functions, resources and disciplines, where managers of individual applications can comprehend only a part of it.

As discussed in the last section, these architectures can be classified as follows:

(a) interfaces between each pair of applications [Chapter-4]

- superdatabases gluing together a pair of databases[18]

- federated database architecture[19]

(b) one integrating application replacing all applications[Chapter-4]

---

[18] Pu C.(1988), Superdatabases for Composition of Heterogeneous Databases, *IEEE 1988 Data Engineering Confference*, pp 548-555.
[19] Heimbigner D., & McLeod D.(1985), A Federated Architecture For Information Management, *ACM Transactions on Office Information Systems*

- logically centralised schema e.g. Multibase, ADDS etc.[20]

(c) <u>a central application intermediating between applications</u>[Chapter-4]

- distributed conceptual schema e.g. Papazoglou's DOODMS[21]

3.6   Problem Of Schema Integration Still Persists

We have seen, in the previous section, that the research for integrating applications of one enterprise can be classified by the way the individual applications are interfaced with other applications. Another way of classifying the research work on integration of disparate application systems can be based on the scale of their operations , as follows:

- integrating two application systems of an organisation, by comparing and matching their schemas, and relating the equivalent objects/entities,

- setting up an organisation-wide integration architecture, where all constituent applications build interfaces using one canonical data model and data manipulation language - so that they appear homogeneous to one another via their interfaces,

- setting up an infrastructure, using CORBA or similar standards, where any participating application needs to comply with the rules for traders or object-request-brokers.

We are still far from the days, when we would have an infrastructure to assemble application systems by using off-the-shelf objects with well-defined interfaces. Applications built under the conditions, prevailing now, need lot of efforts to ensure compliance to the standards like CORBA. Semantics of the data items still need be understood first and the differences in data structures of the same information represented differently on different application bases must be reconciled, before the interfaces can be defined to comply with the infrastructural standards. Until we reach that stage when all participating applications use objects that have standard meaning and standard interfaces, we cannot take advantage of the infrastructural standards like CORBA. The most fundamental problem of schema integration still remains that the same fact can be modelled in many different ways. The same real world can be represented by different modelling structures; depending on how the

---

[20] Breitbart Y. (1990), Multidatabase Interoperability, *SIGMOD Record*, Vol.19, No.3, pp 53-60.

[21] Marinos L., Papazoglou M.P., & Norrie M.(1988), Towards the Design of an Integrated Environment for Distributed Databases, *Parallel Processing and Applications*. North-Holland; Elsevier Science Publishers B.V., pp 283-288.

designer views a phenomenon, it can be modelled as an object type, an attribute or as a set of attributes.

In the next chapter, we shall review the work done so far to solve conflicts among applications with an objective of integrating them.

Papazoglou M.P., & Marinos L.(1990), An Object-Oriented Approach To Distributed Data Management, *Journal Of Systems and Software*, Vol.11, No.2, pp 95-109.

4. REVIEW OF WORK DONE TO INTEGRATE APPLICATIONS

4.1 Introduction

Unlike most other research projects, this project on application integration embraces a wide variety of technological areas and attempts to integrate the knowledge available from heterogeneous domains to achieve the goals of integrating disparate applications. While it is not needed to know everything of various domains of knowledge, it is important to identify the specific information of every domain that matters.

As a wide spectrum of literature had to be scanned, only the essential information that matters for decisions in this project are included in this chapter, while the broad contexts of the terms used in this chapter have been provided in the appendices as follows:

Appendix - IX	Data Replication In Distributed Databases
Appendix - X	Object Oriented Databases
Appendix - XI	Object-Oriented Languages: Eiffel vs C++

In this chapter we shall review various research activities on integration of isolated applications since mid 1970s - where the main aim is to relate the semantically similar objects in the participating applications so that they can inter-operate, and work together as an integrated system.

The scales of operations of these research activities are as follows:

- a limited number of applications, within an organisation or across organisations, where the application schemas are compared to find the matching items and then to link these matching items together,
- an architecture, where all component applications build interfaces using one canonical data model and data manipulation language - so that they appear homogeneous via their interfaces
- setting up an infrastructure, using CORBA or similar standards, where any participating application follows the discipline to comply with the rules for exchanging information with other applications.

The research activities for small-scale integration, infrastructural integration, and reference architectures will be first reviewed in this chapter, and then we shall discuss on current research activities.

In the sections for *Small-Scale Integration*, we shall review a few selected architectures for integrating a limited number of databases within an organisation or across organisations.

In the sections for *Infrastructural Integration*, we shall review Open Distributed Processing (ODP), Common Object Request Broker Architecture (CORBA), and synergies in various developments of ORBs and ODBMSs.

In the sections for *Reference Architecures*, we shall review a reference model for object-oriented distributed systems, and a reference architecture for schema integration proposed by Sheth and Larson.

In the sections for *Current Research Activities*, we shall review *Classification of Semantic Conflicts* as shown by Naiman and Ouksel, *Unifying Semantic Models* proposed by Sudha Ram *for Intelligent Database Design*, *Integrity Merging in an O-O Federated Database Environment* as carried out by Alzaharani R.M. et al, *Integration of Heterogeneous Information Systems using CORBA* as proposed by J.M. Perez, *Autonomous Heterogeneous Information* System: DIME, Mah P.S. and Shin G' s proposal for *Schema Integration for Heterogeneous Distributed Databases*, Dogac A.'s proposal for *A Multidatabase System Implementation on CORBA*, *A Combination of Java Applets & CORBA for Multi-user Distributed Applications*, Cho and Wuthrich's way of combining the information available in the component databases to make decisions instead of getting the same information from the integrated database, *Heterogeneous Interoperable Mediators and Parallel Architecture(HIMPAR)* implemented by Pires P.F. and Mattoso M.L.Q. and Karunaratna's proposal for *Establishing a Knowledge Base to Assist Integration of Heterogeneous Databases*.

In the next sections we shall review the integration techniques, that has been used for small-scale integration of applications involving one organisation or few organisations, which will be followed by review of infrastructural integration that can be applied for lage-scale integration and then current research activities in this area.

4.2 Small Scale Integration

Below we shall consider some of the techniques used to integrate a limited number of applications, within an organisation or across organisations. These are: (1) Superdatabases, (2) Federated Database Architecture, (3) Logically Centralised Schema, and (4) Distributed Conceptual Schema. Then we shall conclude this section by reviewing major features of these techniques/architectures.

4.2.1 Superdatabases

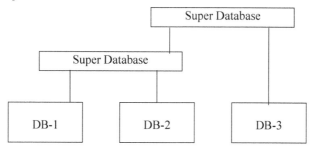

Figure 4.1 The Structure of Superdatabase

Superdatabases show one way of linking databases of applications to be integrated. Application databases need to comply with the rules of the superdatabase, so that they can be composed into the superdatabase, while the superdatabase ensures consistency of updates across the database. In other words, superdatabases ensure that the semantically equivalent objects of the applications being integrated, are maintained in such a way that they always provide the same responses, so that these objects are not only equivalent at a point of time but at any time. Superdatabases link the application's databases to ensure that semantic equivalence of the involved databases is maintained. Two or more databases are composed into a superdatabase[22], which in turn can be treated as an element database for getting composed into a bigger superdatabase. Superdatabases are designed to compose and extend databases, to ensure consistent update across heterogeneous databases.

The element databases that can be integrated into a superdatabase need to satisfy the Composability Conditions, which are

(1) The Interface to the Superdatabase must be declarative and independent of particular implementation. It should be general enough to allow composition of heterogeneous databases and simple enough to minimise adaptation.

(2) To guarantee crash recovery, the element database must understand some kind of agreement protocol, for example, two-phase commit. This requirement is a consequence of distributed control, not of heterogeneity. A transaction of the integrated application, spanning several element databases is termed a *supertransaction*, while the local transaction, participating in a super-transaction, on each element database is called a *subtransaction*. Unless an element database runs strict two-phase commit protocol, there could be only one subtransaction per element database for each super-transaction.

The usual model of a distributed transaction contains a coordinator and a set of sub-transactions. Each sub-transaction maintains its local undo/redo information. The coordinator organises some kind of agreement with subtransactions to reach a uniform decision for committing a transaction. The two-phase commit protocol is most commonly used. In phase one, the coordinator sends the Message "Prepare To Commit" to the subtransactions which respond with votes "yes" or "no". If all votes are "yes", the coordinator enters the phase two and send the message "committed" to all subtransactions. Otherwise the coordinator decides to abort and sends "aborted" to all subtransactions.

(3) To ensure concurrency control, the element database must present an explicit serial ordering of its local transactions. As all major concurrency control methods (two-phase locking, timestamps, and optimistic concurrency control) provide an easy way to capture the serial order, this requirement may not call for excessive modification in the element database. If the element databases maintain serializability of local transactions, the superdatabase has to maintain global serilizability, based on the information of local serial order.

For consistent updates, the element databases must satisfy the above requirements, where an element database may be centralised, distributed, or even another superdatabase. Unfortunately, most distributed databases do not supply the transaction serial order and most centralised databases do not support any kind of agreement protocol. Consequently, these databases need to be modified to have the transaction serial order so that they become composable elements for a superdatabase. Such modifications will ensure extensibility and accommodation of heterogeneity.

The design goals for the superdatabase that glue the composable elements together are:

- composition of element databases with many kinds of crash recovery methods,
- composition of element databases with many kinds of concurrency control techniques,
- recursive composability, i.e., the super-database must satisfy the requirements of an element database.

---

[22] Pu C.(1988), Superdatabases for Composition of Heterogeneous Databases, *IEEE 1988 Data Engineering Conference*, pp 548-555.

The first goal needs only an agreement protocol for crash recovery. The second goal uses the explicit serial ordering of transactions to ensure concurrency control. The third goal requires careful design of the agreement protocol and explicit passing of the serial order.

The superdatabase itself does not contain data, which are stored in element databases. However, it needs to maintain the information to recover from crashes and needs to serialise supertransactions. Therefore, the schema integration is not carried out in the superdatabases, the emphasis is on concurrency control and recovery.

Later, in this thesis, when we would consider having a central integrating application, we would check that the central application co-ordinates the concurrency control techniques of the underlying applications to ensure that semantic compatibility and integrity are maintained.

4.2.2 *Federated Database Architecture*

The main idea behind the Federated Database Architecture is a federation or association of autonomous applications, who would share a list of semantically related data items. Any number of application databases can make a federated database[23], when a federal dictionary is available to support the establishment, maintenance and termination of the federation of those autonomous application databases.

Three schemas are associated with an application database: the private schema, the export schema and the import schema.

The Private Schema describes that portion of the application's data that is local to (stored at) the application. In addition to the application specific data, the private schema contains a small collection of information and transaction relevant to the application's participation in the federation. This information is exported by the application for use by other applications, particularly the federal dictionary.

The federation specific information falls into three categories:

(1) descriptive information about the application, such as the application name and network address;

(2) the primitive operations for data manipulation, such as accessing a type and traversing a map;

(3) the export and import schemas.

---

[23] Heimbigner D., & McLeod D. (1985), A Federated Architecture For Information Management, *ACM Transactions on Office Information Systems, July 1985*

The export schema consists of a collection of types and maps denoting the information, which are semantically related to the information maintained by other application databases and hence can be exported to other applications.

The import schema of an application specifies the information that the application desires to use from other applications. Both application-specific and federation-specific information is specified by a schema derived from the corresponding portions of the export schemas of other applications. An imported type or map has the same properties as an exported type, except that it has no access list and no connection list. In addition, each imported element (type or map) has a derived definition property, specifying how the imported element is derived.

Schema importation is the fundamental information-sharing operation in a federation. The term "importation" refers to the process of gaining access to some elements exported by other applications to suit the specification of its import schema. Before an application enters a federation, it imports nothing. As it enters the federation, it imports built-in information that is enough for functioning within the federation. This level of importation is automatic. Beyond this, all importation of information is at the discretion of the application itself and must be negotiated with the other application.

In order to import information, each application must know or find out what information is available in the federation. This is accomplished in two steps. First, through the federal dictionary each application may discover the names and network addresses of the other applications. Second, each application contacts those applications, using a predefined protocol. At this point an application is in a position to peruse the export schemas of other applications and engage in the schema importation process by negotiation with the exporting application.

Once the schema ie type or map is imported, all subsequent accesses to the contents of the type are carried out directly, without the overhead of negotiation. The actual data transfers occur when the importer attempts to scan the contents of the type. This is exactly same as for a local type except that the data is transferred over a network.

4.2.3 Logically Centralised Schema

If the participating applications are merged into one application, with the logically centralised schema, then the set of semantically equivalent objects across applications is designed as one object only. A logically centralised schema, used by a multidatabase system, is characterised by the following data abstraction architecture[24] :

1. *The global schema* comprises all logical data structure elements resulting from the abstraction and integration process performed on the local database schemata. It presents an integrated view of the distributed database irrespective of the fragmentation, allocation and heterogeneity, if any.

2. *The user schemata* corresponds to the concept of the external schema of the ANSI/SPARC architecture. These schemata comprise all the user view and snapshot definitions.

3. *The local schemata* represents the logical data structures of the underlying local databases to be integrated.

4. *The auxiliary schemata* comprises mapping rules, quantitative and other information supporting multidatabase processing functions to control all other schemata.

In the majority of multidatabase systems the global schema is replicated in all sites of a computer network. This fact and the need to access data residing in distinct, geographically distributed databases creates new problems in the area of database administration and design.

The functional layering of the network of heterogeneous DBMSs consist of three sub-layers:

- the global data manager, or GDM, is the top-most sub-layer that provides services directly to the end users
- the distributed transaction manager, or DTM, is the middle sub-layer that supports the services of GDM, and requires the services of the structured data transfer
- the structured data transfer protocols, or SDTP, is the lower sub-layer that supports the services of the DTM, and requires the services of the file transfer protocol, data presentation protocol, and network inter-process communication protocol.

The Global Data Manager (GDM) of a distributed DBMS performs both the mappings between the global unified view of the data and the local DBMSs, and all relevant I/O operations. If a query or transaction is for an individual DBMS, then it is translated into the local query language and passed to the DTM. If a query or transaction requires integrated, multi-DBMS access, then GDM transforms it into a collection of subqueries or subtransactions, each in a format acceptable to one of the local DBMSs and passes on to the

---

[24] Breitbart Y. (1990), Multidatabase Interoperability, *SIGMOD Record*, Vol.19, No.3, September 1990, pp 53-60.

DBMSs via DTM. When results are returned, the GDM assembles the individual results to produce the answer to the original query.

Functions of the GDM are: (1) global data model analysis, (2) query decomposition, (3) query translation, (4) execution plan generation, and (5) results integration. The global data model is central to functions of the GDM. It provides the global schema, the basis for both the distributed DBMS users' view of the data and the unified data accessing language.

Application integration using the logically centralised schema can be considered as the basis of evaluating the results of application integration using other methods. One major goal of application integration is to create the illusion that the component applications are not disparate systems, but they belong to one system. This method using the logically centralised schema aims to create one integrated application.

4.2.4 *Distributed Conceptual Schema*

In contrast to the Logically Centralised Schema, the distributed object-oriented data management system (DOODMS), proposed by Papazoglou and Marinos[25], aims to build a schema that is distributed over the nodes of the component systems. It maps the data and processing resources of the entire heterogeneous system into a single system-wide object. The unifying o-o data model is termed the distributed object data model (DODM).

Such a unifying view consists of a Distributed Conceptual Schema (DCS) and mappings from its objects to corresponding objects in the conceptual schemas of the underlying component databases. A DCS is virtual schema for which there does not exist any corresponding physical database; rather it provides mapping specifications to define how the distributed conceptual schema is derived from the individual conceptual schemas maintained by the component data bases.

The DCS, defined only once at the pre-integration phase, resides in each individual database site and is operated upon by the DOODMS. All changes pertaining to the DCS are made locally and are propagated by DOODMS to all the sites in the system. A DCS is free to change its logical structure without affecting the structure of its component schemas. This architecture is *semi-decentralised* as changes in DCS is not controlled by any central site.

---

[25] Marinos L., Papazoglou M.P., & Norrie M. (1988), Towards the Design of an Integrated Environment for Distributed Databases, *Parallel Processing and Applications, Elsevier Science Publishers B.V. (North-Holland), 1988*, pp 283-288.
Papazoglou M.P., & Marinos L. (1990), An Object-Oriented Approach To Distributed Data Management, *Journal Of Systems and Software*, Vol.11, No.2, Feb'90, pp 95-109.

For the same reason, local information systems participate only in a loosely coupled association in order to share and exchange semantically related information.

Unlike in Multibase, where users are forced to use a common query language and a global schema, users of the semi-decentralised architecture have the option of using either the query language available at their own site and view the composite database in terms of the locally supported data models or alternatively use the high-level query language for this purpose. Two layers have been proposed in the high-level query language (termed as the system data language):

- the o-o application layer - used by end-users when interacting with the composite system, and
- the interlanguage transformation layer which maps system data language constructs into equivalent ones supported by the local database system.

The front-end extensions, which appropriately enhance the operational features of the existing component DBMS, consist of the following interface modules:

1. The system language components, ie the system language server and the inter-language transformer,

2. The meta-data modules which provide information concerning the distributed application, needed for a conflict-free analysis of the DCS into its constituent objects and properties.

3. The global transaction module which is responsible for the issues of query decomposition and execution plan generation as well as for global concurrency control and recovery.

The DOODMS resides in each site and is sensitive only to global requests, having not to deal with the user actions that are strictly performed locally.

4.2.5 *Summary Of The Small-Scale Integration Architectures*

Out of the four architectures described above, Superdatabase and Federated Architecture do not provide adequate plans for integration of local database schemas, while Multidatabase and Distributed Conceptual Schema approaches attempt to keep track of semantics of all data items in the distributed complex.

A **superdatabase** is similar to a parent coordinating inter-actions between two or more child databases. Superdatabase is suitable mainly for gluing together a number of component databases to ensure concurrency control and recovery (CCR). Though this concept of CCR will be considered in the architecture proposed here, the architecture of Superdatabase is not better than adhoc interfaces between local databases.

Federation is like a trading agency, where any member database has access to the list of data-items available from other databases. Each member database makes its own arrangement to access the data-items. The federated database architecture does not make any attempt to understand the private part of the local databases, but it keeps almost no control on consistency of the databases; each site is responsible for maintaining consistency and avoiding update anomalies.

Logically centralised schema is the result of combining all constituent child databases into one database, where individual databases lose their identities for the identity of the centralised database.

Distributed conceptual schema consists in developing a parent object for each of the child databases, where a parent object knows every detail of its underlying child database; these parent objects interact with one another.

In the logically centralised schema architecture like Multibase, complete tracking is carried out by the global schema; in distributed conceptual schema approach a part of this task is delegated to local DBMSs. Both these approaches involve considerable efforts in understanding the semantics of the whole complex.

Superdatabase proposes synchronous communication among element databases, the other three architectures propose to use asynchronous communication throughout the distributed complex.

In Superdatabase and Federated Architectures, a constituent database accesses data-items directly from another participating database, without caring how these data-items could be fitted together in an integrated schema. Logically Centralised Schema and Distributed Conceptual Schema architectures attempt to keep track of semantics of all data items in the distributed complex. In the logically centralised schema architecture like Multibase, complete tracking is carried out by the global schema; in the distributed conceptual schema approach, a part of this task is delegated to local DBMSs.

The implementation details of architecture of Distributed Conceptual Schema (DCS) is conceived as follows:

- A DCS can be implemented as a set of Local Conceptual Schemas (LCS), each of which is represented as an object on top of a local database, this means that each LCS is different from the others, as it has to map to and from a different local database.

- Distributed Object-Oriented Data Management System (DOODMS) deals with LCSs as its objects, while DODM (Distributed Object Oriented Data Model) is the view of these objects to this application ie DOODMS.

- End-users, at any site, can be given options to invoke the local application or the object-oriented application - DOODMS.

The DCS architecture has an advantage of scales over Multibase architecture in developing the DOODMS. Each DCS has to map the only local database to an object, participating in the DOODMS, while global schema in Multibase needs to have mapping information about all databases.

An architecture can be conceived that draws from the strong points of these four approaches. The architecture of Distributed Conceptual Schema is less expensive to implement than Logically Centralised Schema, as no global schema needs be developed. The complexity of design can be scaled down even further by using the concepts of export and import schemas[26] of the federated architecture, as in most cases only a small fraction of the database is revealed to other databases. If only the public part of local databases are brought under a global system of control, the complexity of distributed schema can be scaled down by the factor of (number of data elements in the export features of a database / number of data elements in the local database). To provide flexibility and modularity to the global schema, the global system can be conceived of as a collection of objects, participating in an application system. This architecture also maps quite well the organisation of tasks in the business. Each object may correspond to a real world manager - if there be any change in the organisation structure, these objects can be redefined and reused to match the new organisation structure. This architecture will be discussed in detail in the Chapter 7, before that it is worthwhile to identify the various issues of a distributed object-oriented system, which is done next in the review of a reference model for object oriented distributed system.

4.3   Infrastructural Integration

Some of the current research work aim to develop an infrastructure for integration, where an individual application can become a member by compliance to certain rules. The examples are CORBA and ODP standards, described below.

4.3.1 Open Distributed Processing (ODP)

Open Distributed Processing [ODP] standards[27] provide the basic ground rules for how applications should be integrated by specifying how a group of applications can

---

[26] The export schema is the schema of the information that can be exported to other participating databases, while import schema is the schema of the information that can be imported.

[27] Poon K (1995), Inside A Trader In Global Trading, *Computer Communications*, Vol.18, No.4, April '95, pp 227-248.

communicate and coordinate the distributed information relevant to an enterprise. The ODP standards state how a consistent body of information is to be viewed and implemented. They describe how the information systems within the enterprise are to operate, keeping in view the design choices and configuration of the system components along with the processes of storage and computation, as well as points of their interconnection. The information specification of the trader is particularly important for linking semantically related objects of various applications - this specification defines the schemas and relations for the information objects such as service types, service offers, matching and selection rules for service offers, trading contexts and trading contracts.

The Reference Model of Open Distributed Processing (RM-ODP) provides a coordinating framework within which support of distribution, interworking, interoperability, and portability can be integrated. The distributed processing environment is analysed from five different viewpoints for various aspects of the system with different priorities. The viewpoints are termed Enterprise, Information, Computation, Engineering and Technology projections. Models are built to describe the different facets of the system.

The *Enterprise Viewpoint* is concerned with the overall operating environment of the ODP system, it shows how and where the ODP system is placed within the enterprise. The enterprise may be the whole of an organisation, or part of it, or may span a number of co-operating organisations. From the enterprise viewpoint, the overall objectives of an ODP system include:

- the roles and activities that exist within the enterprise using the system,
- the interactions between the system and its operating environment,
- the organisational structure of the enterprise,
- what enterprise artefacts are used in what enterprise roles,
- where various processing can be done in the enterprise,
- security and management policies of the enterprise with respect to the roles.

Standards Association Of Australia, *Reference Model For Open Distributed Processing*, ISO/IEC JTC1/SC21/WG7 N755

The enterprise viewpoint can be modelled in terms of objects representing user roles, business and management policies, the ODP system and the environment.

An ODP system in the *Information Viewpoint* is a formal system, whose behaviour is predictable and completely defined by the activities, transitions, and attributes of the enterprise from its conception to the present. The ODP system is represented in terms of information objects and their relationships, where information objects are abstractions of entities that occur in the real world, in the ODP system, or in other viewpoints. The information view of this system should be designed to provide the following items:

- a common basis for understanding the general behaviour of the enterprise,
- structures of information elements that define the information content of the enterprise,
- information flows,
- capabilities to reflect changes in the enterprise,
- quality attributes for information,
- logical partitioning of the ODP system into autonomous parts, and inference over information composed from the parts,
- convenience of the implementors operating in the computing or engineering viewpoints.

An information specification is a schema which defines the possible actions, classes of concepts, and relationships between concepts in some universe of discourse.

The *Computational Viewpoint* of the ODP standards specifies how the application designers view the open distributed systems. From this viewpoint, processing functions (instantiation, assignment, invocation, synchronisation, communication, etc) and data types are visible. From this viewpoint the structuring of applications is independent of the computers and networks on which they run. This viewpoint identifies the transparency requirements. From the computational viewpoint, no distinction is made between the processes that act on information, and containers that store information. If the enterprise has formulated distribution requirements, then this is reflected in the logical structure of the ODP systems by defining suitable interfaces. A computational specification defines in distribution transparent terms:

- the activities that occur in the management application,
- the interactions between components of the management application,
- the structuring of components for interworking and portability.

Operating systems and communication experts look at ODP systems from the *Engineering Viewpoint*. Engineering Viewpoint specifications are concerned with control and transparency mechanisms, processors, memory and communication networks that together enable the distribution of programs and data. The quality of service and transparency requirements visible from the computational viewpoint are used to select the appropriate mechanisms to achieve the required form of distributed processing. An engineering specification provides the following:

- describes the organisation of an abstract infrastructure enabling the execution of the application,
- identifies the abstraction required to manage physical distribution and local system resources,
- identifies and defines the roles of different objects supporting the management application,
- identifies the reference points among different objects.

Those responsible for the configuration, installation and maintenance of the hardware and software of an ODP system look at the system from the *Technology Viewpoint*. The technical artefacts from which the ODP system is built are visible from the technology viewpoints, They include the local operating systems, storage, points of access to communications, etc. A technology specification provides the following:

- expresses the way the computational specifications of the application are implemented,
- identifies the technology relevant to the construction of the management application,
- provides a taxonomy of such specifications,
- expresses the content of statements required from the implementors of the information necessary to support testing of the system.

ODP standards include definitions for *Trading* and the *Trader*, where the trader matches requests for services with service offers based on service type compatibility. The trading function provides service information to clients, so that clients can be configured into an ODP system without prior knowledge of servers that can satisfy their requirements. Three agents are identified in the trading Universe of Discourse, that are:

- **exporter:** an agent whose role is to interact with a trading function to advertise a service offer provided at an interface,

- **importer:** an agent whose role is to interact with a trading function to obtain service offers satisfying some constraints,

- **trader:** an agent whose role is to accept service offers from exporters and respond service requests from importers governed by a trading policy.

A community comprising exporters, importers, and a trading function governed by a trading policy is called the trading policy domain. The trading federation is a community of trading policy domains established for the purpose of making the service offers of each trading policy domain available to the other trading policy domains.

Two major activities in a trading policy domain are:

- **service export:** an interaction between an exporter and a trading function in which the exporter offers a service, to be advertised through the trading function,

- **service import:** an interaction between an importer and a trading function in which the importer requests for a service from the trading function and receives a response.

The description of the functionality of the trader has been progressively formalised in ODP standards in order to provide clear conception and direction to the trader developers through the chaos of the current distributed computing environment.

From the point of view of Application Integration, the *Computational Viewpoint* of the ODP standards help locate the objects that are semantically related, irrespective of their distribution and implementation. The specifications of the trading functions help viewing the applications in terms of import and export of the services offered by the applications.

4.3.2 Common Object Request Broker Architecture (CORBA)

Common Object Request Broker Architecture (CORBA)[28] has been specified by the Object Management Group to provide interoperability between applications on different machines in heterogeneous distributed environments. If semantically related objects of the participating applications can be identified, and their interface definitions are implemented, they can interoperate using this architecture.

The basic operation of CORBA is described in this section. In the Figure 4.2, the *Client* wishes to perform an operation on the *Object Implementation*, which includes both code and data., and a request is sent by the *Client* to the *Object Implementation*. In a group of

---

[28] Object Management Group & X-Open (1991), *The Common Object Request Broker: Architecture & Specification*, OMG Document Number 91.12.1, Revision 1.1
Poon K (1995), Inside A Trader In Global Trading, *Computer Communications*, Vol.18, No.4, April '95, pp 227-248.

applications being integrated, an application can act as a *Client* to request an information, when another application can serve as the *Object Implementation* to provide the information. The Object Request Broker [ORB] provides all mechanisms required to find the object implementation that can service the request, to prepare the object implementation to receive the request, and to communicate the data making up the request. The client need not be aware of the location of the object and its programming language.

The Client can make a request by *Dynamic Invocation* or *IDL stub.* In case of dynamic invocation the client use the same interface without knowing the interface of the target object. In case of an IDL stub, the client uses the specific stub depending on the interface of the target object.

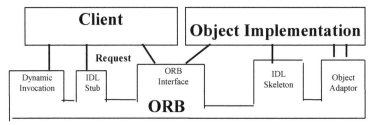

Figure 4.2 ORB receives Client's request and sends it to Object Implementation

The Object Implementation receives a request as an up-call through the IDL generated skeleton. While processing a request, the Object Implementation may need to call the Object Adaptor and the ORB.

The interfaces to objects can be defined by using the Interface Definition Language and/or the Interface Repository:

1) *Interface Definition Language (IDL)* is the language to define the interfaces in terms of the operations to be performed and parameters to these operations. An object implementation uses IDL to advertise what operations are available and how they should be invoked. From the IDL definitions, it is possible to map CORBA objects into selected programming languages.

2) *Interface Repository* provides persistent objects that represent the IDL information in a form available at runtime. Interfaces can be added to an Interface Repository service, whether or not the interface has been defined by using the IDL. Using the information in the Interface Repository, it is possible to encounter an object whose interface was not known when the program was compiled, yet, be able to determine what operations are valid on the object and make an invocation on it.

When the client has access to an Object Reference for an object and knows the type of the object and the desired operation to be performed, it can perform a request for it. The client initiates the request by calling stub routines that are specific to the object or by constructing the request dynamically. Whether invoked by dynamic invocation or IDL stub, a request satisfy the same request semantics, and these two ways of invoking requests make no difference to the Object Implementation that receives the message.

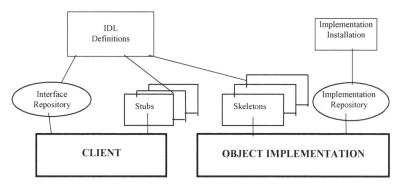

Figure 4.3 Interface and Implementation Repositories

The ORB locates the appropriate Object Implementation, transmits parameters and transfers control to it through an IDL skeleton, which is specific to the interface and the object adaptor. In performing the request, the object implementation may obtain some services from the ORB; depending on the kind of services required from ORB, the Object Implementation may use some Object Adaptor. When the request is complete, control and output values are returned to the client.

Figure 4.3 shows how interface and implementation information is made available to clients and object implementations. The interface is defined in IDL and/or in the Interface Repository; the definition is used to generate the client Stubs and object implementation Skeletons.

The Object Implementation information is provided at the installation time and is stored in the Interface Repository for use during delivery.

In the architecture, the ORB is not required to be implemented as a single component, but rather it is defined by its interfaces. Any ORB implementation that provides the appropriate interface is acceptable. The interface is organised into three categories:

- those operations that are the same for all ORB implementations,
- those operations that are specific to particular types of objects, and
- those operations that are specific to particular styles of object implementations.

Different ORBs may be implemented differently, having different sets of IDL compilers, repositories and Object Adaptors. They may provide a set of services to clients and implementations of objects that have different properties and qualities

There may be multiple ORB implementations, which have different representations for object references and different means of performing invocations. It may be possible for a client to simultaneously have access to two object references managed by different ORB implementations. When two ORBs are intended to work together, those ORBs must be able to distinguish their object references. It is not the responsibility of the client to do so.

The ORB Core is that part of the ORB that provides the basic representation of objects and communication of requests. CORBA is designed to support different object mechanisms, and it does so by structuring the ORB with components above the ORB Core, which provide interfaces that can mask the differences between ORB Cores.

To sum up, in CORBA, clients ask for work to be done and servers do that work, all in terms of tasks called operations that are performed on entities called objects. Applications interact with one another without knowing where the other applications are and how the tasks are accomplished. By using CORBA's model, it is possible to encapsulate applications as a set of distributed objects so that one can plug and unplug those client and server capabilities as they need to be added or replaced in a distributed system. These properties provide the capabilities to handle heterogeneity at the database level. Thus, CORBA provides an infrastructure for implementing a multidatabase system. Semantic interoperability, however, remains to be solved at the application programming level.

4.3.3 Synergies In Various Developments of ORBs and ODBMS

The ORBs (Object Request Brokers) and ODBMSs (Object-oriented DataBase Management Systems) are found to resolve each other's deficiencies rather than creating a redundancy, as M.Reddy[29] observed. Some of the added features made possible by using an ODBMS in conjunction with an ORB are as follows:

---

[29] Reddy M. (1995), *ORBs & ODBMSs: Two Complimentary Ways To distribute Objects*, Object Magazine, Vol.5, No.3, June 1995, PP 24-30,55

Complimentary Data Transfer Mechanism:

From the perspective of an object client, we note that:

    1. In case of an ORB, the data accompanying the request is transferred from the client address space to the object implementation address space.

    2. In case of an ODBMS, the data is transferred from persistent storage to the server address space and from the server address space to the client address space.

    A real-world application demands both these data transfer techniques. Some applications have millions of fine-grained objects; for these applications an ODBMS is the ideal solution because of its inherent capability of providing high-performance, fine-grained persistence. On the other hand, there are lots of situations where it is faster and more convenient to transmit the request from the client to the object; for example a large resource-intensive object capable of running only on powerful machines.

Uniform Treatment Of Persistent And Transient Objects:

In an ODBMS, there are certain operations that can be performed on persistent objects but cannot be performed on transient objects. CORBA has specified a number of services that by definition can be applied to all ORB objects, transient or persistent. So, by using an object database and an ORB together, it is possible to implement an object system where persistent and transient objects can be treated uniformly.

Management Of Both Code And Data:

Given that an object by definition has both state and behaviour, it is obvious that an ORB and an object database used in conjunction can provide a programmer with all the tools needed for the 'complete' object.

Object Interface To Legacy Systems:

By defining a standard interface for object databases in IDL, it will be possible for multiple vendors to provide implementations of these interfaces on a variety of repositories. This will provide a portable way to bring object technology to non-object databases.

4.3.4 Enterprise Application Integration (EAI) Using XML

XML (Extensible Markup Language) is seen by many as merely a presentation standard; it has however the characteristics which may make Enterprise Application Integration (EAI) much easier: 'it is completely open, being under the auspices of the World Wide Web

Consortium, and it separates a document's content from its schema, and both from its presentation'[30].

EAI aims to make one or more disparate applications act as one single application. 'This is a complex task that requires that data to be replicated and distributed to the right system at the right time. For example, when integrating accounting and sales systems, it may be necessary for the sales system to send sales orders to the accounting system to generate invoices. Furthermore, the accounting system must send invoice data into the sales system to update the sales representatives. If done correctly, a single sales transaction will generate the sales order and the invoice automatically, thus eliminating the potentially erroneous manual re-entry of data.' [31]

Some of the methods to accomplish EAI are made easier by use of XML. When integrating applications using messaging, the message formats must be agreed upon by the involved applications. Since two disparate applications are not likely to use similar data structures, interim format capable of handling semi-structured data is needed. XML can make it possible for EAI to easily represent semi-structured data.

XML consists of three important components: an application capable of generating XML-compliant documents, a parser to interpret these documents, and the documents themselves.

XML documents are markedly different from HTML (Hypertext Markup Language). In an HTML document the structure is inseparable from the content - tags scattered throughout the text impose both presentation characteristics and the structure like forms, frames, links to other files and so on. In XML, these components are separated, with document type definition (DTD) carrying the structure and extensible style sheets (XSL) providing the presentation information.

Also XML provides the advantages of its compatibility with Java technology. Because the Java platform supports connectivity to a diverse set of middleware services, such as databases, transaction processing monitors, asynchronous messaging systems, and object request brokers, it makes an excellent tool for developing EAI applications. XML lets developers represent Java object data as it travels in and out of the Java virtual machine and across non-Java technology -based middleware.

---

[30] Chirgwin Richard (1999), *Greater Than The Sum Of Its Parts,* Systems - Enterprise Computing Monthly, July 1999, pp 32-40
[31] Morgenthal J.P, Portable Data / Portable Code: XML & Java Technologies, *The Source for Java Technology; http://java.sun.com/xml/inc;* April 1999.

4.3.5 *Summary Of Integration Infrastructure Activities*

As we have checked in the section on Open Distributed Processing standards, the *Computational Viewpoint* of the ODP standards help locate the objects that are semantically related, irrespective of their distribution and implementation. The specifications of the trading functions help viewing the applications in terms of import and export of the services offered by the applications. However, we need to identify the semantically related objects across applications, so that we can design the trading functions for them.

The XML language provides a data-centric method of moving data between Java technology and non- Java technology platforms. Since CORBA represents the method of interoperability in a process-centric manner, it is not always possible to use CORBA connectivity. In these cases the XML language helps by representing the state of Java objects as they leave and re-enter Java virtual machines.

XML and Java technologies are two most important developments for Internet computing. Whether used together or separately, these two standards help the enterprise to get their applications inter-operate with one another, and use Internet to share and exchange data. However, though XML will help implement the integrating Web application, we would still need to identify the objects of the component applications, and these objects will be involved in the mediation by the integrating Web application.

4.4   *Reference Architecures*

Some of the research activities have helped us getting reference architectures for integration, which can be used for evaluating other architectures instead of developing an architecture.

4.4.1 *A Reference Model For Object-Oriented Distributed System*

After the component applications are integrated, the integrated system will act like a distributed system, whose objects are spread over the network. We like to consider here a reference model for distributed systems. British Telecom Research Laboratory (BTRL) has developed a reference model - the Distributed System Model (DSM) to address the various concerns of a distributed object-oriented system[32]. Objectives of the distributed object-oriented system coincide with those of an integrated systems distributed over a network, in terms of:

- a common reference which could also be used for design and development of new systems, and integration of the existing systems,

- facilitation for reusing software, and this could be used to continue using features of the existing application systems,
- decoupling of system and software design from implementation technology, in order to facilitate interworking between systems and software provided by different manufacturers - this will facilitate integration inspite of technology used.

When a number of disparate applications are integrated, objects from these disparate applications interact with one another. These interactions can be viewed in terms of a few dimensions. In Appendix-XV, we have provided an introduction to the Distributed System Model and how it relates to the architecure proposed in this thesis.

4.4.2 Reference Architecture For Schema Integration

A reference architecture of Federated Database System (FDBS) has been specified by Sheth and Larson to help clarify various issues within a distributed database system. This architecture extends ANSI/SPARC three-level schema architecture to five levels to support the dimensions of distribution, heterogeneity and autonomy.

The five-level architecture of a federated database system[33] includes the following (Fig 4.4):

Local Schema: A local schema is the conceptual schema of a participating application. A local schema is represented in the data model used in the component application, and hence local schemas of different applications may be expressed in different data models.

Component Schema: Local schemas are translated into a data model called the *canonical* or *common data model* (CDM) of the FDBS to derive its component schema. Two reasons for defining component schemas in a CDM are (i) they describe the divergent local schemas using a single representation and (ii) semantics that are missing in the local schema can be added to its component schema. They facilitate negotiation and integration tasks performed when developing a tightly coupled FDBS. Similarly they facilitate negotiation and specification of views and multi-database queries in a loosely coupled FDBS.

The process of schema translation from a local schema to a component schema generates the mappings between the component schema objects and the local schema objects. Transforming processors use these mappings to transform commands on a component schema into commands on the corresponding local schema. Such transforming processors and the component schemas support an FDBS to operate in spite of its heterogeneity.

---

[32] Wright J.H., A Reference Model For Object-Oriented Distributed Systems, *British Telecom Technology Journal*, Vol-6, No-3, July 1988, pp 66-75.

[33] Sheth, A.P. and Larson, J.A. (1990), Federated Database Systems for Managing Distributed, Heterogeneous, and Autonomous Databases, *ACM Computing Surveys*, Vol. 22, No. 3, pp 183-236, September 1990.

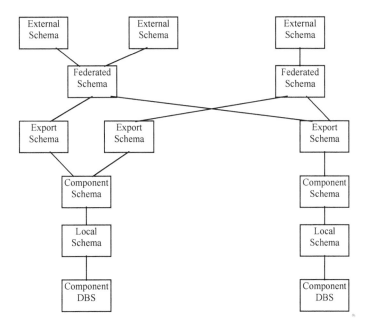

Figure 4.4 Five -level schema architecture for Federated Distributed Database

Export Schema: An export schema represents a subset of a component schema that is available to FDBS. It may include information about access allowed to specific federation users. The purpose of defining export schemas is to facilitate control and management of association autonomy. A filtering processor can be used to provide the access control as specified in an export schema by limiting the set of allowable operations that can be submitted on the correspondent schema. Such filtering processors and the export schemas support the autonomy feature of an FDBS.

Federated Schema: A federated schema is generated by integrating the export schemas. A federated schema may also include the information about how the data is distributed on the local schemas; some systems use a separate schema called a distribution schema or allocation schema to contain this information. A constructing processor transforms the commands on the federated schema into the commands that can be executed on the export schemas. Constructing processors and the federated schema support the distribution feature of an FDBS. There could be more than one federated schemas in an FDBS - one for each group of federation users and/or application programs performing a related set of activities.

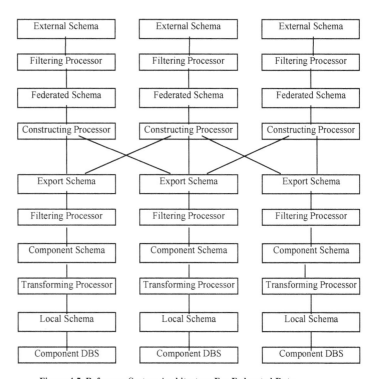

Figure 4.5 Reference System Architecture For Federated Data

External Schema: an external schema defines a schema that is used by a group of users and/or applications. Reasons for using external schemas are as follows:

- If a federated schema is complex and large, a subset of the information of the federated schema can be customised as an external schema to meet the users' needs. If an external schema is in a different data model, then a transforming processor is used to transform the commands on the external schema to the commands suitable to the federated schema.

- External schema may include integrity constraints that have not been specified in the federated schema. A filtering process analyses the commands on the external schema to ensure that they do not violate the integrity constraints of the federated schema
- External schemas may provide access control for using the data managed by the FDBS.

To facilitate integration of local and external schemas, expressed in different data models, all component, export and federated schemas are required to be expressed in the same data model. This data model is called the *canonical* or *common data model* (CDM) of the FDBS. A language associated with the CDM is called an *internal command language*. All commands on component, export and federated schemas are expressed in this internal command language. A CDM may provide a richer semantic constructs than the data models used in the local schemas; a component schema may contain more semantic information than the corresponding local schema.

FDBS schemas need to store the information on mappings, which correlate schema objects at one level with the schema objects at the next lower level. Thus there are mappings from external schemas to federated schemas, federated schemas to export schemas, export schemas to component schemas, and to component schemas to local schemas. The mappings may be stored as a part of the schema information or separate objects in the data dictionaries.

Other important features of the schema architecture are how autonomy is preserved and how access control is managed at the level of component applications and the integrating application. These involve exercising control over schemas at different levels. The local, component and export schemas are controlled by the administrator of the component DBS.

One important function of the component DBA is to define the export schemas that specify the access rights of the federation users to access different objects in the component databases. A federation DBA defines and manages a federated schema and the external schemas related to the federation schema.

4.5   Current Research Activities On Schema Integration
4.5.1 Classification Of Semantic Conflicts

While the interaction among distributed information systems is facilitated by the physical connectivity, the interaction is meaningful only when the systems can identify which information needs be accessed and how this information can be interpreted within the appropriate context. As the information highways connect more and more disparate systems, information is accessed from more and more alien sources, where the conventional static recognition and resolution of semantic conflicts are not possible and dynamic navigation is required. In this open environment, it is essential to understand the different classes of semantic conflicts, so that these conflicts can be resolved. Naiman C.F. and Ouksel A.M.[34] have proposed to classify the conflicts along the dimensions of *naming, abstraction* and *level of heterogeneity* to facilitate systematic interpretations of conflicts during the process of reconciliation.

In the lines of Naiman and Ouksel, we have reviewed in the following paragraphs, the need to classify the semantic conflicts, and to resolve the conflicts incrementally for dynamic schema integration; we have also evaluated Naiman's method of classifying semantic conflicts based on naming and abstraction, and reviewed his ideas of the schematic mapping using the level of heterogeneity.

Need For Classifying Semantic Conflicts

Semantic conflict exists when the communicating parties use different representations or interpretations of the information that is being communicated. Semantic reconciliation is a translation process that resolves the conflict and leads to correct interpretation of the information exchanged. Databases can be heterogeneous on many levels: they can have different data models or different conceptual models, meaning different representation of the same reality, different naming conventions, or different ways to organise the information. Examples of semantic conflicts are structural and representational differences, mismatched domains, and naming conflicts of the facts.

Incremental Resolution For Dynamic Schema Integration

In case of *Static Schema Integration*, semantic conflict in heterogeneous databases is resolved when all of the component database schema and relevant metadata is available. Interoperability is achieved by mapping the component database schemas to a single, global view. Eventhough the full semantic and schematic knowledge are available, the integration process follows an ordered sequence of steps, requiring only a limited knowledge in each step. The next step depends upon, and is determined by, the semantic knowledge that is available at that point; it is this semantic knowledge that provides a *context* within which reconciliation can proceed and further information can be acquired and understood. These context dependencies or *precedence relationships* are well defined in case of static reconciliation and can be pre-determined by the steps of static schema integration. There are cases when static schema integration cannot be achieved, for example, when mapping

---

[34] Naiman C.F., and Ouksel A.M. (1995), A Classification Of Semantic Conflicts In Heterogeneous Database

between the schemas cannot be done because of differences in abstraction of conceptual models for same real world objects.

In case of *Dynamic Schema Integration*, complete semantic knowledge of another database is not static, nor is always available. While the semantic conflicts are the same as those resolved using static integration, the order in which they are detected depends on the subset of full schematic and semantic knowledge available at a point. Thus, the sequence of steps in a dynamic reconciliation process cannot be pre-determined; the dynamic integrator needs the capability to dynamically build the appropriate precedence relationships, depending on the semantic knowledge acquired so far.

The changing business and technological landscape suggests that large-scale static schema integration will be more and more limited and the focus will be shifted towards the incremental discovery process of dynamic integration. The integrator should be able to use whatever semantic knowledge is available in order to determine the next question that should be asked of another information system. By properly recognising and classifying semantic conflicts as they are encountered, the integration system needs to coordinate and sequence various automatic and semi-automatic reconciliation techniques, and it can take advantage of the knowledge that each can render, thereby providing a greater degree of automation.

Desirable Features Of Classification Of Semantic Conflicts

Comprehensive understanding of semantic conflicts is required for achieving schematic mapping. However, because of differences in data models, policies and domains, often semantic integrity differences and other metadata differences are not distinguished among themselves. These may lead to improper recognition of conflicts and hence wrong treatment of fundamentally different conflicts. Also, similar semantic conflicts, such as conflicts that result from aggregation, or homonyms, for example, but occurring at different levels of schematic granularity, are not often recognised as being similar. This can result in redundant treatment of essentially similar conflicts.

Based on the examination of existing classifications, as well as the information requirement of the dynamic reconciliation process, desirable features of classification of semantic conflicts are:

- The classification must capture semantic conflicts, that is, it must capture the abstractions used to represent data in semantic modelling.

Systems, *Journal Of Organizational Computing*, 5(2), 167-193

- The classification must allow the representation of multiple semantic conflicts
- The classification must be *sound*, that is, if given a classification assertion, then there exists a semantic conflict which it represents.
- The classification must be *minimal*, that is, no classification with fewer dimensions or fewer values along the various dimensions can capture semantic conflicts.
- The classification must be *complete*, that is, if a given semantic conflict, there exists a classification assertion or a conjunction of classifications, which represent this conflict.
- The classification must be validated in its use in the dynamic reconciliation process.

Naiman's Method Of Classifying Based On Naming And Abstraction,

As per Naiman, semantic conflicts can be classified along the three dimensions of naming, abstraction, and level of heterogeneity. The semantic relationship between two elements of different databases is represented as an Inter-Schema Correspondence Assertion (ISCA), with the following general form:

Assert [x,y] (naming, abstraction, heterogeneity),

where x refers to an element in the local database schema and y refers to an element in the target database schema. This classification combines the inherent dimensions of semantic conflicts (naming and abstraction) with a structural description that provides for operational integration (level of heterogeneity).

Naming conflicts refer to the relationship between the object, attribute, or instance names. Possible naming conflicts are Synonyms, Homonyms and Unrelated. The naming relationship is commutative, ie if 'x is a synonym of y' then 'y is a synonym of x'.

Abstraction conflicts map the abstraction relationships between two schematic elements. The abstraction relationship is directed from x to y, eg 'x is a generalisation of y'. This relationship is true for all the values in the abstraction dimension except for the value 'class', which represents a commutative relationship. The possible abstraction relationships are Class, Generalization, Aggregation, and Computed Function.

Level of Heterogeneity specifies the level of schematic granularity being compared, this structural relationship is expressed by the pairs: 'object, object', 'object, attribute', 'object, instance', 'attribute, object', 'attribute, attribute', and so on.

The classification provides the criteria by which the semantic conflicts can be distinguished. It indicates the information that is still required to complete the distinction, and propels a search along the naming and abstraction dimensions. Reconciliation begins by searching the remote database on a term from the local query. If a match is not found through this exploration, the query term is expanded along the naming and abstraction dimensions, by searching local knowledge sources to find, for example, synonyms or aggregations of that term. This expanded term is then used in place of the original query term, in an effort to find a match in the remote database. When such an anchor is found, reconciliation techniques are invoked. These techniques trigger further exploration of the remote database (for example, collection of attributes or instances for comparison with local schematic elements), or they require further examination of local knowledge sources (for example, the application of expert knowledge to the newly acquired information). Any new knowledge acquired is examined in the context of previously acquired semantic knowledge; this knowledge is interpreted within the framework of the naming and abstraction dimensions to classify the semantic conflict and map the schematic discrepancy. Uncertainty triggers further exploration in an attempt to collect more naming or abstraction semantic knowledge, and thus corroborate or contradict classification assertions, based on the new evidence gathered.

The Soundness And Minimality Of Naiman's Proposal

The success of the reconciliation process depends on the adequacy of the naming and abstraction dimensions to capture the knowledge needed for the correct schematic mappings and to uniquely represent each semantic conflict that is encountered. The classification is *sound* if, given a classification assertion (naming,abstraction,level), there exists a semantic conflict which it represents. The classification is *minimal* if a semantic conflict cannot be represented with fewer dimensions. The classification provides a minimal set of primitive classes if reducing that set of classes would result in the inability to represent some semantic conflicts. The classification is *complete* if, given a semantic conflict, there exists a classification assertion (naming,abstraction,level), or a conjunction of assertions, which classifies the conflict.

The classification dimensions are shown in the matrix below; each class of conflict is coded by 'S/D' for 'Static or Dynamic', or by 'D' for 'Dynamic only'.

N

A B S T R A C T I O N

A		Class	Generalization	Aggregation	Functional Mapping
M	Synonym	(1) S/D	(2) S/D	(3) S/D	(4) S/D
I	Homonym	(5) S/D	(6) D	(7) D	(8) D
N	Unrelated	(9) S/D	(10) D	(11) S/D	(12) S/D

G

The 12 assertions, that follow, define the domain of semantic conflict in dynamic integration, which is navigated during a well-directed reconciliation process.

1. **Assert** [Id#, SS#] (synonym, class, level)

This is an assertion that Id# and SS# are synonymous terms, representing a synonymous class of elements.

2. **Assert** [Id#, SS#] (synonym, generalization, level)

This is an assertion that Id# is a generalization of SS#, that is, that a social security number is one type of identification number.

3. **Assert** [Id#, digit] (synonym, aggregation, level)

This is an assertion that the terms are synonymous, and that Id# is an aggregation of Digit.

4. **Assert** [Score, Grade] (synonym, functional mapping, level)

This is an assertion that the terms are synonymous and that there is some functional mapping between a Score and its corresponding Grade.

5. **Assert** [Id#, Id#] (homonym, class, level)

This is an assertion that the terms, while identical, refer to different classes of semantic concepts.

6. **Assert** [Id#, SS#] (homonym, generalization, level)

This is an assertion that the two terms are homonyms (they represent different semantic concepts), but their terminology is that of generalization.

7. **Assert** [Id#, digit] (homonym, aggregation, level)

This is possible if the terms themselves are found to have a possible aggregation relationship, but in context they are found to be homonyms (semantically unrelated).

8. **Assert** [Score, Grade] (homonym, functional mapping, level)

This is an assertion that a functional relationship was found between the two terms, but the terms are found to be homonyms in the context.

9. **Assert** [Book, Beer] (unrelated, class, level)

This is an assertion that the terms are terminologically unrelated, and each represents a class of objects.

10. **Assert** [Primate, Author] (unrelated, generalization, level)

Primate is a generalization of Author, but these two terms are unrelated in the context.

11. **Assert** [House, Window] (unrelated, aggregation, level)

This is an assertion that the terms are terminologically unrelated, but that an aggregation relationship exists between them.

12. **Assert** [Sales, Profit] (unrelated, functional, level)

This is an assertion that the terms are terminologically unrelated, but that functional mappings exists between them.

The last four assertions illustrate the cases where the terms are not at all related by real-world semantics, and yet they have a functional relationship, and thus a meaningful semantic mapping.

- The terms Book and Beer each represent a class of objects, which are not meaningfully related.
- Primate is certainly is a generalisation of Author, and the two terms are, technically, synonyms at the level of specialisation (an Author is a Primate, and, thus must be a synonym for that subset of Primate), However, it is unlikely that the two terms would be mapped as synonyms by most reasonable theasuruses.
- There is an aggregation relationships between the terms "house" and "window", but they are not synonyms. Both dimensions are needed to represent the correspondence of these terms and their semantic mappings.
- There may be functional mappings between Gross_Sales and Net_Profit, but they are not synonyms.

In each example of semantic conflict, the conflict cannot be represented in any other way within this classification, without introducing some semantic ambiguity. This demonstrates that the classes are disjoint. From the exhaustive analysis of the disjoint classes of semantic conflict, it is concluded that this classification is sound and minimal, in the environment of dynamic reconciliation.

The Schematic Mapping Using The Level Of Heterogeneity
The naming and abstraction dimensions describe the semantic relationships between two concepts. However, it is the third dimension, the level of heterogeneity, that places the conflict exactly into the context of the database schemas. The third dimension is a structural construct, designed to capture the semantics inherent in the structure of a schema.

The role of context in conflict identification can be illustrated by the following example:

Consider two databases having the relations:

VENDOR(Id#, Name, Address,.....)

CLIENT(C_Id#, Name, Address,.....)

In this example, the two attributes VENDOR.Id# and CLIENT.C_Id# cannot be classified as synonyms, unless we examine them in the context of their corresponding object. If

VENDOR and CLIENT are discovered to be synonymous, this provides corroboration for the assertion of synonymy between the attributes. By using upward propagation, the semantic relationship between VENDOR and CLIENT is discovered - they are both sub-class of the class COMPANY, hence synonyms within that context. Actual schematic mapping of the corresponding attributes can now be done by downward propagation, when VENDOR.Id# can be mapped against CLIENT.C_Id#. The classification, proposed by Naiman, helps the reconciliation process, not only by representing the information, but also by propelling search along the naming and abstraction dimensions, while the level of heterogeneity further directs the search through upward and downward propagation.

The metadata levels of heterogeneity are organised into the successively more general levels of *schema, data model*, and *database*. The *schema level* includes descriptive metadata about the elements of the schema. The *data model level* includes the knowledge about the entire schematic structure and the semantic relationship that can be inferred from that structure. An example of a semantic relationship that may provide knowledge to constrain or direct the reconciliation process is a foreign key or a functional dependency between two entities in a relational database. The *database level* includes information about the nature of whatever general or domain-specific knowledge is available about the domain of the organisation, as well as of the nature of the information stored in the database, irrespective of the data model used. For example, the term 'sheet' may be interpreted differently in the contexts of the steel mill and a hospital. The main purpose of organising semantic metadata into schematic, database, and data model meta data turns focus on to the discovery of the metadata that turns the focus on to the discovery of the metadata that can be useful in classifying semantic conflict.

The Naiman-Ouksel method of classification can adequately represent the range of conflicts described in other classifications. Structural discrepancy is captured in the level of heterogeneity, though it requires syntactic, not semantic investigation. Generalization, aggregation etc are covered in the naming and abstraction dimensions. Some of the conflicts, which are otherwise difficult to classify, can be simply classified in this method. Some of the examples are:

Domain Incompatibility Problems

The conflict in STUDENT(Id#, Name, Address) & TEACHER(SS#, Name, Address) can be classified by examining assertions:

Assert [STUDENT.Id#,TEACHER.SS#] (synonym, class, (attribute, attribute)) and

Assert [STUDENT,TEACHER] (synonym, class, (object,object))

Data representation conflicts for scaling, precision, default values etc can be represented by using computed function in the abstraction dimension.

Naiman C.F. and Ouksel A.M.[35] claim to have checked that all known semantic and schematic conflicts can be classified on the three dimensions of naming, abstraction, and level of heterogeneity.

4.5.2 *Unifying Semantic Model for Intelligent Database Design*

Sudha Ram[36] has prepared Unifying Semantic Model (USM) with the objective of developing an intelligent database modelling toolkit. USM is a specification of the mechanism for describing a Universe Of Discourse, and provides a basis for developing a high-level user interface to one or more databases; this can be constructed as an integrating front end in a heterogeneous database environment, thereby facilitating the process of identifying and retrieving relevant information from the databases of underlying applications.

As per Sudha Ram, a semantic model essentially defines objects, relationships among objects, and properties of objects. Semantic modelling provides a number of mechanisms for viewing and accessing the schema at different levels of abstractions. The USM is based on the abstractions of classification, generalization, aggregation, and association. In particular, it proposes concepts to represent constraints on relationships between subclasses; it also distinguishes between the concepts of Composites and Groups/Aggregates.

---

[35] Naiman C.F., and Ouksel A.M. (1995), A Classification Of Semantic Conflicts In Heterogeneous Database Systems, *Journal Of Organizational Computing*, 5(2), 167-193

[36] Ram S. (1995), Intelligent Database Design Using The Unifying Semantic Model, *Information & Management*, 29, 191-206

Fundamental Concepts In The USM

The USM provides a conceptual basis for capturing the semantics and inter-relationships among objects in the real world. Objects are grouped together into object classes based on some common semantic characteristics.

Two main types of object classes are ENTITY and DOMAIN:

- All real world objects are referred to by the term ENTITY. A collection of entities for which common characteristics are to be modelled is called an ENTITY CLASS. Entity classes may be one of two types: STRONG or WEAK: members of a strong entity class can exist on their own, while members of a weak entity class depend on members of other class(es) for their existence. Entity classes may be considered to be Simple Classes, Interactions, Groupings or Composites.

- A DOMAIN is a symbolic object with a datatype. If two attributes draw their values from the same domain, comparisons between the attributes can be made, otherwise the comparisons do not make sense. A domain can have one of several datatypes: Integer, Count, Measure, Currency, Real, Scaled, Boolean, Enumerated, Name, Text, Datetime, Bit-String, Byte-String etc.

Several types of relationships are defined in the USM:

- Properties,
- Interactions,
- Set/Subset,
- Grouping and
- Composite.

- A PROPERTY RELATIONSHIP relates an entity class to a domain class. A property creates an attribute.

- An INTERACTION or ASSOCIATION RELATIONSHIP refers members of one entity class to one or more other entity classes. Characteristics of interaction relationships are:
  - ⇒ *Participation Cardinality* ie binary or n-ary,
  - ⇒ *Inverse* ie exactly two attributes are created - one in each related entity, and each attribute is the inverse of the corresponding attribute in the other entity.
  - ⇒ *Recursive* - ie the relationship relates a member of an entity class to one or more members of the same entity class.
  - ⇒ *Naming Of Interaction Class* must provide a unique name to a binary relationship, when the relationship has some properties of its own.

⇒ A *Weakness Relationship* is one in which members of one entity class depend on the members of other entity class(es) for their existence.

Attributes: An *attribute* is a characteristic of an entity, ie it is the view possessed by members of an entity class of a relationship to members of some other domain or entity class, or possibly in specific other members of the same class. Characteristics are:

Mandatory/Optional e.g. Tax-file-num could be mandatory in Bank-Account records

Changeable/ Not Changeable e.g. date-of-birth is not changeable

Cardinality e.g. single-valued unique, multi-valued unique, single-valued non-unique etc.

Ordering/Duplicates e.g. BAG (unordered collection, duplicates allowed), SET (unordered collection, no duplicates), or LIST (ordered collection, with or without duplicates),

Derived Attributes i.e mathematically or logically derived from some other attribute,

Composed Attributes i.e, an attribute of an entity class can be related to another attribute using the *matching* concept.

Identifiers e.g. keys

Inter-Attribute Constraints ie Implication, Equivalence, Exclusion, Inclusion, Alternation and Joint Uniqueness.

- SET/SUBSET RELATIONSHIPS: An entity class may be related to one or more other entity classes by means of generalization/specialisation relationship. A generalisation/specialisation relationship between two entity classes defines a super-type/subtype.. The entity, which is a member of a sub-class, inherits the attributes of all its super-classes.

Sub-classes may be defined in one of the three ways:

⇒ Attribute-Defined subclasses inherit all the attributes defined for their super-classes.

⇒ Roster-Defined subclass has membership determined only by examining ie list of members.

⇒ Set-Operation-Defined subclasses are defined as either the difference or the intersection of two or more entity classes.

Three types of relationships can exist among subclasses of a common superclass: equal, mutually exclusive, overlapping. Two kinds of relationships can exist among collections of subclasses of a common superclass: totally exhaustive, and partitions.

- A COMPOSITE relationship defines a new class that has other classes as its members. All such classes are strong. A member of a composite class is a set of members of some other class taken as a whole. The classes that are members may be subclasses of a common superclass, in which case they are said to be homogeneous, else they are heterogeneous. Composite classes have some class attributes that describe a whole class. For example, a composite class *ship-types* may have some properties like *total-number-of-ships*, *fastest-ship* etc. A composite class has at least one attribute called *contents* which refers to members of its class. Obviously, Contents is a multivalued attribute; it may or may not be unique; if it is unique, an entity cannot belong to more than one member of the composite class.

Intelligent Tool For Semantic Modelling,

The prototype system called Unibase-Modeller, at the University of Arizona, runs on a network of IBM PS/2 machines under the Microsoft Windows environment. The software is written using Visual Basic and C.

The components of the tool are:

- Intelligent Dialogue: The user interacts with the Uni-base-Modeller using a graphical user interface. It conducts the dialogue with the user.
- Inference Engine: The dialogue is controlled by an inference engine. In developing a conceptual schema, the user is asked to define entity classes, attributes and relationships.
- Knowledge Base: Intelligence in the system is stored in a knowledge base in three parts: A rule base, an application-specific fact base and an organisation-specific fact base.
- Design Repository: The definition of the schema is stored in the design repository. This is currently implemented using the Paradox relational database management system.

The dialogue is controlled by the inference engine which uses the knowledge base components. The rule base checks the correctness of the schema; e.g. a rule ensures that any time a WEAK entity class is defined, the user specifies the STRONG entity class on which it is dependent. There are other rules to guide the users to define attributes and their properties. The application specific fact base contains information on typical entity classes, their attributes and types of relationships one would expect in a particular application domain. For example, if the user is defining a Hospital application, the system will inform the user of previously defined facts such as Physicians, Nurses, Operations, etc. The user is thus able to start from an existing base of information and modify it as required. The system assists the users to ensure completeness of the schema. The organisation specific facts contain information on synonyms and abbreviations specific to an organisation. The tool performs view integration, assisted by organisation specific fact base.

In short, Unifying Semantic Model is a conceptual model defined to depict the meaning of a real world situation that is to be captured in a database. It provides an abstract information modelling mechanism and can support a means of specifying the universe of discourse(UoD) for exchange of information. When we integrate application systems, it is necessary to specify how the UoDs of these applications overlap, so that the semantically related items of these applications can be identified.

4.5.3 *Integrity Merging in an O-O Federated Database Environment*

The process of resolving conflicts between local integrity specifications is an important aspect of heterogeneous database schema integration. Alzaharani R. M., et al[37] have extended a software tool to cater for heterogeneity in integrity specifications while integrating heterogeneous schemas.

In a homogeneous distributed database, integrity rules can be defined at distributed database (DDB) design time and incorporated into integrity subsystems at local nodes. However, the heterogeneity of federated DDBs makes it difficult to support integrity between global and local levels, because they are designed independently and linked together. Nodal autonomy requires that local integrity constraints are preserved, when the nodes participate in a federation. Processing of global queries, on the other hand, should not be affected by inconsistencies between local integrity rules.

Inter-operability between heterogeneous databases requires a semantically rich canonical model to fully capture the semantics of the local schemas and their associated integrity rules. Object-oriented (OO) techniques could provide a powerful glue within such a context. The notion of inheritance, and thus class hierarchy, in OO models offers an excellent natural basis for implementing integrity constraints. Many types of integrity constraints need to be explicitly specified in relational systems, while they are directly captured by the type system

---

[37] Alzaharani R. M., Qutaishait, M.A, Fiddian N.J. and Gray W.A. (1995), Integrity Merging in an Object-Oriented Federated Database Environment, *Advances In Databases, 13th British National Conference Of Database*, pp 226-248

and the object class hierarchy in OODBs; even some integrity constraints, which are traditionally not represented in DBMSs, could be captured.

Following the ideas of Alzaharani R. M., et al[38] the relevant concepts of integrity merging are:

- A Taxonomy of OO Integrity Semantics
- Specification and Modelling of Integrity
- Merging System Approach
- Derivation of Global Integrity
- Multidatabase Integrity Maintenance
- Global Integrity Utilisation

A Taxonomy of OO Integrity Semantics

This taxonomy is based on whether a constraint spans more than one class or just for constraining instances of a single class of objects.

Intra-class integrity rules: These rules can be further subdivided depending on whether the constraint involves just one instance or more.

Intra-instance integrity rules: Rules that constrains attributes of a single instance.

Inter-instance integrity rules: Rules that constrains attributes of all instances of a class.

Inter-class integrity rules: This category of integrity rules models constraints that involve objects from more than one class.

A canonical model should be expressively rich enough to cater for any type of local constraints. The OO paradigm also supports the attachment of monitors to individual objects. This facility can be utilised in implementing triggers, when the rules are violated.

Specification and Modelling of Integrity

The integrated schema is assumed to be loosely coupled, with any number of homogeneous schemas constructed using the concepts and semantics of the OO data model. Integrity rules can be specified in two different forms, depending on the type of the constraints. Intra-class rules are preferably implemented within the class definition; inter-class rules, on the other hand, can be specified within classes or independently in a schema.

---

[38] Alzaharani R. M., Qutaishait, M.A, Fiddian N.J. and Gray W.A. (1995), Integrity Merging in an Object-Oriented Federated Database Environment, *Advances In Databases, 13th British National Conference Of Database*, pp 226-248

Integrity rules from the different categories, as specified within Taxonomy of OO integrity semantics, can be merged in the following six ways:

1. *Containment*: containment occurs when values restricted by a constraint represent a subset of values restricted by another constraint.

2. *Intersection*: this case is encountered, when the set of values permissible by one constraint overlaps with the set of values permissible by another constraint. Containment is a special case of intersection.

3. *Equivalence*: equivalence is obtained when two identical rules are used in two candidate mergeable classes.

4. *Disjunction*: when two integrity rules constrain two different semantics, or the same real world semantics but using different domains, or the same semantics and domains but allowing disjunctive sets of values, such rules are in disjunction.

5. *Synonymity*: two rules are considered to be synonymous if they model the same real world semantics but use different attribute names.

6. *Negation*: this case arises when two rules model the same real world semantics but use different operators or quantifiers

Merging System Approach

A prototype tool called the Schema Meta-Integration System (SMIS) has been used by Alzaharani R. M., et al[39] to integrate two heterogeneous database schemas into a single homogeneous federated schema by using knowledge-based and meta-programming techniques. SMIS was implemented with the aim of resolving normal schematic conflicts. SMIS is being extended by Alzaharani R. M., et all to cater for integrating heterogeneous integrity specifications. Within the extended version of SMIS, two integration methods are used to cope with different cases, which are as follows:

- Automatic Integration:

Equivalent, synonymous, and the negation-related rules are integrated automatically. For instance the case of two classes *Employee* and *Part-time-employee* could be considered, within the latter contains in addition to the attributes of *Employee* some other attributes. These classes are integrated by making *Employee* the super-class of *Part-time-employee*. As far as integrity is concerned, the constraint *sex = 'm' => age*

---

[39] Alzaharani R. M., Qutaishait, M.A, Fiddian N.J. and Gray W.A. (1995), Integrity Merging in an Object-Oriented Federated Database Environment, *Advances In Databases, 13th British National Conference Of Database*, pp 226-248

< 60, is modelled automatically in the federated schema by attaching to the super-class Employee.

- Semi-automatic Integration

This method is applied when two integrity rules are only partially mergeable. This is the case with containment-related rules. With this method of integration, the user (or DBA) is asked to conform or overrule the decision proposed by the system. To show how integration of rules is accomplished, consider two synonymous classes *Doctor* and *Consultant* which have the same set of properties and the two constraints *experience* > *4* and *experience* > *5* respectively. The system integrates the two classes by creating one global class (say *Doctor*). By default the system will choose the relaxed constraint *experience* > *4* and ask its user to confirm this decision or modify it according to his understanding of the real world semantics (RWS). In each case, the system will automatically attach a *hidden alerter* to the global integrity rule indicating the site that does not conform to the global rule completely.

Derivation of Global Integrity

Class mergeability cases are grouped into the augmented SMIS system in various integrity groups. Two representative groups are presented by Alzaharani R. M., et al[40] , which are as follows:

- *Integrity group of strongly equivalent or strongly synonymous classes*

When two local classes are strongly equivalent or strongly synonymous, they are represented in the federated schema by creating a single class (with a proper name) having the attributes of these classes. Their integrity rules are modelled globally using the classification as follows:

Containment: By default, the more relaxed constraint among the two is chosen. However, the designer can instruct the system to change this selection in a semi-automatic manner.

Intersection: The system automatically attaches the two local rules to the appropriate federated class. An implication IC (Integration Constraint) format is used to model the rules at the global level.

Disjunction: This case is handled as in the intersection case.

Equivalence: Here one of the two rules is automatically used at the global level.

---

[40] Alzaharani R. M., Qutaishait, M.A, Fiddian N.J. and Gray W.A. (1995), Integrity Merging in an Object-Oriented Federated Database Environment, *Advances In Databases, 13th British National Conference Of Database*, pp 226-248

Synonymity: Not applicable, since the classes are identical, with the same set of properties and integrity constraints.

Negation: Either of the two rules is automatically chosen for the global level, with preference given to the one with fewer operators (or comparators).

- *Integrity group of classes that share a common set of attributes*

Classes that share a common set of attributes are modelled in a homogeneous federated schema by creating an inheritance hierarchy in which the common set of attributes are represented by a superclass. The rest of the attributes in each class are left in their respective subclasses. For example, the local classes Car and Truck, which have some common attributes, are represented globally by creating the superclass Vehicle with its two subclasses Car and Truck, each having their own attributes that are not in the superclass. As far as their associated integrity constraints are concerned, various types of rule mergeability require different processing depending on classes of *Containment, Intersection, Disjunction, Equivalence, Synonymity* and *Negation*.

Multidatabase Integrity Maintenance

In a multidatabase system, each local node contributes to the federated system under the conditions of being able to determine what data it will share with other sites, what global requests it will service, and when it will join or stop participating in the multidatabase. Local processing has the top priority at local nodes. Furthermore, local nodes are not affected by global requirements. This is the ideal case. In practice, however, local nodes have to contribute some of their capabilities to serve global users' requests. The authors regard autonomy as being satisfied if multidatabase transactions are processed by the local DBMSs as if their local requests. This implies that they are handled through a user/application interface which guarantees local nodes full control over their low level processing of global queries. Global rules should ensure that no updates are propagated to nodes that are not directly involved in a query, because these side-effects make global rules violate local autonomy, due to the existence of interdependencies between database objects. Whenever global updates are allowed in a MDB environment, some form of global control is required to ensure that global updates are accurately executed in a concurrent way.

In multidatabases, local autonomy gives DBAs the freedom to change local schemas without referring to the global DBA. An automatic tool should take the role of propagating changes in local schema and integrity rules to the global levels.. This tool must be complimentary to a federated schema maintenance tool. However, an automatic integrity monitoring tool is expected to make some compromises in local autonomy.

Global Integrity Utilisation

Global optimisation has been considered by Alzaharani R. M., et al[41]. Even simple distributed queries can have many execution plans which can be evaluated at different costs. Syntactic knowledge of operations and storage details help generate efficient queries, but semantic processing adds a relatively new dimension to the query optimisation by exploiting available knowledge about the data. This knowledge-based query optimisation gains processing efficiency by making use of the semantic integrity constraints.

To sum up, Alzaharani R. M., et al[42] have provided a taxonomy of integrity semantics in the OO model. as well as the implementation of a generic tool that examines integrity rules to resolve their inconsistencies and create heterogeneous integrity rules while generating a federated schema. Global homogeneous integrity rules are also utilised in optimising global transactions.

4.5.4 *Interconnecting applications Using CORBA*

Perez J.M[43] has addressed the problem of managing large quantities of data of diverse nature - alphanumeric, audio, graphics, video, etc in an integrated manner. The two main approaches in the area of integration of information systems are: *Structural Integration* and *Operational Integration*. Structural Integration approach creates a global schema starting from the schemata from the underlying systems that are going to be integrated. Perez J.M. has followed the Operational Integration approach - the data reside in any place of the heterogeneous systems and a set of operations allow the management of the data.

Though three possible alternatives have been considered by J.M.Perez for solving the communication problem among the components of the system: Sockets, RPC and CORBA, we opine that the Sockets and RPCs are too low-level tools to be compared against CORBA. However, the architecture, considered by J.M. Perez for using CORBA, shows how to access data and processes, distributed over several machines, in an integrated manner.

---

[41] Alzaharani R. M., Qutaishait, M.A, Fiddian N.J. and Gray W.A. (1995), Integrity Merging in an Object-Oriented Federated Database Environment, *Advances In Databases, 13th British National Conference Of Database*, pp 226-248
[42] Alzaharani R. M., Qutaishait, M.A, Fiddian N.J. and Gray W.A. (1995), Integrity Merging in an Object-Oriented Federated Database Environment, *Advances In Databases, 13th British National Conference Of Database*, pp 226-248

Following J.M. Perez's lines, we may review briefly how Sockets and RPC can be used for integration of systems.

Sockets are implemented by a set of system calls to communicate with a set of network protocols. The programmers, using sockets, maintain a total control on the parameters of the communication. This contributes to the efficiency of the system, since one can adapt them to the necessary requirements. But this implies that the programmer requires to have the detailed knowledge of all communication processes of the components of the system.

RPC, ie Remote Procedure Call, is a general facility for the programs to execute services in remote hosts. The remote services could be incorporated as function calls within an application. From the point of view of client, a RPC function is identical to a normal function, except that it is executed in a remote server. RPC is a powerful and useful tool in order to extend the notion of service of being basically a compact program (a black box) called by related functions.

The server executes the function utilising the given arguments as the parameters and it returns the result of the function to the client. The client and the server could be in the machines of different types with different native representations (of elementary data) for the parameters and the result. In order to operate correctly in a heterogeneous environment, the client and the server should agree in the common representation for the arguments and the result. RPC provides greater abstraction than using sockets, within RPC the services behave like normal functions. However, it is still necessary to specify several parameters of the connection, such as the localisation of the server.

CORBA

CORBA (Common Object Request Broker Architecture) is a specification for the definition and construction of distributed systems with client/server architecture. Using CORBA, the effort of development is focussed on the construction of the system, ie the services that it provides, not in the details of the communication. Its high level definition allows to make abstraction of the platform, operating system and programming language that are utilised in order to develop and install the new system. It provides a language called IDL (Interface Definition Language) independent of any programming language (although it is close to C++) for the definition of the servers, the data types that it utilises, the services it provides, etc. Also it defines a set of rules for implementing the services defined by means of IDL in a classic programming language (generally C, C++, Common Lisp, Modula etc).

---

[43] Perez J.M.(1995), Integration Of Heterogeneous Information Management Systems Using CORBA,

Because of the level of abstraction available from CORBA, the programmer need not know the details of communication between the processes, it is the task of CORBA to ensure that the processes communicate to one another. Even it is not necessary to know where the defined servers reside; the client applications behave in the same manner whether they reside on the same host or they are separated in a series of remote hosts so long they are accessible through a network.

The main advantage of using CORBA instead of low-level tools are:

- CORBA permits greater levels of abstraction, which benefits the programmer as it provides higher level primitives for the communication among several modules;
- It is independent of the platform, operating system, and programming language, so it allows to construct systems that are easily portable. In theory, it could be implemented in any programming language (now only in C, C++, Common Lisp and Modula) on whatever operating system; and

It is specially conceived in order to construct distributed systems with client-server architecture. It is also possible to utilise RPC for these systems, but with CORBA it is not necessary that the client knows where the server resides; in RPC, location of the server is required during compilation/parsing time.

Suitability of CORBA for inter-communication

J.M.Perez has weighed pros and cons of three approaches using Sockets, RPC and CORBA, and selected CORBA for establishing communication amongst the heterogeneous application systems; because:

1) With sockets, it is necessary to keep track of the type of machines and operating systems to be used and their compatibility with the network.

2) With RPC mechanism, a higher level of abstraction is attained. Detailed knowledge of the features of the communication is not necessary, but the programmer must assign them unique identifiers (number and version), which is not easy to register them global in a network.

3) CORBA appears with a greater level of abstraction. With CORBA, the services behave like those in the case of RPC, that is, like normal functions. But also, it is not necessary to create identifiers for this services - CORBA is the one in charge of the communications among the processes. The only requirement is to register the services like CORBA services, which is carried out by using functions provided by CORBA.

The Architecture proposed by J.M.Perez

The figure 4.6 shows the J.M.Perez's architecture that permits solving the communication problem of the integration of information system on Oracle Server, Sybase Server, vi-Edit Server, grep Server, Cadence Server, and AutoCAD Server.

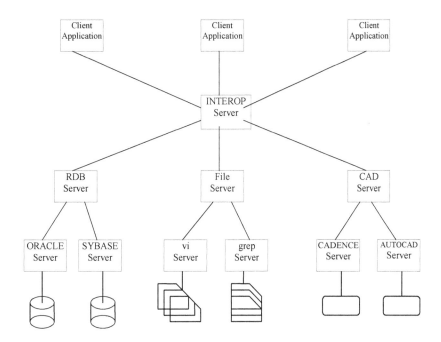

Figure 4.6 The Resulting Architecture Proposed By J.M.Perez

In the lower level there are modules that deals directly with the data. There exists a module for each data model and management system to utilise: ORACLE databases, SYBASE databases, ascii files (vi), CAD files (CADENCE), etc. In the following level there are a series of modules that share characteristics, as it is the case of the module for CAD systems. In the upper level exists the main module of the system - INTEROP module, which is capable of accessing all the data using the modules of the lower level.

Due to the modular design, it is easy to expand the system with new components. For example, if audio data management system needs be included, at most two modules need be included. One of these modules would access to the audio data, and the other located in the higher level to the previous one would manage the audio data type family.

The above architecture has shown how to access and manage data and processes, distributed over several machines, in an integrated manner. Though this architecture shows how to avoid communications between individual disparate systems by establishing communications to the integrating module INTEROP, this solution is restricted to *syntactical heterogeneity* only, the solution does not show how the integrating module INTEROP will decipher the meaning of the messages sent across and solve the problems related to *semantic heterogeneity*.

4.5.5 Autonomous Heterogeneous Information System: DIME

Very large distributed database systems can be constructed by integrating local database systems (LDBSs), that exist as isolated systems, into one global system or a federation. But, the LDBSs could be heterogeneous, using different data models, database languages, concurrency control and recovery schemes. Therefore a mechanism is needed to map each LDBS in a heterogeneous distributed database system (HDDBS). It is not desirable to modify the LDBSs, so that design autonomy, in terms of the original design of the data model and the protocols used by individual LDBS, is maintained in the HDDBS.

The major aim of some of the HDDBSs developed in last two decades, for example MULTIBASE, Proteus, ADDS, DATAPLEX etc. is to resolve the heterogeneities of local data models and local database languages. However, these systems, except DATAPLEX, do not provide global update operations ie automatic updating of data stored at different LDBSs. In those systems, updating data stored at different LDBSs is either impossible or allowed to execute only in a restricted manner as off-line updates. Again, all the systems including DATAPLEX cannot deal with the heterogeneity of local concurrency control schemes (LCCSs). For example, DATAPLEX restricts the local concurrency control only to the strict two-phase locking scheme.

Cho H., Kim Y.S., Moon S.[44] has described the design and implementation of an autonomous HDDBS, named Distributed Information Management (DIME) in which heterogeneity among LCCSs exist but complete site autonomy is guaranteed.

DIME is claimed to have achieved the following advantages:

- DIME allows both global update operations and global retrieval operations where different LCCSs are used in different LDBSs. This is achieved by a unified concurrency control scheme developed by Cho H., Kim Y.S., Moon S.

- DIME implements international standard protocols on the distributed transaction processing and the remote database access. With the standards, DIME can alleviate the complexity of integrating different LDBSs.

- DIME provides distribution transparency to assist users access data. Users can generate not only single site queries (including remote site queries) but also inter-site queries without considering data distribution in LDBSs. This results from an efficient handling of the distributed catalogs.

Because the main thrust of DIME is to support a global concurrency control scheme where the heterogeneity of LCCSs exists, DIME does not consider heterogeneities of local data models. DIME can only be applied to LDBSs each of which support relational data model with SQL interface. It is assumed that there are no data incompatibilities between LDBSs. This results in simplifying the schema integration procedures, which are not the main focus of the current version of DIME. Cho H., Kim Y.S., Moon S. contemplate to resolve, in the next version of DIME, the problems of data incompatibilities, such as naming conflicts, data representation conflicts, differences in data structures, data scaling conflicts, and conflicting data values.

4.5.6 *Schema Integration for Heterogeneous Distributed Databases*

Mah P.S., and Shin G[45] have proposed a schema integration method using a *unified data model*, which is basically a relational model with object-oriented features, as the global model for integrating schemas of multiple databases in the relational, hierarchical, and network models. The unified data model is designed to satisfy the two main objectives - (1)

---

[44] Cho H., Kim Y.S., Moon S. (1996), *Design and Implementation of an Autonomous Heterogeneous Distributed Database System: DIME*, Document Supply Service, Yonset University, Seol, Korea
[45] Mah P.S., and Shin G. (1997), Schema Integration for Heterogeneous Distributed Databases, *Proceedings of the International Symposium on Future Software Technology '97, 29-31 Oct 1997, Xiamen, China*, pp 173-180.

the model needs subsume other data models, and (2) the query language should be easily translated to the languages of other data models. If a full-fledged object-oriented data model is chosen as the global model, expressive power of the model helps translating the schemas from other data models to o-o data model, but the query translation becomes difficult. on the other hand, if a relational data model is chosen as the global data model, the schema integration process becomes difficult, though the query translation becomes easy. The unified relational and object-oriented model, or simply unified data model, is adopted as a compromise.

The unified model is an extension of the relational model, that allows *nested tables* (nested classes), the *set of values* (multivalued attributes), *procedures* (methods), and *hierarchies* (class hierarchy and inheritance). Furthermore, the syntax of the unified model query language SQL/X is upwardly SQL-compatible. The unified model includes a set of modelling concepts of the object-oriented model that are fundamental and widely used. But the model does not include all the concepts of the object-oriented model. For example, it does not include the ordering in a set, bags, inverted functions etc.

The main features of this integration method are proposed to be as follows:

- The conversion of each local schema into a unified local schema to remove the difference in modelling is systematic.
- The various data and schema conflicts (domain mismatch problems) occurring during the schema integration can be resolved using object-oriented features.
- The global query can be translated into equivalent SQL/X queries for the unified local schemas systematically.
- The resemblance between the SQL/X and SQL in syntax facilitates the translation of a global query into the equivalent SQL queries for local relational databases. Moreover, the path expression of the SQL/X query can be exploited to specify the sequence of access paths in the network and hierarchical models during the query translation.

The task of decomposing a global query into a set of site queries become complex if one considers the query with explicit join conditions on multiple classes. The query optimisation problem in this extended query model is proposed to be researched further.

4.5.7 A Multidatabase System Implementation on CORBA

A multidatabase system, METU Interoperable DBMS (MIND)[46], has been based on OMG's distributed object management architecture (OMA), CORBA and COSS. The OMA defines a Reference Model identifying and characterising the components, interfaces, and protocols that compose a distributed object architecture. CORBA is the core communication mechanism which enables distributed objects to operate on each other. COSS provides a set of standard functions to create objects, to control access to objects and to keep track of objects and object references.

In MIND, there is a generic Database Object defined in CORBA IDL and there are multiple implementations of this interface, one for each of the local DBMSs, namely Oracle8, Sybase, Adabas-D and MOOD (METU Object-Oriented Database System). The current implementation makes unified access possible to any combination of these databases through a global query language based on SQL. When a client application issues a global SQL query to access multiple databases, this global query is decomposed into global subqueries and these subqueries are sent to the ORB (CORBA's Object Request Broker) which transfers them to the relevant database servers on the network. On the server site, the global subqueries are executed by using the corresponding call level interface routines of the local DBMSs and the result is returned back to the client via the ORB. The partial results returned from the related servers are merged if necessary. This approach hides the differences between the local database and the rest of the system. Thus, what the clients of this level see are homogeneous DBMS objects accessible through a common interface.

MIND implements a four-level schema architecture that addresses the requirements dealing with distribution, autonomy, and heterogeneity in a multidatabase system. This schema architecture includes four different kinds of schemas:

1) Local Schema: is the schema managed by the local database management system, and is expressed in the native data model of the local database; hence different local schemas are expressed in different data models.

2) Export schema: is derived by translating local schemas into a canonical data model. The process of schema translation from a local schema to an export schema generates mappings between the local schema objects and the export schema objects.

3) Derived (Federated) Schema: combines the independent export schemas to one or more integrated schemas. A federated schema also includes the information on data

---

[46] Dogac A., et al (1996), asuman@srdc.metu.edu.tr, *A Multidatabase System Implementation on CORBA*, 0-8186-7289-7/96 @1996 IEEE, pp 2-11

distribution that is generated when integrating export schemas. the global query manager decomposes a command on the federated schema into a set of commands on one or more export schemas.

4) External Schema: defines a schema for a user or an application, it can be used to specify a subset of information in the federated schema that is relevant to the users. Additional information and integrity constraints can be specified in the external schema.

The classes in export and derived schemas behave like ordinary object classes. They consist of an interface and an implementation. But unlike ordinary classes, which store their objects directly, the implementations of the classes of these schemas derive their objects from the objects of other classes.

Since CORBA handles heterogeneity at the platform and communication layers, MIND development is focussed on the upper layers of the system such as schema integration, global query execution and global transaction management, which reduced the development effort dramatically. It is possible for MIND to become an integral part of a broad distributed object system that not only contains DBMSs but may also include objects of different kinds such as file systems, spreadsheets, workflow systems, etc.

4.5.8 JAVA Applets and CORBA for Distributed Applications

The Java language environment, World Wide Web, and Common Object Request Broker Architecture are complementary software technologies for developing and deploying multi-user distributed applications. Evans E., and Rogers D[47] has shown an approach to building an easy-to-use client software as WWW-downloadable Java applets, which use CORBA to interact effectively with remote software and thus coordinate and control access to a set of shared resources.

Evans E., and Rogers D. have used this approach to reimplement a portion of an existing multi-user distributed application that had been built using the WWW Common Gateway Interface (CGI), and found this approach superior to the widely used CGI approach, as well as to a conventional CORBA approach that does not exploit the WWW.

In these multi-user distributed applications, users need to invoke operations that are implemented by server software residing on remote host computers. The user is not logged into the server host, but interacts with the client software running on a desktop computer. The client software may provide a graphical user interface (GUI) that accepts user requests

---

[47] Evans E., and Rogers D. (1997), Using JAVA Applets and CORBA for Multi-User Distributed Applications, *Internet Computing*, May-June 1997, pp 43-55

and displays information. The server software provides the bulk of the application services based on data, executable resources, or devices that are shared among users. In the Java/CORBA approach, all of the user-side client software is implemented as Java applets, which in turn use CORBA for most remote operations with the rest of the application's software components. The users transparently download the applets when they are needed, thus removing the need to manually distribute and install any application-specific software. The applet executes within the browser's Java runtime and presents a GUI to the user. The user makes requests via the GUI, some of which may result in the applet's invoking methods on the remote objects via the ORB. These remote objects may be instantiated in remote object server programs running on the server host. The applet receives the results of its remote invocations and may display some of these in the GUI. The scenario could be more complex too; for example, the remote objects might in turn act as clients to other remote objects on other hosts, or, the applet itself could contain a remote object, whose methods could be invoked by a software executing on the server side.

In addition to the WWW-based deployability and platform independence of clients, the Java/CORBA approach offers several advantages over both CGI and a traditional CORBA approach: (1) it allows greater flexibility and control over GUI design, (2) remote method argument can be actual types, including structured types and even classes, (3) server-side software is less complex, (4) client and server programs can exploit both multi-threading and the continuous execution state., (5) resources needed by the server programs are more efficiently used and managed.

However, one major pre-requisite of this approach is that, we need to know which client object is semantically linked to the server object, so that an applet may invoke the appropriate method in the server object.

4.5.9 Representing Knowledge of The Entire Database From That Of The Components

When decisions need be made from the information available in a set of data sources, one option is to integrate all the sources into one and use the integrated information for decision making, another option could be to depend on one of the sources without integrating all sources into one. Cho V. and Wuthrich B[48]. proposed for integrating only the relevant information from individual sources, so that the decisions from the relevant information

---

[48] Cho V., and Wuthrich B.(1998), Towards Real Time Discovery From Distributed Information Sources, *Second Pacific-Asia Conference On Knowledge Discovery*, April 1998, pp 376-377

would be close to the decision made from one integrated source. As the decision involved in Cho and Wurthrich's project was discriminant analysis between credit-worthy and non-credit-worthy, they proposed to generate one rule from each data source, and then bring the individual rules together to represent adequately the knowledge of the entire database. This mining approach provides a faster way to arrive at an equivalent decision without the need to physically merge the individual data sources.

4.5.10 HIMPAR - Heterogeneous Interoperable Mediators and Parallel Architecture

The HIMPAR system, as implemented by Pires P.F. and Mattoso M.L.Q.[49], is based on the architecture of Mediators - where specialised Mediators are created for each specific application domain. No unified integration schema is required; each Mediator represents a customised view that is intended to meet the needs of a specific group of users.

The Mediator is one of the following categories into which Pires and Mattoso have classified various projects concerning HDDSs according to their autonomy degree and the strength of coupling:

- HDDSs with Global Schema - Creation and maintenance of a unified global integration schema, as followed in projects Pegasus[50], UniSQL/M[51], Mermaid[52], and IRO-DB[53], becomes increasingly hard to manage as the number of component systems increase.

- Federated Database - Problems associated with creation, maintenance and storage of unified global schema are eliminated. But, the integration of schemas via import and export schemas[54] is static, and the alteration of local schemas and the addition of new information sources require the import schemas to be changed accordingly. Therefore, when a large number of information sources are integrated, scaling and maintenance of such systems are difficult.

---

[49] Pires P.F.., and Mattoso M.L.Q.(1997), A CORBA Based Architecture for Heterogeneous Information Source Interoperability, *25th Technology of Object-oriented Languages and Systems*, 1997, pp 33-49
[50] Du W. and Shan M.(1996), Query Processing in Pegasus, Object Oriented Multibase Systems, A.O.Bukhres and A.K. Elmagarmid ed., Prentice Hall, USA, 1996, pp 449-471
[51] Kim W. et al, (1993), *On Resolving Schematic Heterogeneity in Multibase Systems*, Distributed and Parallel Databases, Vol.1, No.3, 1993, pp 251-279
[52] Templeton et al.(1987), *Mermaid - A Front End to Distributed Heterogeneous Databases*, Proceedings of the IEEE, May 1987.
[53] Gardarin G. et al, *IRO-DB: A Distributed System Federating Object and Relational Databases*, Object Oriented Multibase Systems, A.O.Bukhres and A.K. Elmagarmid ed., Prentice Hall, USA, 1996, pp 684-712
[54] Heimbigner D., & McLeod D. (1985), A Federated Architecture For Information Management, *ACM Transactions on Office Information Systems, July 1985*

- Multibase Query Languages - Systems based on multibase query languages, as in projects MRDSM[55], OMNIBASE[56] and CALIDA[57], have no integration schema; the database interactions are accomplished by using multibase query languages. However, this approach does not provide a transparent data access and users need information about the distribution and semantics of the data in order to formulate queries.

- Distributed Object Management (DOM) - Resources of the system are represented as a collection of objects which provide service interfaces and implementation of services, as in MIND - METU Interoperable DBMS[58] and Jupiter[59]. In the MIND system, the integration of local sources is done by constructing a global schema, while Jupiter uses the multibase language approach.

- Mediators - Integration of information sources involves the use of Mediators in projects TSIMMIS[60], GARLIC[61], DISCO[62], and DIOM[63]. These projects intend to integrate structured and non-structured (with no data schema) data sources.

The HIMPAR architecture has the same advantage as the other systems based on Mediators, additionally the approach is strongly based on standards. The data model is based on the ODMG[64] standard, and the interoperability of the architectural components is achieved through CORBA[65] standard. The communication between two Mediators and between a Mediator and a Wrapper uses a standard query language, the OQL (Object Query Language). The use of new standards is intended to ease the integration of new data sources. The use of the CORBA standard at the interoperability layer favours the system's

[55] Litwin W., and Abdellatif, *An Overview of the Multi-Database Manipulation Language MDSL*, Proc. IEEE, Vol.75, No.5, May 1987, pp 621-632

[56] Rusinkiewicz M. et al (1989), *OMNIBASE: Design and Implementation of a Multibase System*, Proc. Annual Symposium on Parallel and Distributed Processing, Dallas, May 1989

[57] Jacobson G., et al (1988)., *CALIDA: A Knowledge-based System for Integrating Multiple Heterogeneous Databases*, Proc. Intl. Conf. Data and Knowledge Bases, Jerusalem, Jun.1988

[58] Dogac A., et al (1996), *Building Interoperable Databases on Distributed Object Management Platforms*, Communications of ACM, Sep.1996

[59] Murphy J. and Grimson J.(1995), *The Jupiter System: An Environment for Multidatabase Interoperability*, Information and Software Technology, Vol 37, 1995, pp 503-513

[60] Papakonstantinou et al. (1995), *The TSIMMIS Approach to Mediation: Data Models and Languages*, Proc. NGITS workshop, 1995

[61] Carey M.J., et al, *Towards Heterogeneous Multimedia Information Systems: The Garlic Approach*, Tech Report, IBM Almaden Research Center, USA

[62] Tomasic A. et al (1995), *Scaling Heterogeneous Database and the Design of DISCO*, Tech Report, n*2704, INRIA, France,Nov.1995

[63] Liu L. et al (1996), *An Adaptive Approach to Query Mediation across Heterogeneous Databases*, Proc. Intl.Conf. Cooperative Information Systems, IEEE Computer Soc. Press, Los Alamitos, Calif., 1996, pp 144-156

[64] Cattel R.G.G. and Barry D. (1997), *The Object Database Standard 2.0*, Morgan Kaufmann Publishers, USA, 1997

[65] Object Management Group & X-Open (1991), *The Common Object Request Broker: Architecture & Specification*, OMG Document Number 91.12.1, Revision 1.1

implementation, since both the Wrapper and the Mediator modules can be implemented in any programming language, according to the preference of each user group.

However, HIMPAR architecture provides the way of using new standards to integrate the heterogeneous applications, but does not deal with how to identify the semantically related items across applications, so that these items can be linked.

4.5.11 Knowledge Base for Integration of Heterogeneous Databases

Karunaratna et al.[66] have proposed for a knowledge base [KB] that can be evolved incrementally, by analysing metadata of the databases that join a federation, leave a federation or have their views changed. The KB is organised as a semantic network of concept clusters; four layers of KB have been proposed: a concept layer, a view layer, a meta-data layer, and a DB layer. A concept is thought of as a unit of knowledge representation that guides the process of classifying objects into clusters, which are considered as logical grouping of schema objects. Concepts may be related to each other via binary relations (*links*). As in schema structures, links have properties. In addition to *strength* and *link-type* properties, they also have an essential property named *frequency*, whivh specifies how many times the corresponding link occurred in the federation and is being used in user views. In the concept layer, link strengths represent how closely concepts are related in the federation. The link prpoerty *link-type* takes values from the set {aggregation, isA, positive-association}. Thus, KB records concepts and their inter-relationships defined in the schema and also their frequency of occurrence in the federation, and is used both as a semantic dictionary and as a basis to enrich schemas semantically during the detection of relationships among schema components when creating user views. However, the proposal of KB is based on the assumptions that a set of common terms are used as schema object names and their attribute names, when the schemas are developed to represent similar real world objects, and therefore semantic relationships can be identified from the meta-data of component databases. We suggest that meta-data information needs to be examined by checking their real world counterparts, and also it may not be necessary to consider the entire meta-data of the component databases, we may consider only those meta-data that are for the semantically linked concepts.

---

[66] Karunaratna D.D., Gray W.A., Fiddian N.J., Establishing a Knowledge Base to Assist Integration of Heterogeneous Databases, *Proc 16th British National Conf on Advances In Databases,July 6-8,98, pp 103-118*

4.5.12 Summary of the Current Research Activities

The papers, reviewed above in the previous section, show that schema integration is still of paramount importance in establishing inter-operability of databases. Naiman and Ouksel have worked on identification and classification of the conflicts; this provides us a way to identify the conflicts that need be resolved and classify them along the dimensions of naming, abstraction, and level of heterogeneity. Sudha Ram has specified a Unifying Semantic Model for describing the universe of discourse in a common canonical data model, so that participating applications can be integrated. Alzaharani has explored the role of integrity constraints in the process of schema integration, and provided a systematic analysis of how local and global integrity constraints are to be maintained. J.M.Perez has established that though CORBA is suitable for interconnecting applications for an organisation, it does not address the problems of semantic heterogeneity caused by differences in schema design for same real world objects. Again, in the work carried out by Cho H,.et al, only the heterogeneity of local concurrency control schemes is resolved, the problems of schema incompatibilities have not been covered in the current version of the system. Mah P.S. and Shin G. have attempted to test the unified data model as the canonical data model for integrating schemas; however object-oriented data model serves well in translation of schemas, particularly when the component schemas are non-relational or object-oriented. The unified data model will be suitable only when the component databases are relational, hierarchical or network. METU Interoperable Database (MIND), as researched by A Dogac et al, uses the CORBA infrastructure for implementing a multidatabase system, while the paper by Evans E. and Rogers D. is for facilitating interoperations in multi-user applications by using Java/CORBA approach. In these approaches, however, the semantic interoperability remains to be solved at the application programming level. Similarly, HIMPAR architecture shows how the applications can be integrated using new standards of open systems, but what items from component applications can be linked still need to be identified. Karunaratna et al. have shown how a knowledge base can assist integration of evolving and heterogeneous databases, where we suggest that meta-data information needs to be examined by checking their real world counterparts, and also we may consider only those meta-data that are for the semantically linked concepts.

4.6   Conclusion from Literature Review

The goal of an integrated system is to achieve transparency like a well-planned distributed system, so that the resulting system behaves like one system, that knows all data items maintained by the underlying systems. The main challenge in designing such a system is that it is too complex for the designer to understand the semantics of each underlying system. Yet, most architectures for small-scale integration, so far, attempted to understand the semantics of all data items in the distributed complex and hence proved too difficult to be implemented. However, an architecture can be designed using the strong points of SuperDatabase, Federated Database, Logically Centralised Schema and Distributed Conceptual Schema. The concept of export schemas of the Federated Database architecture, would lead us to consider only those data items that matter in the integrating schema, while the idea of distributed conceptual schema would lead us to model objects using the items in the export schemas, so that these objects could inter-operate with one another in an integrating application.

CORBA-like standards have been developed to achieve infrastructural integration, where any participating application needs to comply with the rules for traders or object-request-brokers. Though we look forward to the days, when systems can be assembled by using off-the-shelf objects with well-defined interfaces, applications built under infrastructure, prevailing now, need lot of efforts to ensure compliance to the infrastructural standards like CORBA. At this point, CORBA can be used to establish a mechanism for communication among applications, but semantics of the data items still need be understood to achieve compliance with the CORBA-like infrastructural standards. Differences in data structures of the same information represented differently on different application systems need be identified and their semantic correspondences asserted until we get to the stage when all objects have standard meaning and standard interfaces, to facilitate infrastructural integration.

As we have seen in the section on Summary Of Current Research Activities, work is still on to classify the semantic conflicts, to describe the overlapping universe of discourse in a common canonical data model, to solve problems of global concurrency control and integrity management while maintaining local autonomy, to explore various ways of interconnecting applications, and to use various modelling techniques to improve compatibility of component applications. to achieve improved communication facilities for interoperations in multi-user applications by using Java/CORBA approach. However, none of the reviewed research directions fully address the problem of establishing semantic links amongst the objects of various applications.

The most fundamental problem of schema integration still remains that a real world object can be modelled in many different ways. The same fact may be seen from different levels of abstraction, or represented using different properties. Depending on how the designer views a phenomenon, or on what is permitted by modelling constructs, the same real world object can be modelled as an object, an attribute or as the composition of several attributes. Considering the problem of our sample Customer Relationship Management system, we need to identify the semantically related objects in the involved banking applications and model this semantic relationship, so that these applications can meaningfully interact with one another. Only after the semantic relationship between objects across inter-operating applications are identified, these relationships can be expressed by using CORBA-like mechanisms for defining the interfaces. In the next chapter, we shall concentrate on the conflicts and correspondences between objects of different applications, so that we can explore the ways to resolve the conflicts.

5. INTER-APPLICATION CONFLICTS & CORRESPONDENCES

5.1 Introduction

The major task of linking semantically related objects shared across applications is to identify the conflicting definitions ie the cases where (a) the same real world objects have been defined differently in the applications and where (b) different real world objects have been defined identically in the applications. Conflicting definitions of objects in different applications can be broadly defined as the schema conflicts and the data conflicts. These conflicts need be reconciled to achieve integration of applications.

Schema Conflicts are caused by the fact that different designers may model the same piece of reality in different ways, because the data models may support different equivalent constructs for the same concept and/or different designers may have different perceptions of the real world. If we consider the example of integrating banking applications, we may find that more than one application maintains the address of a customer. In one of them the address could be considered as an attribute of the object customer, and stored as literals. In another application an address could be maintained as a row in the address table, while the object customer maintains a pointer to one row in the address table.

Conflicts in their actual data contents are defined as *Data Conflicts.* When two objects are semantically equivalent, they provide identical responses to the same queries. But, even if two objects are modelled in the same way, and no schema conflicts exist, they would still provide different responses in case of data conflicts, ie when instances of one object are not identical to the instances of the other object. For example, one banking application may provide real time update of the balance, while another shows last batch run figure of the same balance; sometime during the day these two applications provide different responses to the same query.

Some issues like *domain mismatch* and *schematic discrepancy,* cannot be covered in the broad classification of Data and Schema Conflicts. *Domain Mismatch* occurs when two apparently identical schemas may not match each other in respect of the domain of possible values of their corresponding data items. *Schematic Discrepancy* occurs when data in one application corresponds to metadata in another.

In the next few sections, a comprehensive analysis of the schema and data conflicts have been carried out. Schema, data and other conflicts among applications can be attributed mainly to the differences in the contexts of those applications. The application which sends information and the application, that receives it, may operate with different contexts. As the real world objects are represented in their schemas, the contexts of the sources and the receivers of information are captured in the respective schemas. We can find ways either to eliminate the conflicts in the schemas or we may support the conflicting representations found among various schemas, without altering them, but by specifying which items of one application can be matched with some items of another application, and by linking these semantically related objects in a central application.

5.2 Schema Conflicts

Schema conflicts are the cases when the same real world objects or the semantically equivalent objects have different schema definitions in the component applications. There are two basic causes of schema conflicts.

One, the different structures could be used for the same information - say, entities or objects in one case and attributes or features in another case. For example, some component databases may represent a *publisher's address* as an attribute of the entity *publisher*, while another may have the *address* as a separate entity, and the key of the entity *address* is kept as an attribute of the publisher.

Two, the different specifications could be used for the same structure; these include different names, data types, and constraints for semantically equivalent entities/objects and/or attributes/features. Because the relational model uses either entities or attributes to represent information, schema conflicts within the model can be classified[67] by enumerating combinations of different structures used to represent information and all possible specifications of the structures. The same classification can be extended to the object models, using object class and features in place of entities and attributes.

Entity-versus-attribute conflicts result from the use of entities in some component databases and attributes in others to represent the same information. Many-to-many entity conflicts and many-to-many attribute conflicts are due to different numbers of entities or attributes representing the same information. Entity-structure conflicts arise when semantically equivalent entities have different structures, that is, different numbers and/or kinds of attributes. When all component databases use the same structure for the same information, all user-definable elements within the structures can be enumerated and all conflicts as either one-to-one entity conflicts or one-to-one attribute conflicts.

---

[67] Kim W., and Seo J. (1991), Classifying Schematic and Data Heterogeneity in Multidatabase Systems, *IEEE Computer, December 1991*, pp 12-18.

SCHEMA CONFLICTS:
  A. Entity-versus-entity conflicts
    1. One-to-one entity conflicts
      a. Entity name conflicts
        1) Different name for equivalent entities
        2) Same name for different entities
      b. Entity structure conflicts
        1) Missing attributes
        2) Missing but implicit attributes
      c. Entity constraint conflicts
    2. Many-to-many entity conflicts
  B. Attribute-versus-attribute conflicts
    1. One-to-one attribute conflicts
      a. Attribute name conflicts
        1) Different names for equivalent attributes
        2) Same name for different attributes
      b. Default value conflicts
      c. Attribute constraint conflicts
        1) Data type conflicts
        2) Attribute integrity constraint conflicts
    2. Many-to-many attribute conflicts
  C. Entity-versus-attribute conflicts

DATA CONFLICTS
  A. Wromg data
    1. Incorrect-entry data
    2. Obsolete data
  B. Different representations for the same data
    (same representation for different data)
    1. Different expressions
    2. Different units
    3. Different precisions

Figure 5.1. Data and Schema Conflict Classification[68]

5.3 *Data Conflicts*

Data conflicts are of two types: (1) wrong data, and (2) different representations for the same data.

---

[68] *Adapted from* : Kim W., and Seo J., Classifying Schematic and Data Heterogeneity in Multidatabase Systems, *IEEE Computer*, pp 12-18, December 1991.

Wrong Data could be either incorrect data or obsolete data. For example, if the birth date of an employee in one component database is different from that maintained in another component database, then at least one of the database has incorrect data for the birth date of the same employee. If the same data is maintained in more than one database and subjected to different update cycles, data maintained in some database could be obsolete. For example, two databases may maintain different salary of the same employee, because one of them has been recently updated, while the other has not been.

Incomplete Information[69]: Missing and incomplete information is often represented by null values in relational databases. Null values may or may not be allowed in some tables, even some databases may not allow null values. Moreover, the meaning of the null values may be different in different databases.

Recording Errors: These could be due to typographical mistakes or variations in measurement. Typing errors may occur with names involving similar phonetics, e.g. *Smith*, *Schmidt*, and *Smythe*.

Surrogates: Surrogates are system generated identifiers, used in different databases. They could have the same domain and meaning, but be otherwise unrelated.

Asynchronous Updates: These happen when data items, replicated in different databases, get updated at different points in time and become inconsistent. these are more likely if the data items are inherently varying with time, such as a person's age, weight or salary.

Different Representation Of The Same Data could happen because of differences in expression, units, precision, and domain mismatches[70] - some common fact could be treated in different ways by different domains in different databases.

Examples of differences in expression are as follows:

- Different types for the same data: The same attribute may have incompatible type definitions in different databases. For example, social security number could be of type *character* in one database and *numeric* in another. Similarly, an attribute may be single-valued in one database, while set-valued in another.

- Different formats for the same data: Different databases may use different formats for the same data item, for example date in day/month/year vs month/day/year. For a date like

---

[69] Chatterjee A., and Segev A. (1991), Data Manipulation In Heterogeneous Databases, *SIGMOD Record*, Vol.20, No.4, December 1991

[70] Kent W. (1991), Solving Domain Mismatch and Schema Mismatch Problems with an Object-Oriented Database Programming Language, *Proc. of the 17th VLDB Conference, Barcelona, September 1991*, pp 147-160

01/02/03, interpretations could be 2nd January 2003 or 1st February 2003 or 3rd February 2001.

- Different words for the same data:

  New South Wales, N.S.W., NSW

- Different strings for the same data:

  123, Coronation Blvd, Ste 555, Stratfld, NSW

  123, Coronation Boulevard, Suite 555, Stratfield, New South Wales.

- Different codes for the same data: Codes are used for various reasons, such as saving storage space. Codes are often local to the databases, and therefore non-uniform even when referring to the same domain.

*****	A	Excellent	1	5
****	B	Good	2	4
***	C	Fair	3	3
**	D	Poor	4	2
*	E	Bad	5	1

Examples of differences in units are as follows

- When the conceptual territory is a measured quantity, such as weight, the different domains in the group would simply be different representations expressed in different units; this mismatch is easily reconciled by arithmetic. Similar is the case of amounts maintained in different currencies eg AUD, GBP, USD, INR etc. Period could be maintained in number of weeks in one database, while in number of days in another, which means 2 units of the first database is equivalent to 14 units of the second database.

  More complex discrepancies arise when the same conceptual territory is perceived as being populated, or partitioned in different ways. The concept of "job" might be common to several databases, yet each database may have a different notion of what the specific jobs are. In one database the jobs might include engineer, secretary, administrative assistant, and customer representative, while the other database may have its jobs as technician, designer, engineer, secretary, administrative assistant, and customer representative. The same conflict may arise with the set of skills one might possess in different jobs in different databases. Other examples might include different palettes of colours covering the same spectrum, different grading systems at different schools, different rating systems for restaurants, terms in different languages for the same or similar concepts, different kinds of geographic units.

  The existence of different domains is not a problem unless there is a need to see these domains in some integrated way. The treatment of domain mismatch can be separated into two parts:

- Mapping between domains
- Integrator facilities which use such mappings.

Currency conversion represents mappings between different domains, which is the different ways of representing money values. This mapping is independent of usage. Integrator facilities depend on how the domains are used. The paradigm for reconciling stock prices may differ from reconciling salaries in different currencies, even though same currency conversions are used - for stock prices the averages may be relevant, while for salaries the annual total.

When there is a difference in precision among databases, domain size varies with the precision. For example one database specifies the weight_of_ship as 'heavy', 'middle', 'light' and 'ultra-light'; so the domain size of weight_of_ship is four. Suppose another database specifies weight_of_ship as integers from 1 to 1,000,000 then the domain size of weight_of_ship is a million. Similarly, if one database maintains only dollars for the transaction amount, while the other maintains dollars and cents, then the two transactions of $55.45 and $55.40 will appear to be of equal value in the first database, while different in the second database.

Mappings among domains have a wide variety of characteristics:

- Domain mappings could be multi-valued; for example, a job in one company may correspond to a set of possible jobs in another company.

- Domain mappings may depend on contexts or usages, involving auxiliary rules for integrating domains. For example 85% might mean 'B' for an undergraduate course, but 'A' for graduate courses.

- The mapping might be arithmetic-based, like currency conversion, or it may be arbitrary based on some rules, like mappings between jobs or colours, or the mapping from the numeric grades to letter grades. It might be only an estimate, say from letter grades to numeric grades: A=95, B=85, so as to facilitate statistical computation over large sets of students receiving both letter and numeric grades.

- If the mapping is not 1:1, then it does not have a (single-valued) inverse. There is no natural inverse of mapping from numeric grades to letter grades. If an arbitrary estimate is introduced to serve as the inverse, then value may not be preserved when inversed: a 90 may map to an A, then map back to a 95.

- Mappings might be provided only among existing domains, or a new domain might be introduced as a common denominator. For example, ECU or European Currency Unit might be common denominator, different systems of grading restaurants may be converted into a Low-Medium-High scale.

- Domain mappings might be extended to yield auxiliary information besides a target domain value. The result might also include information about the source domain, or about the mapping process. Thus a conversion to dollars might yield the result <55.45,GBP,1.85>. ie a dollar value, the original currency and the exchange rate used for conversion.

- The problem of maintaining mappings does not arise, if the domains are fixed and the mappings are totally defined, e.g. by a computation on data values. This is the case for units conversions, or string mappings based on concatenation or similar operations. The maintenance problems often arises from changes in the source or target domains. Things might be added to the source domains or things might be removed from the target domains - which may lead to non-existence of matching values in the target domain for some values in the source domain. The general problems of maintaining mappings are to determine (i) when and how such population changes are detected and the necessary adjustments initiated, (ii) how the corresponding elements in the other domain can be discovered or created, (iii) how the mappings are adjusted.

5.4 Schematic Discrepancy Between Data And Metadata

Schematic discrepancies[71] arise when data in one database correspond to metadata in another. This problem can be illustrated by the following example, related to the interest-rate in housing loan market, showing three interest-rate databases: A, B and C. In all three of them there is information about the interest rate of each bank on a day.

Database - A   (one relation per Bank with one tuple per day)

ANZ:		Westpac:		NAB:	
Date	Interest-Rate	Date	Interest-Rate	Date	Interest-Rate
950408	14.18	950408	13.47	950408	12.50
950409	14.20	950409	13.50	950409	12.15

Database - B

(one relation Day_Bank_Rate or DBR with one tuple per day per Bank with its interest rate)

Database - C

(one relation Day_ANZ_WPAC_NAB or DAWN with one tuple per day & one attribute per Bank - which is the interest rate of that Bank)

DBR:		
Date	Bank	Interest Rate
950408	ANZ	14.18
950408	Westpac	13.47
950408	NAB	12.50
950409	ANZ	14.20
950409	Westpac	13.50
950409	NAB	12.15

DAWN:			
Date	ANZ	Westpac	NAB
950408	14.18	13.47	12.50
950409	14.20	13.50	12.15

In the above example, it can be seen that the values of the attribute 'Bank' in *Database-B* corresponds to:

- names of attributes in *Database-C*
- names of relations in *Database-A*

Data in Database-B corresponds to *metadata* in databases C and A.

We can observe that the schema of *Database-A* is a specialisation of the schema of the *Database-B*, because each relation in of *Database-A* corresponds to a subclass of the relation in *Database-B*. Conversely, the relation in *Database-B* can be seen as a generalization of the relation in *Database-A*. If the federated schema is to have a relation like DBR: in *Database-B*, then the schema of *Database-A* can be transformed by the discriminated union of its three relations ANZ, Westpac and NAB. The discriminant attribute may be renamed to change its name from *discriminant* to *bank*. Conversely, the *Database-B* can be partitioned by the attribute *Bank*, so that three relations are created corresponding to the three values of the attribute Bank, namely ANZ, Westpac and NAB, these new relations may be named as ANZ, Westpac and NAB respectively and they would not contain the attribute. This partitioning by attribute will result into schemas like *Database-A*.

A schema such as the one of the Database-C is an aggregation of Database-B - each tuple in Database-C is the (cartesian) aggregation of values in Database-B. Reciprocally, tuples in the Database-B can be seen as decomposition of those in Database-C. This kind of schematic discrepancies can be solved by operations along aggregation/decomposition dimension. If federated schema is to have a relation schema like the one of DBR: in Database-B, then the schema in the Database-C is transformed into appropriate schema, by the decomposition. If, however, the federated schema is to have schemas like the one for Database-C, the Database-B database schema is transformed into this form by the composition operation.

Thus, by defining extended relational operations: *discriminated union and partition by attribute*, along the generalisation/specialisation dimension, as well as *decomposition and composition* along the aggregation/decomposition dimension, metadata may be transformed into data and vice versa, in the relational context. These operations may be applied at different levels of a federated architecture, to solve different cases of schematic discrepancies.

There are other examples of having the data instances in one database to correspond to the schema elements in another. For example, jobs can be modelled as an attribute of a person in one database, while as a type in another database: 'Sam's job = Engineer ' in one database is equivalent to 'Sam is an instance of the type Engineer'.

---

[71] Saltor F., Castellanos M.G., and Garcia-Solaco M. (1993), *Overcoming Schematic Discrepancies in Interoperable Databases*, Universitat Politecnica de Catalunya, Pau Gargallo 5, E-08028 Barcelona, {saltor,castellanos,mgarcia}@lsi.upc.es

5.5 The Role Of Context In Integration

Some of the typical schema and data conflicts presented in preceding sections can be explained by the differences of contexts. When real world objects are represented in the application systems, some features of the objects are not explicitly specified, because they are obvious in the context of the applications and assumed as a matter of course. However, contexts could be different in another application, where those obvious assumptions may not hold good. These differences in contexts are reflected how the applications differ in identifying objects, defining which attributes are relevant in their definitions, naming their attributes, and so on, as explained below:

Identification differences: - How an application system would identify an object depends on the norms used in the context of the application. In some application system abbreviated names may be used to identify objects, while another may allot numeric codes, while some other may use generated object identifications.

Attribute Naming Difference: - The same attribute may be named differently in different applications, depending on the names they are accustomed to.

Definitional Difference: -The same term may be defined differently in different applications. Within generally accepted accounting principles, there are many variations of interpretations of depreciation rules and tax rules. Some features of an object may not be relevant to an application, and hence they are not included in the specifications, while others could be obvious and there is no need to specify them explicitly.

Interpretational Differences. - The same term may be interpreted differently by different functional groups. For example, the term `Diet` is a patient's diet requirement for the *Nurse* user group, while the *Dietitian* user group may regard the same term as patient's `Treatment`. It represents a basic difference in semantic interpretation of the two user groups. `Diet` of each group may mean different sets of objects and different sets of attributes of those objects.

Differences in abstraction level. - Different user groups require data to be presented in varied depth and format, the level of detail required may be different for different user groups. For example, to the user group *Nurse,* while managing a chemotherapy patient, the name of the drug and the dosage frequency may be sufficient. However, the *Oncologist* user group would need to know the full details of the patient's treatment program. On the other hand, the *Pharmacist* user group may just need information about number of chemotherapy patients being treated with a particular drug, as a guideline for reordering the drug.

Differences in association. -The nature of a user's specialisation has direct impact on the association links between the data, and symbols that represent the data. For example, the term Diagnosis could signify to a *Surgeon* the information like CAT-SCAN reports, tumour size, etc. However, an *Oncologist* might associate the same term Diagnosis with information associated with detail of oncological treatment, drug dosage monitoring, and so on.

Difference in Interdatabase Instance Identification: - Different participating applications may use slightly different name of the same object instance, but they would appear different by any computerised comparison. For example the same company may be called as 'Ford Motor Co' , ' Ford Motor Co.', 'The Ford Motor Company' 'Ford Motor USA' and so on.

In order to integrate information from various participating applications, it is important to know the context of the information at the source system and the context of its interpretation at the receiving system.[72]. A context is the collection of implicit assumptions about the meaning of the information and its quality, and these implicit assumptions are not included in the schema of the object, nor they are shown as data values in the instances of the objects. Context may not be explicitly stated, because it may be more efficient to communicate the information without the details of context. Also, the context could be so obvious in the source environment, that one may not anticipate any different interpretation, but when the information is sent from one context to another, the interpretations at the receiving site could be different from the source site.

Context may vary in three major ways as follows:

- *Geographical difference* - The way things are interpreted in USA is different from that in Australia, France or China.
- *Functional difference* - Different functional areas may interpret and use the same information differently, even within the same organisation.
- *Organisational difference* - The information used in the same function, in the same country can have different meanings for two companies. The way a credit rating is defined by Westpac could be different from the way the Commonwealth Bank does the similar things.

Autonomous applications may evolve independently in semantics, quality and content of data. Not only the stock prices are changing continuously, even the definition of the

---

[72] Madnick S.(1997), Database in the Internet Age, *Database Programming and Design, January 1997*
Srinivasan U., and Ngu A.H.H. (1995), Information Re-engineering in Co-operative Clinical Information Systems, *Working Paper, School of Computer Science and Engineering*, University of New South Wales, Australia

stock price may change, for example the Paris stock exchange may express the price in ECU (European Currency Units) instead of Francs. Keeping the associated contexts in view, it is necessary to match the information items of various applications, a conversion function may be introduced, where necessary. When the semantically related objects or information items from various applications are identified, in spite of their differences in interpretations, and insufficiency of specification of contexts, these related items could be linked together to integrate the applications.

5.6 Correspondence Assertions To Link Semantically Related Objects

We have seen in the preceding section that because of contextual differences, same real world objects are defined differently in different applications. If we need to integrate applications, without modifying their schemas, we have to link semantically related objects of the applications in spite of their conflicting representations in the schemas; we need to identify, in the component applications, the objects that share related information and assert correspondence between these related objects.

Two main steps to resolve the problem of linking the semantically related objects are:

• to find out whether and to what extent the component applications share related objects,
• to model the related objects to design the schema of the related objects.

While some automatic tools may be available for searching the various schemas to locate related objects by finding matches both at schema and instance levels, the related objects need be reviewed from the context or perspective of the user or the integrated application to ensure that the match will always be there in future. Automatic tools may help investigation, trying to find out which objects from two schemas show enough similarity in terms of names, domains, components, relationships to other objects, etc to be a candidate for a match. The system integrator is to confirm or deny the match with reference to those object-attributes, which are relevant to the user of the integrated application. This information can be recorded as correspondence assertions[73]: Each particular assertion states some relationships between two objects and their instances in two applications. The knowledge expressed by these assertions can be used either to model mappings between corresponding objects, or to appropriately merge these objects into an integrated schema.

Let us suppose that two designers model the same real world or universe of discourse (UoD) by using the same data model, they can still choose different constructs to represent the common UoDs. In object-oriented models, for instance, a designer willing to describe a component X in the object O, may choose between creating a new object X (and include a reference to X in O) or adding an attribute X to the object O. This situation where two related UoDs are represented using different data structures is called a schema conflict or a structural conflict.

The data model used may contribute in generating some structural conflicts. The more constructs a data model supports, and the more complex these constructs are, the more potential for conflicts will exist. In the ER approach, for example, the designer can represent a real world object as an entity, a relationship or an attribute. In object-oriented models, there are various possible ways of representing an association between two object classes: embedding one class as an attribute to the other, using single or cross referencing, and creating an additional object to represent the association.

Two different representations compatible with the same real world object - a library - is shown in the figure 5.2. The viewpoint represented in the schema *S1* considers *Authors* as a multivalued attribute of the entity type *Book*. Conversely, the viewpoint represented in *S2* considers *Books* as a multivalued attribute of the entity type *Author*.

If correspondence assertions are limited only to relate comparable constructs ie an entity type from one schema compared to an entity type from another schema, or an attribute from one schema compared to an attribute from another schema, a relationship type from one schema compared to an relationship type from another schema, then no assertions can be made between the schemas S1 and S2. However, it would be incorrect to merge S1 and S2 as they are. The integrator may choose to replace S1 with S2, or S2 with S1. Alternatively, the integrator may replace both schemas: by replacing S1 with S1' and S2 with S2'. In both cases the initial specifications are abandoned to make the integration possible. The reason to modify the input schemas in case of structural conflicts, is the inadequacy of mapping capabilities, between corresponding objects or among input schemas and the integrated schema. If S1 and S2 refer to the same UoD, the following two assertions describe the correspondences between their objects:

Book ≡ Author.Books with corresponding attributes: title=title, ISBN=ISBN

Book.Authors ≡ Author with corresponding attributes: name=name, birthdate=birthdate

---

[73] Spaccapietra S., Parent C. and Dupont Y. (1991), Automating Heterogeneous Schema Integration, *Technical Report, Ecole Polytechnic Federal*, Lausanne, Switzerland

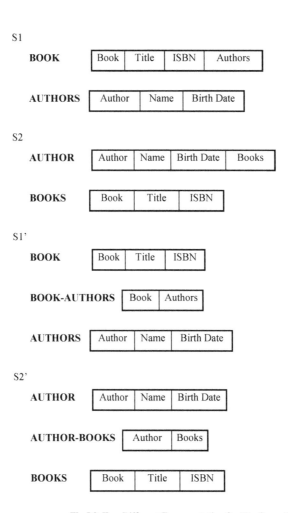

Fig 5.2 Two Different Representation for The Same UoD [74]

---

[74]   The correspondence of BOOK and AUTHORS in schema S1 respectively with BOOKS and AUTHOR in schema S2 can be asserted, irrespective of the data model chosen to represent the schemas. The figure 5.2 shows the representation of relational tables, but we could also use classes of objects to assert the same correspondence.

These assertions state that: (i) there is a structural conflict in the representation of books and authors; (ii) there is no semantic conflict concerning books and authors, (iii) there is no descriptive conflict, as books, and authors have the same attributes in both schemas.

Structural conflicts imply that a correspondence may exist between two schema objects, whether they are an object class, an attribute, a relationship etc. Assertions may thus be classified as:

• *Correspondence assertions between the objects of the same type:*

Example (S1' - S2'):   Book ≡ Books   Authors ≡ Author

• *Correspondence assertions between the objects of different types:*

Example (S1 - S2):   Book ≡ Author.Books   Book.Authors ≡ Author

These assertions state that the real world represented by the entity type *Book* in S1 is the same as the one represented by the attribute *Books* in S2. Similarly, the real world represented by the entity type *Autho*r in S2 is the same as the one represented by the attribute *Authors* in S1.

S3:

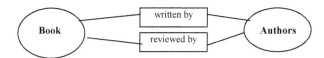

Fig 5.3 Different Links Between Same Entities

• *Correspondence assertions between links:*

The term link is used here to refer to a connection between two objects in a schema, irrespective of the data model. Depending on the data model, it may be a connection between an attribute and its parent object, a connection between two object types through a reference, or a connection between a relationship type and an entity type through a role.

Object correspondence assertions are not sufficient to completely define commonalities between two schemas. For instance, the following correspondence assertions for S1-S2:

Book ≡ Author.Books   Book.Authors ≡ Author

do not imply that the association between books and authors is the same. It could be the case that S1 talks about authors having written the associated books, while S2 describes books reviewed by each author. The integrated schema in that case will be S3 as shown in Fig 5.3. This is the schema which could be derived from the two previous assertions describing the correspondence between the objects of S1 and S2.

S4:

Fig 5.4 Same Link Between Two Entities

If, however, the semantics of the book-author links in S1 and S2 be the same, then this identity has to be explicitly stated by an assertion about links:

Books - authors ≡ books - Author

This additional knowledge leads to the integrated schema S4 in Fig 5.4.

By having correspondence assertions relating two objects from heterogeneous schemas, it can be specified whether and to what extent the inter-operating applications share related information.

5.7 Existing Conflicts In Component Databases

Some conflicts could already exist in the participating databases; in this section we evaluate our modelling-shared-data approach in terms of resolution/aggravation of these existing conflicts.

The schematic and data conflicts are mostly due to differences in representing concepts in the participating applications. Since a data repository is defined by its schema and data, conflicts can be broadly classified as either **schema** or **data** conflicts. Schema conflicts result from the use of different schema definitions in different component databases. Data conflicts are inconsistencies of data, when there are no schema conflicts. Domain mismatch problems may often be responsible for data conflicts. Figure 5.1 summarises the framework for the enumeration and classification of schema and data conflicts.

More than one system may maintain the same information separately, if two objects maintaining the similar information are semantically equivalent, they provide identical responses to the same queries. If there be different values and update cycles for the same data item maintained in different databases, they cannot be considered equivalent. If a data item can be accessed from more than one database, the item is already replicated, the object in the integrating model has to resolve the conflict. If the two sources provide different values of the same information, we may treat them as two different data items, as they are now, by qualifying the data item with the prefix of the source database.

In the following chapter, we would explore how these different classes of conflicts can be identified and resolved in the integrating schema. Here, we can see that these conflicts do not pose any extra problems in our modelling-shared-data approach of schema integration, rather we need to deal with only a subset of conflicts, which are relevant to the data items exchanged across databases.

6. WAYS TO RESOLVE CONFLICTS IN DISPARATE APPLICATION SYSTEMS

6.1 Introduction

An integrated information system can be constructed by interconnecting a set of existing disparate systems so as to enable cooperation among these systems. One way of achieving interoperability among the component systems is by transforming the schemas of the existing systems to increase their similarities and then by merging the transformed schemas. The other way of achieving interoperability is to identify the correspondence among the related elements of the schemas involved and specify these inter-schema correspondences by suitably modelling these related elements; the original schemas are allowed to continue as before. In this chapter we shall explore how we can enhance the second approach by identifying the correspondences between the export schemas only, as the data items, which are private to an application, need not be considered for integration.

In this chapter, we have structured our discussion as follows:

In the Section 6.2, we shall discuss on how to standardise the schemas to be integrated by applying a number of schema transformations, so that similarities between the schemas are increased to facilitate the process of schema integration.

In the Section 6.3, we shall discuss the other way of schema integration by identifying correspondence between conceptual schemas of the component applications. Inter-schema correspondences can be used to identify the elements that have to be inserted in the integrating schema, to find out where these elements are distributed in the local databases, and how the elements from the integrating schema can be mapped into initial schemas and vice versa.

In the Section 6.4, we shall report on some recent research work that aims to discover the concepts common to the component application systems, and identify correspondence. Based on a numerical measure of similarity, objects can be grouped into clusters ie collections of objects where intra-cluster similarity is high and inter-cluster similarity is low.

In the Section 6.5, we shall introduce an architecture of integration where the correspondences are identified only in the export schemas of the component applications, which makes the task of integration much simpler.

Section 6.6 presents conclusion that leads to detailed proposal of this architecture in the next chapter.

6.2 Schema Transformation To Increase Conformity and The Integration
6.2.1 View Integration and Database Integration

Schema integration is the process of integrating schemas of related applications into one integrated schema, so that semantically similar concepts from different schemas are mapped against one another[75]. This process includes both *View Integration* and *Database Integration*..

View integration methodologies are used when the component views are based on the same data model. Records in the database are stored as schemas, not as views; views cannot be created/deleted/modified without creating/deleting/modifying the schemas they are derived from. Programs, that use the view, access the objects as per the schema, a part of which is expressed in a view.

Database integration, on the other hand, is meant for cases where local schemas are based on different data models, have an associated extension ie. actually stored in a database, support a number of application programs, and implemented in an existing DBMS.

The most fundamental problem of schema integration is that the same real world objects can be represented by different modelling structures; depending on how the designer of an application views a phenomenon, it can be modelled as an object, an attribute or as a set of attributes. Also different applications may consider different sets of attributes of the same real world objects as relevant to them.

The schema integration process[76] can be divided into the phases of

- Schema Comparison,
- Schema Conforming and
- Schema Merging.

Schema Comparison is the phase of identifying the corresponding concepts from the involved schemas. Main activities in this phase are (1) *Name Comparison*, (2) *Structure Comparison* and (3) *Identification of Supertype-Subtype Relationships*.

Name Comparison identifies synonyms and homonyms; in case of synonyms the same fact is represented by different names while in case of homonyms different objects are represented by the same name.

Structural Comparison identifies whether the same real world aspects have been modelled using different constructs. For example, the relationships between objects can

---

[75] Batini C., Lenzerini M. and Navathe S.B. (1986), A Comparative Analysis of Methodologies for Database Schema Integration, *ACM Computing Surveys*, Vol.18, No 4, pp 323-364

either be modelled directly as attributes, or indirectly by introducing objects to tie associated objects together. The relationship of marriage can be represented by a single attribute *married_to* between the objects MAN and WOMAN, or an additional object MARRIAGE can be introduced to connect to MAN and WOMAN by attributes wife and husband. Name and Structural comparison identifies the cases where exactly the same information is represented in two schemas, by using different names and/or different structures.

Supertype-Subtype Relationships are correspondence between two schemas, when the object in one schema is the subtype of an object in the other, so an attribute in one schema is derivable from a set of attributes in the other.

Schema conforming is the second phase of transforming schemas to increase their similarities. Homonyms and synonyms are renamed, structurally different but semantically equivalent constructs are replaced by a common construct.

Schema merging is the third phase of merging multiple schemas into one. Discrepancies in names and structures have been already removed in the schema conforming phase, same concepts of different schemas are super-imposed in this phase. However, some errors, which have not been detected so far, could be revealed in this merging phase, necessitating adjustments to the comparison and conforming phases. Thus schema integration is a iterative process, moving back and forth between comparison, merging, restructuring, error analysis and redesign.

Before the integration assertions can be made, the schemas need be transformed so that it is possible to express any relationships between the schemas as simple relationships between two object or two attributes. This translation process will eliminate the cases when one object need be compared against the attribute of another object. Though the schemas are normally modified after the schema comparison has taken place, sometimes the schemas need be modified to facilitate comparison.

---

[76] Johannesson P.(1993), Schema Integration, Schema Translation, And Interoperability In Federated Information Systems, *Doctoral Thesis, Department of Computer and System Sciences, Stockholm University*, Printed by Akademitryck AB, Edsbruk

6.2.2 The Frame of Reference For Schema Integration

The schema integration process is usually massive and complex; a frame of reference is required to make this process manageable, and to verify the semantic correspondence between the schemas. The following issues need be considered in the frame of reference[77]:

1) *We require a data model with clear formal semantics that can express semantics expressed in all involved data models.* Because of higher expressive power of object-oriented data models, the schemas designed in any other data model can be expressed in the object oriented data model without any loss of information.

2) *A formal specification for relationships between different schemas should be available.* We consider the following four relationships between two objects, X_1 and X_2, from two different schemas :

- The assertion that X_1 and X_2 are equivalent, is expressed as: $X_1 \equiv X_2$
- The assertion X_1 contains X_2 ie X_1 is a superset of X_2, is expressed as: $X_1 \supseteq X_2$, where all instances of X_2 are instances of X_1, but an instance of X_1 is not necessarily an instance of X_2.
- The assertion that X_1 and X_2 intersect, is expressed as: $X_1 \cap X_2 \neq 0$
- The assertion that X_1 and X_2 are disjoint, is expressed as: $X_1 \neq X_2$.

The objects X_1 of schema S1 and X_2 of schema S2 can be expressed as $S1.X_1$ and $S2.X_2$ to show the schema, an object that belongs to the schema.

3) *The notion of conflicts between schemas should be formalised.* Conflicts between the two schemas will be specified in terms of objects of the schemas, and when two objects are compared, the conflict between the objects will be specified in terms of the attributes of the corresponding objects.

4) *The notion of correspondences between schemas should be formalised.* Correspondences between the two schemas will be specified in terms of objects of the schemas, and when two objects are compared, the correspondence between the objects will be specified in terms of the attributes of the corresponding objects.

---

[77] Johannesson P.(1993), Schema Integration, Schema Translation, And Interoperability In Federated Information Systems, *Doctoral Thesis, Department of Computer and System Sciences, Stockholm University*, Printed by Akademitryck AB, Edsbruk

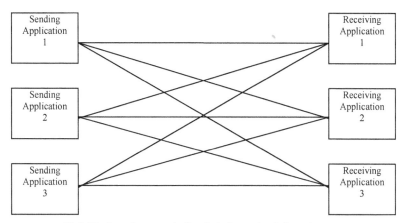

Fig 6.1 Each sender converts directly to the receiver's format

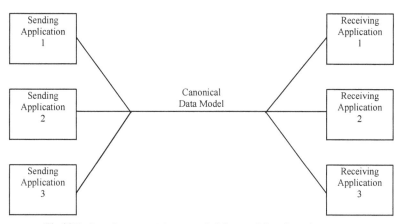

Fig 6.2 Each sender converts to a canonical data model, each receiver

converts from the canonical data model to its native data model.

6.2.3 Translation to a Canonical Data Model

When many different data models exist in a federation, it is necessary to adopt one canonical data model, so that translation can be carried out between the canonical model and the native models of the participating databases. This is necessary to obviate the need of translation from one native model to other native models. Figures 6.1 and 6.2 explains the advantage of having one canonical data model, number of inter-model translations are reduced in geometric proportions.

In order to ensure that the semantics of the participating schemas are expressed in their translations to the canonical data model, the canonical data model must have an expressive power which is not less than that of any native model in the federation. Most of the traditional data models have limited expressive power, while some of the semantics are hidden in the system specifications, application code, organisational assumptions etc. Therefore the canonical model must be rich enough to represent the semantics expressed in the local schemas as well as additional semantics captured through knowledge acquired from the application codes etc. Thus the transformation from the native data models to the canonical data model is not just a syntactic transformation, but structural and behavioural enrichment as well as to increase their semantic contents.

Another important characteristic of canonical data models is simplicity; a canonical data model should contain as few basic constructs as possible. This requirement makes an ER model inadequate as the canonical data model of the federation. When converting a local schema from its native model to an ER model, a decision must be made for each type or class to determine whether it should be an entity type or a relationship type. Again, the schema comparison is complicated, because the same fact can be modelled as an entity type

in one schema, while as a relationship type in another schema. These kinds of problems are avoided in the data models that provide just one basic construct, such as the relational data models or object-oriented data models.

Translation from traditional to conceptual models can also help Reverse Engineering, if components and relationships of an existing system need be explored. Reverse engineering usually also explores the semantic information not contained in the original system. A large number of legacy systems are still in operation, where the exact understanding of the data and procedures has been lost after years of system evolution, and reverse engineering attempts to provide that understanding, whether or not the system needs to be integrated with other systems.

6.2.4 Federation of Autonomous Applications

If, in a decentralised system, the nodes are autonomous, a central authority cannot control the co-operation and interaction among the application systems. Instead, the interaction has to be managed by means of decentralised communication and bilateral agreements between the component application systems. Each node needs to maintain knowledge about the rest of the federation, it needs to keep track of the names and addresses of other nodes, and it must be able to find out what information other nodes are prepared to export and the agreements needed for export of information.

A contract[78] is a bilateral agreement where one node, the *exporter*, is committed to make a subset of its schema available to another node, the *importer*, according to a set of contract terms. The contract refers to, from the export schema of an exporting node, the set of objects, which are made available to other nodes. The importer bases its request for import on the contract, while the exporter uses the contract to validate the import requests and monitor access to domain objects. The difference in contexts of the importer and the exporter, if any, needs be specified in the contract.

The rules by which a set of objects are made available to an importer are specified in the terms of a contract, which include: the time from the event of establishing of a valid contract to the event of terminating the contract, the method of granting access to domain objects, the deviation from expected behaviour allowed, the procedure for verifying a partner's identity, the cost for establishment and use of the contract.

The process of contract establishment consists of four phases: Announcement, Bidding, Negotiation and Commitment. *Announcement* is sent by the exporter node to a set of nodes specifying the objects for which contracts are requested, and the proposed terms of the contract. *Bidding* is the response to the announcement, with suggestion for modifying the proposed terms of contract. *Negotiation* comprises of the exchanges between the announcer and a selected bidder to make the terms acceptable. The negotiation ends when a response is a definite affirmation or denial. In the final *Commitment* phase, a contract is established in case of affirmation, otherwise the establishment process is terminated.

---

[78] Johannesson P.(1993), Schema Integration, Schema Translation, And Interoperability In Federated Information Systems, *Doctoral Thesis, Department of Computer and System Sciences, Stockholm Universit*, Printed by Akademitryck AB, Edsbruk

6.2.5 Different Forms Of Autonomy

The organisations that manage different information systems are often autonomous, ie the systems are under separate and independent controls. Different forms of autonomy can be identified, for example design, communication, and execution autonomies. *Design autonomy* means that each component database can be designed by independent choices of the data model, query language, data representation, integrity constraints, and implementation. *Communication autonomy* refers to the ability of a component system to decide how it will communicate with other systems - when and how it will respond to requests from other component systems. *Execution autonomy* indicates that a system should be able to execute its local operations without interference from operations initiated by other component systems - this implies that no external system can enforce an order of execution on a system with execution autonomy.

Based on the concepts of distribution, heterogeneity, and autonomy information systems can be classified into different types. A *centralised* information system consists of a single information system located on a single computer. For *decentralised* information systems, two alternative approaches can be taken: the composite and the federated, or multidatabase approach. In the *composite* approach, a global schema is maintained to define the inter-relationships between the schemas of the databases of component applications. A universal language is used to express access and manipulation operators, which are mediated through the global schema. Using this schema, users and applications of the component systems get the illusion of a single, centralised information system; they do not find any system or semantic heterogeneity, since all conflicts are resolved in advance. The major disadvantage of the composite approach is that it may be very expensive and time-consuming to construct a global schema, and the construction has to be repeated every time a local schema is changed or added.

In the centralised approach, local schemas are replaced by one central schema, while in the decentralised approach, local schemas continue while they are mapped to a central schema, or a number of schemas. In either of the two decentralised approaches - composite or federated, local schemas are maintained, as before integration. In the composite approach, a global schema is prepared, and mapped with the local schema, while in the federated approach, a schema is designed to integrate two inter-operating schemas. The next section shows how the schemas can be integrated, on the basis of inter-schema correspondence, by using a binary strategy i.e two schemas are integrated at a time, while the resulting schema can be again integrated with another schema.

6.3 Integration using Inter Schema Correspondence[79]
6.3.1 Inter Schema Correspondence

Whether and to what extents two schemas describe the same real world objects, and how to match their descriptions can be determined from the perspectives of the user or the application that will use the information from the schemas. Automated tools may help in evaluating some degree of similarity between two schemas, mainly based on names, structures and pattern of usage of the objects/attributes.

The knowledge of inter-schema correspondences needs be provided by the system integrators, who are conversant with representation of real world objects in the applications. Their task is to identify in each schema the objects which describe the same real world objects and state what correspondences exist among the objects in terms of their structure and population, ie schema and data contents. Following Naiman's proposal, as detailed in section 2.4.1, semantic and schematic conflicts can be classified on the three dimensions of naming, abstraction, and level of heterogeneity; this will help identify correspondences.

A correspondence assertion may be defined here as a declarative statement, asserting that some object in one schema is semantically related to some object in another schema. Correspondence assertions may be classified on the class of objects they relate:

- objects described with the same modellling concept, for example two relations (in relational schemas), two classes (in object-oriented schemas), two entity types or two relationship types (in ER schemas), two attributes;

- objects described with the different modellling concepts, for example relations vs attributes (in relational schemas), class vs attribute (in object-oriented schemas), any combination of entity type, relationship type and attribute (in ER schemas);

- links between objects, stating that a connection between two objects in a schema has the same semantics as the connection between two corresponding objects in another schema .

Correspondence assertions are declared, keeping in view the real world counterparts of the schema-objects. The objects, value attributes and reference attributes are focussed on, irrespective of data-models used.

---

[79] Some ideas presented in this section have been adapted from the following work:
Spaccapietra S., Parent C. and Dupont Y. (1991), Automating Heterogeneous Schema Integration, *Technical Report, Ecole Polytechnic Federal*, Lausanne, Switzerland

6.3.2 *Integration Based On Correspondence Assertion*

A correspondence assertion asserts the semantic relationship between some object in one schema and some other object in another schema, by specifying how their real world counterparts are related. Relationships between two objects, X_1 and X_2 can be specified as one of the four usual set relationships: equivalence, inclusion, intersection, and exclusion (ie disjointness). More assertions can be specified for the corresponding attributes of the objects, so as to clarify which attributes are compared and which attributes are totally unrelated.

Set relationships used in the assertions can be illustrated by examples of an enterprise considering integration of several local databases, as follows:

- The *product catalog*, describing all the products sold by the enterprise, may appear in various local databases. The *product catalog* is the same for all departments, all instances in the *product catalog* of one department, also appear in the *product catalog* of another department, so the *product catalog* is semantically the same to all the departments and to the application systems used by those departments, even if the *product catalog* may be modelled differently in these departments. Therefore, an *equivalence* assertion will relate the *product catalogs* together.

- Each local application database may maintain a file of department *employees*, using the same format, but an *employee* working for one department is exclusive for that department and cannot work for any other department; the object *employee* will be asserted as corresponding but *disjoint*.

- Each department may maintain a *customer* file, where some of the *customers* may appear in the *customer* files of more than one department; the object *customer* will be related by an *intersection* correspondence.

- Each department may have a file of *suppliers*, where *suppliers* are chosen from a file of pre-approved *suppliers*, maintained at the head office. The object *supplier* in local databases may intersect with each other, but the object *supplier* in each local database will be asserted as *inclusion* correspondence with respect to the *supplier* in the head office database.

As we see in the examples above, the level of semantic correspondence depends on the domain, ie possible values of instances, of the similar objects in different databases. A correspondence assertion between two objects, X_1 and X_2 from two different schemas may be asserted as follows:

The assertion that X_1 and X_2 are equivalent, is expressed as: $X_1 \equiv X_2$

The assertion X_1 contains X_2 ie X_1 is a superset of X_2, is expressed as: $X_1 \supseteq X_2$

The assertion that X_1 and X_2 intersect, is expressed as: $X_1 \cap X_2 \neq 0$

The assertion that X_1 and X_2 are disjoint, is expressed as: $X_1 \neq X_2$.

6.3.3 Corresponding attributes assertions:

Whenever a correspondence assertion is considered between two objects, it is necessary to specify which attributes of these objects are corresponding, so that semantic relationship can be checked in terms of those attributes. One to one mapping can be established between each of these relevant attributes of one object and its corresponding attribute in the other object. These corresponding attributes could be value attributes or reference attributes of the object.

Corresponding value attribute assertions:

Let us consider that there is a correspondence assertion between two objects, X_1 and X_2,

where $A_{11}, A_{12}, ...A_{1i},.. A_{1n}$ are the value attributes of X_1,

and $B_{11}, B_{12}, ...B_{1i},.. B_{1n}$ are the value attributes of X_2.

Assertion between corresponding objects means that each A_{1i} corresponds B_{1i} or $f_{1i}(A_{1i})$ corresponds B_{1i}, where f_{1i} is a conversion function.

S3:

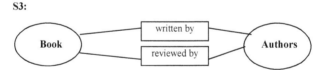

Fig 6.3 Different Links Between Same Objects

Path correspondence assertions:

The analysis of schema relationships also depends on the correspondence among the paths or reference. Suppose, the following two assertions describe the correspondences between their objects:

Book $\equiv$ Author.books with corresponding attributes: title=title, ISBN=ISBN

Book.authors ≡ Author with corresponding attributes: name=name, birthdate=birthdate. eventhough 'Book' in one schema is equivalent to 'books' in the other schema and 'authors' in one schema is equivalent to 'Author' in the other schema, this does not imply that the association between books and authors is the same. It could be the case that one talks about authors having written the associated books, while the other describes books reviewed by each author.

The integrated schema in that case will be S3 as shown in Fig 6.3.
If, however, if there is a path correspondence assertion :

        Books - authors ≡ books - Author

This additional knowledge leads to the integrated schema S4 in Fig 6.4

S4:

Fig 6.4 Same Links Between Same Objects

6.3.4 Integration Process:
The schema integration process is required to define, for each object in the initial schemas,

- what objects have to be inserted into the resulting schema
- the distribution information attached to these objects, showing on which local database which subset of the corresponding population may be found.
- the mappings between the initial schema and the integrated schema.

The mappings will support translation of global queries against the integrated schema into local queries against the local schemas.

6.3.5 Integration of the corresponding attributes of two equivalent schemas:
While establishing semantic links between two application schemas (say, S1 and S2), we need to identify the corresponding objects of these schemas - say the object O1 of the schema S1 and the object O2 of the schema S2. We also need to identify which attributes of these objects are comparable.

If it is asserted that $O1 \equiv O2$, with corresponding attributes A1 and A2, then the integration of attributes A1 and A2 will result in an attribute A, such that:

- its name is A, which could be chosen to be A1, A2 or any other name
- its domain should include the union of the domains of A1 and A2
- number of possible values would depend on set relation between A1 and A2, as follows:

  - If A1 = A2, or A1 $\supseteq$ A2, then the minimum number of possible values of A is same as that of A1, and the maximum number of possible values is same as that of A1.

  - If A1 $\cap$ A2 $\neq$ 0, then the minimum number of possible values of A is the higher of the two minimum number of possible values of A1 and A2, and the maximum number of possible values of A is the sum of the two maximum number of possible values of A1 and A2.

  - If A1 $\cap$ A2 = 0 ie A1 $\neq$ A2 , then the minimum number of possible values of A is the sum of the two minimum number of possible values of A1 and A2, and the maximum number of possible values of A is the sum of the two maximum number of possible values of A1 and A2

If A2 = f(A1), then the distribution information associated to A will state that

  - A appears as A1 is on database S1, and

  A's derived attribute A2 appears on the database S2.

6.3.6 *Integrate-join of two objects:*

In the last section, we considered correspondence of two objects, based on only one attribute A. Let us consider semantic proximity[80] of the object O1 of the database schema S1 with the object O2 of the database schema S2, when O1 has the multiple value attributes $(A_{11}, \ldots , A_{1m}, B_1, \ldots B_n)$ and O2 has the multiple value attributes $(A_{21}, \ldots , A_{2m}, C_1, \ldots C_o)$, and O1 $\in$ S1, O2 $\in$ S2, such that O1 $\equiv$ O2 with corresponding attribute pairs (A_{11}, A_{21}) .... (A_{1m}, A_{2m}).

The integration of the objects O1 and O2, will result into the new integrated object-type O, whose attributes will be the union of attributes of O1 and O2, defined as follows:

  - attributes $(B'_1, \ldots B'_n)$ for each of attributes $(B_1, \ldots B_n)$ of O1, for which there is no correspondent attribute in O2; the domain and number of possible values of these attributes will be equal to those of $(B_1, \ldots B_n)$,

---

[80] By semantic proximity, we mean how close is the smantic relationship between the objects - equivalence, inclusion, intersection or disjoint.

- attributes $(C'_1,..... C'_o)$ for each of attributes $(C_1,..... C_o)$ of O2, for which there is no correspondent in O1; the domain and number of possible values of these attributes will be equal to those of $(C_1,..... C_o)$,

- attributes $(A'_1,..... A'_m)$ for each pair of correspondent attributes of O1 and O2 ie $(A_{11}, A_{21}) .... (A_{1m}, A_{2m})$.

The population of O will have one instance for each instance of O1 and O2, where each instance will have attributes $(A'_1,..... A'_m)$, $(B'_1,..... B'_n)$ and $(C'_1,..... C'_o)$ as specified above.

Correspondence assertions relating O to O1 and O2 are as follows:

$O \equiv O1$ with corresponding attribute pairs $(A'_1, A_{11}) .... (A'_m A_{1m})$, and attribute pairs $(B'_1, B_1) .... (B'_n, B_n)$,

$O \equiv O2$ with corresponding attribute pairs $(A'_1, A_{21}) .... (A'_m A_{2m})$, and attribute pairs $(C'_1, C_1) .... (C'_o, C_o)$,

Mapping from/to O to/from O1 and O2 are as follows:

O is split into vertical fragments, where

$(B'_1,..... B'_n)$ can be mapped from $(B_1,..... B_n)$ from database S1,

$(C'_1,..... C'_o)$ can be mapped from $(C_1,..... C_o)$ from database S2, and

$(A'_1,..... A'_m)$ can be mapped from $(A_{11}, ..., A_{1m})$ from S1 or from $(A_{21}, ..., A_{2m})$ from S2.

6.3.7 Integration of objects that appear on only one schema:

Suppose, an object O1 of schema S1 has no correspondent object in another schema, then it is to be added to the integrated schema as an object O, where the type of O is same as that of O1.

Correspondence assertion : $O \equiv O1$

Mapping: $O = O1$

Distribution : O is O1 on database O1.

6.3.8 Integration Of Two Links:

Let two linked objects A1 and B1 in database schema S1, correspond to two linked objects A2 and B2 in database schema S2, with the following correspondence assertions:

$A1 \equiv A2$

$B1 \equiv B2$

$A1—B1 \equiv A2—B2$

let A be the integrated object corresponding to A1 and A2 in the integrated schema,

let B be the integrated object corresponding to B1 and B2 in the integrated schema,

then the integration of A1—B1 and A2—B2 links is a link A—B. The type of the link depends upon those of A and B:

- if A or (and) B is a value attribute then A—B is an attribute link

- if A and B are objects then A—B is a reference link; a reference attribute named B is added to A and vice-versa.

As the three correspondence assertions are equivalence ones, the integrated link A—B will have the same number of possible values as the links A1—B1 and A2—B2.

Correspondence assertions:

$$A—B \equiv A1—B1$$
$$A—B \equiv A2—B2$$

6.3.9 Integration of two paths:

A path is a series of links between two elements in a schema. For example, if E_1, E_2, ... E_n be elements of schema S_1, such that E_1 is linked to E_2, E_2 is linked to E_3, ... E_{n-1} is linked to E_n, then the series of links E_1–E_2–E_3–.....–E_{n-1}–E_n is a path between E_1 and E_n.

If F_1, F_2, ... F_p be elements of schema S_2, such that F_1 is linked to F_2, F_2 is linked to F_3, ... F_{p-1} is linked to F_p, then the series of links F_1–F_2–F_3–.....–F_{p-1}–F_p is a path between F_1 and F_p.

Suppose, there is a correspondence between E_1 and F_1, and between E_n and F_p, such that $E_1 \equiv F_1$ and $E_n \equiv F_p$. Now, we integrate the schemas S_1 and S_2 into the integrated schema S having the elements G_1 and G_n, so that $G_1 \equiv E_1 \equiv F_1$ and $G_n \equiv E_n \equiv F_p$.

We now need to consider the path between G_1 and G_n.

A path is a series of links. When integrating two paths, we need to find out, if each path bears any different information, or it can be deduced from the other.

A path E_1–E_2–E_3–.....–E_{n-1}–E_n has some extra information only if one of the elements in the path has any attribute, or maximum cardinality in one of the links E_1–E_2–E_3–.....–E_{n-1}–E_n is more than one, otherwise the path is equivalent to a direct link between E_1 and E_n.

Similarly, a path F_1–F_2–F_3–.....–F_{p-1}–F_p has some extra information only if one of the elements in the path has any attribute, or maximum cardinality in one of the F_1–F_2–F_3–....–F_{p-1}–F_p is more than one, otherwise the path is equivalent to a direct link between F_1 and F_p.

If the path between E_1 and E_n is information bearing, then it needs be modelled in the integrated schema S. Similarly, if the path between F_1 and F_p is information bearing, then it needs be modelled in the integrated schema S.

6.3.10 Integration Of An Object And An Attribute

Let X_1, with value attributes $(A_{11}, ... , A_{1m}, B_1,.....B_n)$ be an object of schema S_1, and X_2 be a complex attribute of object E_2 of schema S_2 where value attributes of X_2 are $(A_{21}, ... , A_{2m}, C_1,.....C_p)$.

The correspondence assertion here maps an object X_1 to a complex attribute X_2:

$X_1 \equiv X_2$ with corresponding attribute pairs $(A_{11}, A_{21}).... (A_{1m}, A_{2m})$.

Let E be the object corresponding to E_2 in the integrated schema.

The objects in the integrated schema resulting from the integration of X_1 and X_2 are an object X, and a reference link between E and X, such that:

- the value attribute X_2 of E_2 is transformed into X'_2 referencing X; number of possible values of X'_2 are equal to that of X_2,

- the name of X is arbitrarily chosen,

- the structure of X consists of the union of X_1 and X_2 attributes as defined by the integrate-join of X_1 and X_2.

 Correspondence assertions relating X to X_1 and X_2 are as follows:

$X \equiv X_1$ with corresponding attribute pairs (A_1, A_{11}) .... (A_m, A_{1m}), and attribute pairs (B'_1, B_1) .... (B'_n, B_n),

$X \equiv X_2$ with corresponding attribute pairs (A_1, A_{21}) .... (A_m, A_{2m}), and attribute pairs (C'_1, C_1) .... (C'_p, C_p),

Correspondence assertions relating to reference links are as follows:

$S_1— X_1 \equiv E_2— X_2 \equiv E— X$

Mapping between X   and X_1 and X_2 are as follows:

 X is split into two vertical fragments, where

 $[A_1,..... A_m, B'_1,....,B'_n]$ can be mapped from $[A_{11}, ..., A_{1m},B_1,...,B_n]$ from database S_1, and

 $[A_1,...., A_m, C'_1,...,C'_p]$ can be mapped from $[A_{21},..., A_{2mj},C_1,..,C_p]$ from database S_2,

 The E— X link is on database S_2 only.

The effect of applying the above rules of relating an object to an attribute of another object can be seen from the example below:

S1:   Class Car   Car# : ....

                       Colour: ....

                       Horsepower: ....

                       Owner tuple < id#: ...., name: ...., sex: ...., birthdate: ....>

S2: Class Person Id# : ....

                       name: ....

                       sex: ....

                       Birthdate: ....

                       Cars set {car tuple < car#: ...., colour: ...., horsepower: ....>}

Correspondence assertion, here, maps Car.Owner to Person, and also Person.Cars to Car.

The integration of S1 and S2 results in classes S3 and S4:

S3: Class	Person	S4: Class	Car
	Id#:		Car#: ....
	name:		Colour: ....
	sex:		Horsepower: ....
	Birthdate:		Owner reference Person
	Cars set {car reference Car}		

6.4 Conceptual Clustering To Identify Correspondence

The purpose of cluster analysis[81] is to place objects into groups, such that objects in a given cluster tend to be similar to each other in some sense and objects in different clusters tend to be dissimilar.

In order to establish a cluster of objects, each object is characterised by a set of variables. The variables are chosen such that they are good indicators of both the structure and usage of the database objects and also serve to establish similarity measures among the objects that are clustered. For example, data used in the clustering process could be gathered at three different levels:

a) data relating to structure such as *Number of attributes* and *Number of foreign keys* may be gathered from the data dictionaries of each individual component system,

b) data relating to usage such as *Number of users* and *Number of categories of users*,

---

[81] Srinivasan U., and Ngu A.H.H. (1995), Information Re-engineering in Co-operative Clinical Information Systems, *Working Paper, School of Computer Science and Engineering, University of New South Wales,* Australia

Srinivasan U., Ngu A.H.H and Gedeon T. (1995), Concept Clustering for Cooperation, *IFIP DS-6 Conference, Atlanta, Georgia, May 1995*

c) data relating to maintenance/updates of the database such as *Update frequency* and *Number of tuples.*

A clustering algorithm can be used to partition these objects into clusters using the values of the variables. The clusters thus formed are meaningful in such a way that each cluster actually represents a generic concept in the application domain.

These concept clusters, labelled as appropriate generic concepts, can serve as the starting point in providing a customised external view to different user groups. The set of concepts meaningful to a given User Group, called Group Data Objects, is a subset of the common generic concepts discovered using the discovery process outlined above. The interpretation differences between different user groups is supported by providing appropriate context-labels to the Group Data Objects. These context-labels thus represent concepts that are meaningful to a particular User Group.

6.5 Integration By Identifying Correspondence In Export Schemas Only

Integration by identifying correspondence among schemas is more easily implemented than integration by schema transformation and schema merging, because the work required for schema transformation to increase the similarity between schemas increases in geometrical propotions when the number of applications increases. Moreover some features of the integrated application are expected to be different from those of the component applications, while integration by identifying correspondence among schemas allows the schemas of the component applications to continue as before.

An integration architecture can be designed by considering only the sharable features of the individual application systems, where correspondence can be asserted between the sharable features of two component applications. The benefits of this approach are:

- inter-schema correspondences and differences among the applications in representing the same real world objects need be reconciled only for the shared data items, i.e for a subset of all data items involved; data items which are private to one application only need not be considered.

- complexity of schema transformation and designing a global schema need not be addressed, as the integrating application need to consider only selected parts of the underlying schemas.

- the local schemas of the component applications will remain unchanged as they are used independently of other participating applications, except that a part of each underlying schema will be modelled in the integrating application.

6.6 Conclusion & Integration With Shared Data Only

The approach of *Integration Based On Correspondence Assertion,* as shown in this chapter is based on the following major considerations:

- Resolution of structural conflicts resulting from different representation of the same real world objects,
- Conflict resolution without modifying the initial schemas,
- Applicability to a variety of data models.

Structural conflicts necessarily arise from user requirements, as different needs exist in the real world. Instead of forcing schemas to conform to a unique representation, mapping facilities need be provided to map initial schemas to the integrated schema, and vice-versa. By having model independent integration rules, one can ensure that the integration strategy is consistent over various models. Moreover, it becomes feasible to allow description of inter-schema correspondences directly on the existing schemas, without requiring a preliminary step to translate all existing schemas into their equivalent schemas based on some common model. The resulting system can be made user-friendly through support of multi-model interface, allowing each user to interact the integrated database through the preferred data model.

This approach can be implemented even more economically, if identification of interschema correspondences is restricted to only the data items that are relevant for integration, ie the data items that are shared between more than one applications; this means - only a subset of the conflicts need be considered; the conflicts that are not related to any shared data need not be modelled. Therefore, the number of conflicts that need be resolved, is less than that in an approach where all data items of the application are considered.

If the integrated schema is based on an object-oriented model, then the mapping problems, described in Chapter 5, are not encountered at all, because it is convenient to map objects at any level of granularity. For example, an object may contain another object, while both the container object and the contained object can be mapped to a third object; but it may not be feasible to treat an entity and its attribute in the same manner.

One of the objective of this integration is to ensure that the integrated schema represents at least as much information as provided by each of the original schemas; since the proposed method allows the component systems to continue as before, the information of the original schemas remain available to the users.

7. THE PROPOSED ARCHITECTURE

7.1 Introduction

We have reviewed, in chapters 5 and 6, how the same real world objects are represented differently, while different real world objects appear to be the same in the schemas of the inter-operating applications. We have also checked how these conflicts of similarities and differences can be resolved to integrate these applications. In this chapter, we propose an approach to simplify this integration process by identifying a subset of objects of each involved application, so that the integration of the component applications can be achieved by integrating only the selected subsets of objects from these applications. We shall propose the rules of selecting these subsets, and check that subsets, selected by these rules, are not only necessary for inter-operation between applications, they are also sufficient for this purpose and no other objects need be considered. We shall also evaluate the obvious advantages of working with the subset of objects than modeling all objects of all involved applications. We shall compare the advantages of having an object-oriented application as the integrating application with those of having an application using a relational database. Finally, we shall review the architecture, proposed in this chapter, with one reference architecture and other approaches of application integration.

While reviewing the work done so far to solve inter-application conflicts, we have seen that the research has been carried out to suit different scales of operations ie. (1) integrating two applications of an organisation, by comparing and matching their schemas, (2) setting up an architecture, where many applications build interfaces using one canonical data model and data manipulation language - so that they appear homogeneous, and (3) setting up an infrastructure, using CORBA or similar standards, where any participating application needs comply with the rules for traders or object-request-brokers. We have seen that the problem of schema integration still persists. In spite of the attempts to build the infrastructure for open systems, most of the existing application systems and a major part of the applications being developed are not in a position to comply with infrastructural standards.

We have identified that one problem of application integration, is that only a part of the real world object is represented in an application, while the context of each application explains the parts which are not represented. Also, the same piece of reality may be modelled differently in different applications, either because the data models support equivalent constructs, or because designers have different perceptions of the reality. We have seen in chapter 5, broadly two classes of conflicts need be reconciled in order to achieve integration of applications, which are schema conflicts and the data conflicts. In this chapter we propose an approach to solve schema conflicts only; we would briefly consider resolving data conflicts when there is no schema conflicts, by matching object instances in two applications, when those instances belong to equivalent classes of objects.

The process of schema integration has the objectives of linking the semantically related objects in spite of their structural differences. This can be achieved mainly in two different ways - one involves transformation of schemas used by different applications, while the other aims to establish correspondence without transforming the schemas. The second approach is preferred, because changes and disruptions in the existing applications are less, autonomy and organisation of the local applications are less affected, and local database management systems, if any in the component application, need not be replaced by a distributed database management system encompassing all applications.

The first approach involves schema transformation to increase similarity between conceptual schemas of the component applications, schema comparison to identify correspondences and achieve compatibility, and integration of the local schemas into one integrated schema for the integrating application.

The second approach aims to get the best of the both worlds - different applications are allowed to use different data models and database or file management systems, and to enjoy complete autonomy as regards the design of the applications. Correspondence is asserted between elements at different hierarchical levels of schemas of component application systems, which again may use different data models. The initial schemas are not modified, but facilities to map between the integrated schemas and initial schemas are provided.

In this chapter, we like to build on the second approach, by concentrating on only the information that matters, ie, the information shared across application systems, while the information, that concerns an individual application system only, need not be considered for modelling into the integrating application. Three main ideas that provided inspiration to the proposed architecture are (1) use of only the export schema rather than the entire schema, (2) correspondence assertions between elements of the export schemas, (3) object modelling to hide the details of the schema not appearing in the export schemas.

(1) The idea of *Export Schema* has been developed from the concept of federated database architecture[82]. Our definition of shared data items has been expanded to include also the

---

[82] Heimbigner D., & McLeod D. (1985), A Federated Architecture For Information Management, *ACM Transactions on Office Information Systems, July 1985*

identifiers or keys to the information exchanged and data items involved in constraints with the data items actually exchanged.

(2) The idea of *Model-Independent Assertions* for correspondence between objects of the participating application systems has been developed from the work carried out by Spaccapietra S., and Parent C., Dupont Y.[83]. But application of this technique has been restricted only to the shared objects or data items, instead of the entire schemas of participating applications. Also, model independent assertions have been simplified by using object-oriented modelling.

(3) The concept of a central application intermediating between applications has been discussed in section 3.4.5 of Chapter-3, and also in the discussion on distributed conceptual schema e.g. Papazoglou's DOODMS[84]. A central integrating application can be designed to consist of *objects* on top of each application.

Each of the objects, in the integrating application, need know only the public parts of the database maintained in the underlying application, as published in its export schema. This integrating O-O application will model interactions, ie messages and responses between objects. Since each application needs interact only with the integrating application, and not other participating applications, translation of schemas and data manipulation statements are required only from and to one DBMS/OS environment hosting the integrating O-O application.

7.2 The Major Challenges of Integration

The major challenges in designing an architecture to integrate heterogeneous applications are from the differences in the implementation of the applications.

(1) The same real world objects are often represented differently in the applications, because some features of the real world objects are not represented in the applications, but implied in the contexts of the applications.

(2) Incompatibility of the underlying applications in terms of data models and data manipulation procedures has introduced different ways of representing the same fact.

---

[83] Spaccapietra S., and Parent C. (1993), View Integration : A Step Forward In Solving Structural Conflicts, *IEEE Transactions on Data and Knowledge Engineering, 1993*
Spaccapietra S., and Parent C., Dupont Y. (1992), Model-Independent Assertions for Integration of Heterogeneous Schemas, *Very Large Databases Journal*, 1(1), July 1992
[84] Marinos L., Papazoglou M.P., & Norrie M. (1988), Towards the Design of an Integrated Environment for Distributed Databases, *Parallel Processing and Applications, Elsevier Science Publishers B.V. (North-Holland), 1988*, pp 283-288.
Papazoglou M.P., & Marinos L. (1990), An Object-Oriented Approach To Distributed Data Management, *Journal Of Systems and Software*, Vol.11, No.2, Feb'90, pp 95-109.

(3) If a central integrating application is designed, a global schema that combines all component schemas is often too complex.

(4) There is a need to maintain the local schemas so that component applications can continue to be used in the same way as they are used independent of other participating applications,

(5) There is a need to have facilities to map the integrated schema to the original local schemas.

7.3 *The Proposed Solution*

An architecture can be conceived to avoid the major challenges of application integration by considering only the sharable features of the individual application systems. An object can be developed on top of each application to export only those features, which the application can share with other application(s). Let us term these objects as *export objects*. These export objects will form a homogeneous set and participate in the integrating application system. The benefits of this approach are: (1) differences among the applications in representing the same real world objects need be reconciled only for the shared data items, ie for a subset of all data items involved, (2) incompatibility of the participating applications will not be visible, as the information and features shared among participating applications will reside within one object-oriented application, (3) complexity of a global schema need not be addressed, as only selected parts of the underlying schemas need be considered in the integrating application, (4) the local schemas of the component applications will remain unchanged as they are used independently of other participating applications, except that a part of each underlying schema will be modelled in the integrating application, (5) the export objects on top of each application provide facilities for mapping between the original local schemas and the schema of the integrating application.

This idea can be stated as follows[85]:

Each of the application systems, participating in a system of heterogeneous but inter-operating application systems, can view every other application system as an object or a collection of objects. One or more objects can be built to control each of the participating application systems. These controlling objects can then participate in a homogeneous

---

[85] Ghosh P. (1996), Integration of Application Systems by Modelling Information Shared among Applications, *Proceedings of the 31st Annual Convention of the Computer Society of India, 30th October to 3rd November, 1996, Bangalore, India*, pp 297-305.

application environment, in spite of the differences in the hardware/software/database management systems of the underlying local application systems. The export schemas of the underlying applications will be used to build an export object on top of each application. These export schemas will include only those objects that are shared across the application boundaries. These objects will form a homogeneous set and participate in an object-oriented application system, i.e. each application A_i will have an export object C_i. All export objects i.e. C_is will form a homogeneous set. These export objects C_is [i=1,2,..n] will be linked together in an integrating object-oriented application. This integrating application will model the export objects from the participating applications and the corresponding attributes of these export objects, depending on the semantic closeness or correspondence among those objects.

7.4 An Overview of The Architecture

How various components work in this architecture (Figure 7.1) is analysed as follows.

Let applications involved in a set of inter-operating and distributed applications be symbolised as $A_1, A_2, \ldots, A_i, \ldots A_n$. An object will be developed on top of each application system (say A_i), let us call this object as *Export Object* (say C_i). All communications to and from the application A_i will be via its export object C_i. Each application system A_i will view every other application, via the export object C_i as an object, or a collection of objects, which means C_i will communicate with another export object C_j, which in turn query/update the corresponding application A_j.

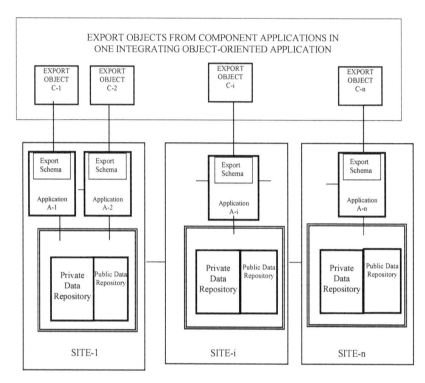

EXPORT OBJECTS FROM COMPONENT APPLICATIONS IN
ONE INTEGRATING OBJECT-ORIENTED APPLICATION

Figure 7.1 Integration Architecture Based On Export Schemas

N.B. The figure shows several sites SITE-1, SITE-2, ...SITE-i, ...SITE-n.

Each site contains data repositories, and applications A-1, A-2, ...A-n are run on these sites. There could be several applications on the same data repository. Each application has its own schema for the data stored in the underlying repository. Each application determines what parts of the data repository are private and what parts are public. For the sake of simplicity, rigid boundaries are shown between public and private parts.

What each application shares with other applications, is specified in the export schema. The export object C-i is built from the export schema of the application A-i.

Export objects C-1, C-2, ...C-n form an object-oriented application that integrates the applications A-1, A-2, ...A-n.

Correspondence between one export object C_i and another export object C_j can be asserted as one of the following: $\equiv$ (equivalent), $\neq$ (not equal), $\subset$ (subset of), $\supset$ (superset of), $\rightarrow$ (refers[86]). When two export objects are compared for being asserted as equivalent, not-equal etc, they will be compared in terms of a set of attributes common to these objects.

Each C_i may be modelled to be aggregation of other objects, say C_{i1} ....C_{ik}.

C_is could be linked to C_js at any level of granularity, ie, corresponding counterparts of C_i in the underlying application could be a table in one case, a row of a relation in another, or even the DBMS itself.

An application A_i can be on any hardware, under the control of any operating system and DBMS /file management systems. All C_i's must form a homogeneous set, ie on compatible hardwares, under the control of same operating system and DBMS. All C_i's, will be linked into an object-oriented application system, which could be supported by suitable DBMS or ODBMS.

Every application A_i would communicate to its export object C_i only for the export and import features of the application, where the export features are those what A_i can make available for C_i and the import features are those what C_i can make available for A_i. A_i is a black box to C_i, except for the export and import features of A_i, so is C_i to A_i.

At any stage of development or modification/enhancement of the application A_i, C_i knows only those features that it requires to query/update, that is C_i will be open and closed at the same time - C_i will be open and functioning with existing export/import schema of A_i, but can be closed and reused in C_i', which would be developed to include new export/import features of A_i.

Depending on the need for including new export/import features or dropping existing features, the integrating application may or may not need to modify its view of export/import schema of A_i. Accordingly, the schema of the integrating application system may be loosely or tightly coupled.

Each of the controlling objects C_1, C_2, ..., C_i, ... C_n may start a process with its underlying application at the same time when another controlling object is interacting with its corresponding application, ie these controlling objects may be operating in parallel.

Depending on the business needs of the integrating and participating applications, communications between each pair of A_i and C_i could be designed as synchronous or

---

[86] C_i refers C_k as one of its attributes.

asynchronous. Asynchronous communication is expected to provide flexibility in order to avoid any deadlock or confusion because of delays in getting replies/acknowledgment from the underlying applications. However, the communications between each pair of A_i and C_i can be designed to be synchronous, when (i) each pair of A_i and C_i and the link between them are always active, (ii) each A_i maintains updated and consistent information (each A_i updates its information at real time or maintains update cycles that is consistent with the business) and (iii) each A_i maintains a transaction management procedure (ie for concurrency control and recovery).

7.5 Main Ideas In The Proposed Architecture

As we see the integration architecture in Fig. 7.1, the integrating application is composed of the controlling/export objects, built on top of the component applications. These export objects are modelled from the export schemas of these applications, while the other private parts of the application schemas are not considered. Modelling of the integrating application is based on how the export object of a component application is related to export objects of other component applications. Data modelling language used for the integrating application needs to be expressive enough to represent the models from the underlying applications.

Main ideas of the proposed architecture, therefore, are (1) Export Schema instead of the entire schema, (2) Correspondence Assertions between elements of the Export Schemas, (3) Encapsulation to hide the details of the schema not appearing in the Export Schemas, (4) Canonical data model of the integrating application.

7.5.1 Export Schema instead of Entire Schema

In order to integrate application systems that run on different DBMS or file systems[87], we propose to model only the data items / objects that are shared across applications. This involves selecting an export schema of shared data items from each component application.

---

[87] If the component application maintains its data on file systems, it is required to identify the fields of the records, that the application is ready to share with other applications. The export object on the top of this application will access these sharable fields of the application records. This export object, in turn, will be modelled in the integrating application.

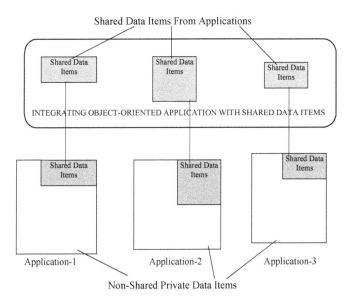

Shared Data Items From Applications

INTEGRATING OBJECT-ORIENTED APPLICATION WITH SHARED DATA ITEMS

Shared Data Items

Shared Data Items

Shared Data Items

Shared Data Items

Shared Data Items

Shared Data Items

Application-1   Application-2   Application-3

Non-Shared Private Data Items

Figure 7.2 Selection of Export Schemas from Component Applications

This sub-schema has to be independent of the rest of the schema of the underlying application. If an instance of a data item is added, deleted or modified in the subschema, it should not be necessary to update any data item in the rest of the schema to ensure consistency and integrity of information. Hence, it would not be necessary to model the rest of the schema in the integrated schema. This sub-schema, however, has to include some extra data items in addition to those being exchanged across the applications; these extra data items are those which are involved in access and/or update of the data items actually exchanged. *Shared data items*, as conceived in the proposed architecture of integration, are defined below. By the term *Data Item*, we mean the type of data or the class of objects, not the value of the data item or the instance of the object.

Shared Data Items include:

(a) Data items exchanged across application boundaries – these are the data items that are directly accessed by other applications,

(b) Data items, which are involved in a constraint with data items, directly accessed by other applications

(c) Data items which are keys ie identifiers for the data items, directly accessed by other applications, or keys ie identifiers for the data items, which are involved in a constraint with those directly accessed data items

If a shared data item is involved with a second data item, such that the latter is either a key for accessing the shared data item or is involved in a constraint with the shared data item, then the second data-item has to be included in the list of shared data items. When this second data-item is included, checks are to be made again for its involvement with any other data-item, if any, which needs be included too. This step will be repeated with every new data-item added until there is no other data-item to be included.

A schema of shared data-items[88] is a subset of the entire schema of a participating application. Iterative steps of picking up all data items involved with the shared data items ensures that the export sub-schema is independent of what is left out in the rest of the data-items of the entire schema.

A set of shared data-items is sufficient, if we get no different information by adding any extra item. As we have included all data-items that are related to the shared data items, any other items is unrelated and would convey no extra information.

All the items in the set are necessary, if removal of an item from the schema of the integrating application leads to inaccessibility of information about a required data-item. Those items, which are supposed to be shared across applications, need to be present in the integrating application; therefore we cannot delete any of those items from the schema of the integrating application. We cannot delete the key of data items exchanged across application boundaries, because the relevant data items cannot be accessed without using the keys. We cannot delete any item that is involved in the integrity constraints because we need ensure

---

[88] By the term *Data Item*, we mean the type of data or the class of objects, not the value of the data item or the instance of the object.

that the integrity constraints are maintained, when the concerned shared data item is updated.

7.5.2 Correspondence Assertions between Objects of the Export Schema

Each application represents some *Real World Objects;* to each of these applications, an object is a collection of attributes. Each application has its own set of attributes for the same real world object. Two applications may represent the same or semantically related *Real World Objects,* but different sets of attributes of the same real world object are relevant to different applications.

Two objects are same/different from the perspective of the applications, depending on which attributes are relevant to an application. An object of one application can be equivalent to another object of another application, in terms of certain attributes, relevant to the application - application integration needs to link the semantically related objects of two applications.

Again, some of the application objects are private, these objects are not visible to other applications. Only those objects, which are shared with other applications, are public and visible to other applications. These objects are included in the export schema of the application. Public objects of one application could be semantically related to public objects of another application. We propose to integrate applications by linking semantically related public objects on the respective export schemas.

When we design an integrated schema to assemble the export schemas of the component applications, we need to identify how the objects in one export schema are related to the objects in another export schema. If we go down to the level of objects in each component schema, we need to identify in each schema the objects which describe the same real world objects and ascertain correspondences among them in terms of their structure and population, ie schema and data contents. Semantic and schematic conflicts between objects can be classified on the three dimensions of naming, abstraction, and level of heterogeneity in order to identify correspondences [Chapter 4, section 4.5.1]. Possible *naming conflicts* are synonyms, homonyms and unrelated. *Abstraction conflicts* are to check if one object is a generalisation, aggregation, or computed function of another, or of a different class. The *level of heterogeneity* specifies the level of schematic granularity being compared ie whether the comparison is between two objects, between an object and an attribute. A correspondence assertion[89] between the objects of two export schemas is to specify how their real world counterparts are related. The relationships between two objects[90], X_1 and X_2, can be specified as one of the four usual set relationships: equivalence, inclusion, intersection, and exclusion (ie disjointness). Correspondence assertions between objects are specified in terms of the relationships of the corresponding attributes of the objects, these assertions clarify which attributes are compared and which attributes are totally unrelated.

Set relationships[91] used in the assertions are illustrated below by examples of an enterprise considering integration of several local databases. These relationships are captured by object oriented modelling of the related objects for the integrating application.

- **Equivalence** - All services provided by the enterprise are shown in the service catalogue, and this catalogue may appear in various local databases. The service catalogue is the same for all departments, so an *equivalence* assertion will relate the service catalogues together.

- **Disjoint** - Local applications may use the same format for department employees, but an employee works only for one department; the employee will be asserted as *disjoint*. While integrating local applications, we need to introduce one attribute to show the implied context of the department; if the value of this attribute is different, then the object employee is different. The object employee in the schema of one departmental application is disjoint from the object employee in the schema of a different departmental application, because the corresponding attribute department is different in the two objects.

- **Intersection** - Each department may maintain a customer file, where some of the customers may appear in the customer files of more than one department; the object customer will be related by an *intersection* correspondence. The object customer of each department will include an attribute which is a list of departments the customer could be possibly associated; the object customer of one departmental application will intersect the object customer of a different departmental application, when this attribute - a list of departments - intersects. If however, the list-attribute associated to customers of one department does not intersect with the list-attribute associated to customers of a different department, then the object customer of these two departments do not intersect.

---

[89] Spaccapietra S., and Parent C., Dupont Y. (1992), Model-Independent Assertions for Integration of Heterogeneous Schemas, *Very Large Databases Journal*, 1(1), July 1992

[90] One may call the real world objects as external objects, and their computer representations as internal objects. In this thesis, by the term object we mean the class of external objects whose behaviour is modelled in the applications.

- **Inclusion** - Each department may have a file of suppliers, where suppliers are chosen from a file of pre-approved suppliers, maintained at the head office. The object supplier in local databases will be asserted as *inclusion* correspondence with respect to the supplier in the head office database. If an attribute of approved-supplier-flag is introduced for the object supplier of a departmental application, value of this attribute in any department, will be inherited from the attribute approved-supplier-flag, of the object pre-approved supplier of the head office.

When the export schemas are modelled together for the central object-oriented application, the assertions are incorporated in the model in terms of generalisation and specialisation of classes. For example:

1. The assertion that objects ie classes X_1 and X_2 are equivalent, is expressed as: $X_1 \equiv X_2$, where X_1 and X_2 will be merged into a single object/class in the schema of the integrating application. For example, if Services of Department-A are identical with Services of Department-B, we may merge them into the single object Services, referred by both Department-A and Department-B.

2. The assertion that X_1 and X_2 are disjoint, is expressed as: $X_1 \neq X_2$, where X_1 and X_2 will be generalised into a superclass, where X_1 and X_2 each will include one attribute, which is of different values in X_1 and X_2. For example, Employees of Department-A are disjoint from Employees of Department-B, when the attribute Department is considered, because employees can belong to only one department. However, they can be generalised as Employees of the Organisation, if Department-A and Department-B belong to the same Organisation.

3. The assertion that X_1 and X_2 intersect, is expressed as: $X_1 \cap X_2 \neq 0$, where X_1 and X_2 will have a common subclass for the intersection.

4. The assertion that X_1 contains X_2, is expressed as: $X_1 \supseteq X_2$, where X_2 will inherit some properties of X_1, and modelled as the subclass of X_1.

Since the central integrating application is object-oriented, X_1 and X_2 can be at different hierarchical levels in the underlying applications, a common design methodology can be applied to the objects at any level of granularity. Unlike in relational data models, an object can have another object as its component.

When two objects are asserted as corresponding, further assertions are required to specify the corresponding attributes in the objects, so that one to one mapping can be established

---

[91] In the section 1.7 in the Chapter 1, we have provided definitions for semantic equivalence, semantic disjoint, semantic intersection and semantic inclusion.

between each attribute of an object and its corresponding attribute in the related object. These corresponding attributes could be value attributes or reference attributes of the object.

Corresponding value attribute assertions:

Let us consider that there is a correspondence assertion between two objects, X_1 and X_2,

  where A_{11}, A_{12}, ...A_{1i},.. A_{1n} are the value attributes of X_1,

  and B_{11}, B_{12}, ...B_{1i},.. B_{1n} are the value attributes of X_2

Assertion between corresponding objects means that each A_{1i} corresponds B_{1i} or $f_{1i}(A_{1i})$ corresponds B_{1i}, where f_{1i} is a conversion function.

Path correspondence assertions:

 The analysis of schema relationships also depends on the correspondence among the paths or reference. The following two assertions describe the correspondences between objects of two schemas [Shoe, persons] and {Person, shoes]:

  Shoe ≡ Person.shoes with corresponding attributes: size=size, Model=Model

  Shoe.persons ≡ Person with corresponding attributes: name=name, birthdate=birthdate.

These value attribute assertions do not imply that the association between shoes and persons is the same. It is possible that the reference in one schema is about *Persons* having made the *shoes*, while, in the other schema, the reference describes *Shoes* worn by each *person*.

If, however, if there is a path correspondence assertion:

  Shoe ⇔ persons ≡ shoes ⇔ Person,

then the association is same in both schemas, not *made_by* in one and *worn_by* in another.

   After similarities and differences among the export schemas are determined in the above lines, these export schemas will be integrated into a schema for the central application. The central schema will consist of objects showing: a set of objects, a list of super-objects[92] in which the object can be generalised into, a set of attributes that distinguish one object from another, keys that uniquely identify each instance of the objects, relationships of an object with other objects, domains of the attributes. The schema integration process is required to define, for each object in the initial export schemas: (i) what objects have to be included in the resulting schema for the central object-oriented application, that comprises export objects on top of each application, (ii) the distribution information attached to these objects, showing which subset of the corresponding population

---

[92] Super-objects are defined here as superclasses of objects.

may be found in which underlying application. (iii) the mappings between the initial schema and the integrated schema, and vice-versa.

The mappings will support translation of queries, raised from any of the underlying application, into global queries to suit the integrated schema, and again translation of queries on the integrated schema into local queries to suit the local schemas of the underlying application.

7.5.2.1 Correspondence Assertions Between Instances of Application Objects
In the previous section, we have discussed how we can relate application objects from one export schema to those in another export schema, and how these relationships can be modelled in the integrating application. These relationships among application objects can be modelled in terms of their structure or schema; but can be also evaluated for population, ie data contents. When we assert correspondence between an object of one application, to an object in another application in terms of data contents, we need to identify the instances of one application object that match the instances of another application object. The instance of the object in each of the application needs to be identified by a unique key or identifier, we need to establish correspondence between these unique keys or an abstraction or a computed function of the key. For example, let I_1 be instance of the object O_1 of the application A_1, where I_1 is identified by the unique identifier K_1, and let I_2 be instance of the object O_2 of the application A_2, where I_2 is identified by the unique identifier K_2.

We may specify the condition of equivalence between the instances I_1 and I_2 is as follows:

$K_1 = K_2$, or $K_1 = f(K_2)$, ie the value of K_1 can be derived from that of K_2. Once we establish correspondence between one object instance from one application and another object instance from another application, then values of other attributes of the object instance can be deciphered from the instance identified by the equivalent key. Suppose, we need to compile details of one person, who maintains accounts with different banks and credit unions. We need to establish, that these accounts, though maintained by different banks, belong to the same person, and his assets and liabilities can be determined by evaluating the accounts related to the same person. If both banks maintain the attribute of Tax-File-Number for the person, semantic equivalence of the two person-instances can be asserted, when the attribute Tax-File-Number has the same value in both banks' applications.

It may be of some interests here to consider equivalence of two application objects in terms of data contents, then we need to consider whether the two objects have the same attributes *always* or *only on a certain special occasion*. If they need to be equivalent on all occasions, then we need to consider maintenance of data values of the instances over time - take care of complexities caused by replication of the objects at different sites, transaction management[93], synchronous/asynchronous communication to ensure all replicas maintain same values.

7.5.3 Encapsulation to Hide Non-Export Details

The integrating application can be designed to consist of *Export Objects* for each application. Each of the export objects C_i for applications A_i needs to know only the public interface of the database maintained in the corresponding application A_i. The integrating application will model interactions, ie messages and replies between objects.

This solution provides the following advantages:

- Implementation differences among underlying data repositories of applications A_i need not be resolved, as export objects C_i only care for its interfaces with other objects C_j, but need not care how the methods are implemented in those other objects C_j.

- Those data items of the underlying applications that do not appear in the export schemas, need not be modelled in the integrating applications, and the schema of the integrating application does not care about non-export details.

- Semantics of relationships between various data-items in the applications are captured with more precision in the object-oriented data model, at all levels of granularity.

- Since the objects are designed only on the sharable (or the export) features of the individual applications, no expensive data modelling is required to capture the entire semantics of individual applications.

7.5.4 Canonical Data Model of the Integrating Application

When many different data models exist in a set of applications to be integrated, it is necessary to adopt one canonical data model for the integrating application, so that translation can be carried out between the canonical model and the native models of the

---

[93] Data replication in distributed databases, has been discussed in Appendix-IX. In Appendix-XVI, we have discussed on (1) operations in the system, integrated as per the proposed architecture, and (2) co-operations in distributed transaction processing. The integrating object-based application has been reviewed, in the Appendix-XV, in terms of the object interaction dimensions of a reference architecture for distributed systems.

participating applications. This is necessary to obviate the need of translation from the native data-model of one underlying application to the native data-models of other underlying applications. Figures 6.1 and 6.2 in the Chapter-6 explain the advantage of having one canonical data model; number of inter-model translations is reduced in geometric proportions. Each of the heterogeneous applications, in the proposed architecture, communicates to only the central application hosted on one dbms/os environment. There is no need to care about the dbms/os of other participating applications.

To achieve syntactic compatibility between the central application and the participating applications, we need a canonical data model into which any other data model, used by the participating applications, can be translated. Two data models are *structurally equivalent* if each database schema designed in one model can be put into a one-to-one correspondence with the equivalent schema designed in the other model (and vice versa), with matching data manipulation procedures in each data model. However, no such canonical data model is available, because *structural equivalence* between two different data models (between the canonical data model and the component data model in this case) cannot be guaranteed[94]. However, *operational equivalence* can be achieved in object-oriented data models, by guaranteeing the same response to the same message. Object-Oriented data models thus qualify as canonical data models for their operational equivalence. The features of information hiding enable an object to integrate the individual applications by sending a message and getting a reply, without any need to know how the reply is implemented.

7.6 Necessary and Sufficient Data Items for Integrating Schema
7.6.1 Necessity Of Shared Data Items

All data-items as per the definition of shared data-items are necessary because:

(a) Data-items, accessed from one system by another system, are necessary, because values/status of these items are relevant and required to be retrieved.

(b) Keys ie identifiers to access data-items in (a) are necessary, because without them we would not know where the data-items in (a) belong and hence these data-items cannot be accessed.

---

[94] Kalinichenko L.A.(1990), Methods And Tools For Equivalent Data Model Mapping Construction, *Proceedings Of International Conference on Extending Database Technology, Venice, Italy, March 26-30, 1990*

(c) Data items in constrained relationship are not necessary, only if the whole system is available in read-only mode, ie no system can change values of any item. If, however, values /states of the data-items in (a) can be altered, and this forces values/status of constrained items, these constrained data-items are necessary.

7.6.2 Sufficiency Of Shared Data Items

The subschema of shared data items includes all data items that are exchanged across applications, plus all data items related by constraints or navigational requirements. If we add one or more data-items in the list of shared data-items as per above definition, those extra items are unrelated to the data-items we are interested; hence the would convey no extra information. This proves the sufficiency of the shared data items, as per definition cited above.

7.7 Integrity Constraints In Identifying Shared Data Items

Integrity constraints are regarded as parts of the semantic definition of schema elements, and hence they should be complied with. If the constraints involve a data element in the set of shared data items with another data element from the schema but outside the set of shared data items, then the constraints may not be honoured when this data element is modified in the integrating application. Therefore, the set of shared data items needs to be expanded by inclusion of other data items, which form the basis of integrity constraints. Depending on whether a constraint spans more than one class or it just constrains instances of a single class of objects[95], we may or may not need to include any extra data items in the list of shared data items. Different types of constraints have been classified below to check whether or not some extra data items need be included in the list of shared data items to guarantee that the constraints are satisfied.

The proposed architecture will enforce these integrity constraints, so that the assertions of the integrating applications would not allow the underlying applications to break the rules set up by these constraints. For example, in one underlying application, the height of an object is greater than its width. If the height of the object is available to other applications, the height is modelled in the integrating application. Since we need to check that the height is always greater than the width, the width also needs to be modelled in the integrating application. The integrating application will also provide assertions to enforce

---

[95] Alzaharani R. M., Qutaishait, M.A, Fiddian N.J. and Gray W.A. (1995), Integrity Merging in an Object-Oriented Federated Database Environment, *Advances In Databases, 13th British National Conference Of Database*, pp 226-248

that height exceeds the width. If any of the component applications attempts to reduce the value of the height below the value of width, that transaction will be rejected. How different assertion rules need be modelled in the integrating application depends on the how the integrity constraint spans different classes and different instances. Some rules are illustrated below.

Intra-class integrity rules: These rules can be further subdivided depending on whether the constraint involves just a single instance or multiple instances - *Intra-instance* or *Inter-instance.*

Intra-instance integrity rules constrains attributes of a single instance, for example:

- Constraints specifying legal values in a domain; eg. *colour in [red, green, orange]; age< 65.*

- If the set of shared data items includes *colour* and/or *age,* no other extra data items are included, because if *colour* takes a value as specified in the list *[red, green, orange],* or if *age* takes a value which is < *65* no other data items should be affected as per this constraint.

- Constraints specifying inter-dependencies between data values; for example *status = 'top secret' =□ storage_city = 'Plymouth'*

- If both implicating and the implicated data items are included in a local schema, and one of them is in the sub-schema of shared data items, then the other data item needs be included in the sub-schema of shared data items.

- Constraints restricting property values of an object, for example an employee cannot be his own manager : *employee.name not = employee.manager_name*

- If one of the properties, say *employee.name* is included in the sub-schema of shared data items, then the other property ie *employee.manager_name* needs be included in the sub-schema of shared data items.

- Time-related constraint: this type of constraints ensures that the newly entered values for certain attributes satisfy certain conditions relative to their previous values, for example; *new salary > old salary*

- If *salary* appears in the sub-schema of shared data items, no other data item need be included, as this constraint can be verified by checking the value over time.

Inter-instance integrity rules must be checked for violation against all instances of a particular class, while updating any instance of that class. Examples of these rules are:

- Computational Constraints: in this category, a computation is required on some value of all instances of a class, for example *Average Salary of all employees in a department cannot exceed $50000*

- If Computational Constraints involve only the values of one data item only, then no other data item need be included. However, suitable assertion clauses need be included in the integrating application to enforce this constraint.

- Non-computational Constraints: these are constraints that span more than one instance. For example, the organisational rule that the manager of an employee is an employee can be asserted in the integrating application as: *for all instances of Employee, the attribute Manager of the Employee is same as the attribute Name of another instance of the Employee.*

- If both *Manager* and *Name* of the object *Employee* are included in the sub-schema of shared data items, no other data items need be included, but if only one of them is included, then the other need be included too.

- Uniqueness Constraints enforces every object of a certain class to have unique value for some attribute(s). For example, the rule that the patient number is the unique identification of a patient, can be formulated as follows:

  The attribute Patient_No of any instance of Patient is not same as the attribute Patient_No of any other instance of Patient

  - In order to enforce this constraint in the sub-schema of shared data items, no other data item is required, if the data item *Patient_No* is included.

Inter-class integrity rules specify constraints that involve objects from more than one class, and are divided into four groups: *Referential Integrity, Multiplicity Integrity, Inverse Relational Integrity* and *Navigational Integrity.*

- Referential Integrity: these ensure that a reference to an object in a database is always valid. Reference validity means that after deleting an object, no reference remain in the database for that object, for example an appropriate constraint could be:

  On delete of Address a, there would be no Person p such that p.address = a

- If both *Address* and *Person.address* are included in the sub-schema of shared data items, no other data items need be included, but if only one of them is included, then the other need be included.

- Multiplicity Integrity: association between two classes takes different multiplicities according to the role it plays. It can be 1:1, 1:n or m:n. For example, a rule that, a student must enrol in at least 3 courses, can be expressed as: *count(student.courses)* $>= 3$.

- If *student.courses* is included in the sub-schema of shared data items, no other data items need be included; the constraint however needs be specified.

- Inverse Relational Integrity: these can be exemplified by the temporary relationship between a course and a teacher. In relational systems, a separate table would be created to model this relationship; relational integrity is modelled in some OODBs by using a inverse construct which identifies the inverse of a property. For example, the attribute *taught-by* in the class *Course* is the inverse of the attribute *teaches* in the class *Teacher*. Explicitly such a relationship can be expressed as follows:

    For any Course c, there exists no Teacher t such that t = c.taught_by and not in t.teaches.

- If both *Course.taught_by* and *Teacher.teaches* are included in the sub-schema of shared data items, no other data items need be included, but if only one of them is included, then the other need be included.

- Navigational Integrity: this category includes integrity rules that involve navigation through the composition hierarchy of a class. For example, the rule: employees working in a department that manufactures materials with risk greater than 5 must be at least 35 years old, is represented as;

    employee.dept.manufactures.risk $> 5 => age >= 35$.

- If both *employee.dept.manufactures.risk* and *employee.age* are included in the sub-schema of shared data items, no other data items need be included, but if only one of them is included, then the other need be included.

The above examples show how inclusion of some data item in the sub-schema of shared data items, makes it necessary to include related data items, so that the integrity constraints can be verified in the sub-schema.

7.8 *Extreme Conditions In Modelling Shared Data Items*

Two extreme conditions of data items being shared are the cases when:

(a) No data items are shared by an underlying application/database -

> If no data items of an underlying application/database is shared, that database need
> not participate in integration. If no data items of any of the underlying databases
> are shared, then there is no need for integration.

(b) All data items are shared by an underlying application/database -

> If all data-items of one participating application are shared, we need to model them
> in the integrating application, but still we need to model only a subset of data-
> items from other application.

If, however, all data-items of all participating applications are shared, we need to model all
data-items, say by following Distributed Conceptual Schema[96] approach.

Most of the participating applications will be between these two extreme conditions.

> If data items are withdrawn from the export schema of an application, the number of
data items removed from the integrating application will not be always equal to the number
of data items withdrawn from the export schema of an application. Similarly, the number of
data items added to the integrating application will be greater than or equal to the number of
data items added to the export schema of an application.

7.9 Changes in Configuration of the Integrating Application

The configuration of the integrated application may change over time. Some applications
may be added, some deleted, and some modified. The integrated application may encompass
more sites, or it may be withdrawn from some sites.

If a new application is added, we need to identify its export schema, which will be included
in the model of the integrating application. We also need to check, if any extra item needs to
be included in the export schema, because that item is needed to access one of the export
schema item, or that item is involved in a constraint with one of the export schema item.
After all items in the export schema of the new application have been identified, we need to
identify semantic correspondence, if any, of these items with the items in the schema of the

---

[96] Papazoglou M.P., & Marinos L. (1990), An Object-Oriented Approach To Distributed Data Management, *Journal Of Systems and Software*, Vol.11, No.2, Feb'90, pp 95-109

integrating application. These correspondences will be modelled into the addendum to the existing schema of the integrating application.

If one application is withdrawn from the integrated application, we need to identify the items, which were in the export schema of the withdrawing application. These will include the items shared with other applications, plus those items which were included because they are either involved in constraints with the shared data items or they are required for accessing one of the shared data items.

If an existing application is modified, some more data items may be added, and some data items may be deleted from the entire schema. Similar to addition of applications, we need to find out exactly how many other items need be added, because of their involvement in accessing the data item, or in a constraint with other export items.

If a new site is introduced in the configuration, it needs to be introduced transparently to the existing system. This means communication and site failures need to be taken care of so that all component applications appear to be at the same site. If the new site introduces a new application, or add more objects to an existing application, we need to take care of changes in an existing export schema, or addition of a new export schema. As discussed before, changes in export schemas may involve addition/deletion of items, which are involved in constraints with the items in the schema increments/decrements.

Further complications are involved when replicas of some objects are available in more than one site. Suitable mechanisms of concurrency control and recovery need be introduced to take care of such complex situations.

7.10 Advantages Of Modelling Only Shared Data Items

In the proposed architecture, the complexity of design is scaled down by using the concepts of export and import schemas of the federated architecture, as in most cases only a small fraction of the schema is revealed to other applications. As only the export schemas i.e. the public parts of the schemas of the component applications are brought under a global system of control, the complexity of distributed schema is scaled down by the factor of (number of data elements in the export schema of an application / number of data elements in the local application). This is illustrated in the following section.

7.10.1 Comparison Of Modelling Efforts In 3 Different Approaches

Two major approaches of schema integration, discussed In Chapter 4, are

- Logically Centralised Schema Approach and

- Distributed Conceptual Schema Approach.

In this section we like to compare, for an equivalent task of application integration, the modelling efforts required by these two approaches with that required by using the proposed architecture. For example, let us consider the task of integrating 20 application schemas with 50 data-items in each.

Total number of data-items = 20 X 50 = 1000.

LOGICALLY CENTRALISED SCHEMA APPROACH:

For our estimates, let us assume that all 1000 data-items need be modelled, and each of these data items can be related to every other data items ie 999 other data items.

No. of possible binary relationships = 1000 * 999 / 2 = 499,500

In practice, much smaller number of meaningful relationships will be possible. But if every data-item is related to every other data-item, then the number of possible relationships is equal to the number of combinations of two items taken from the 1000 items. Since we cannot guess the exact number of meaningful relationships, we can compare the figures on the basis of maximum possible number of relationships.

DISTRIBUTED CONCEPTUAL SCHEMA APPROACH (DCS):

In this approach, data items of each application schema are separately modelled in its distributed conceptual schema [DCS], then data items in the integrating application are modelled.

No. of possible relationships in for 50 data items in each distributed conceptual schema [DCS] = 50 * 49 / 2 = 1,225

Total no. of possible relationships in 20 DCSs = 20 * 1,225 = 24,500

Assuming only 10% of all data items are in the integrating application, number of relationships in the integrating application = 100 * 99 / 2 = 4,950

Total no. of relationships = 24,500 + 4,950 = 29,450

PROPOSED ARCHITECTURE OF THE O-O APPLICATION WITH

10% SHARED DATA ITEMS [Chapter 7 Section 7.3]:

Data items of the participating databases need not be modelled. Only the data items, in the integrating application, are modelled.

No. of relationships in the integrating application = 100 X 99 / 2 = 4,950

Integration Architecture	No. of possible Relationships
LOGICALLY CENTRALISED SCHEMA	499,500
DISTRIBUTED CONCEPTUAL SCHEMA	29,450
O-O INTEGRATION WITH SHARED DATA	4,950

Figure 7.3 Modelling efforts in different architectures

7.10.2 Cost Of Modelling Only Shared Data Items

Suppose, there are n databases D_1, D_2,.......D_n; and a database D_i has m_i non-sharable and s_i sharable data items. In other words,

the database D_1 has m_1 non-sharable and s_1 sharable items,

the database D_2 has m_2 non-sharable and s_2 sharable items,

....

....

the database D_i has m_i non-sharable and s_i sharable items,

....

....

the database D_n has m_n non-sharable and s_n sharable items.

Total non-sharable items = $(m_1 + m_2 + ... + m_i + ... + m_n)$

Total sharable items = $(s_1 + s_2 + ... + s_i + ... + s_n)$

Modelling Shared Data Items Only :

Since each sharable item is used at least by two databases, maximum number of data items in the model = $\Sigma (s_i) / 2$

At the other extreme end, if each sharable item is used by all databases, then the minimum number of data items in the model = $\Sigma(s_i) / n$

Modelling All Data Items :

Similarly, if all items ie $(s_i + m_i)$ from the database D_i are modelled, each item is used at least by two databases, maximum number of data items in the model = $\Sigma(s_i + m_i) / 2$

At the other extreme end, if each item is used by all databases, then the minimum number of data items in the model = $\Sigma(s_i + m_i) / n$

If a data model is prepared with N data items, the number of possible relationships =

$$^NC_2 = N * (N-1) / 2$$

This means if N is sufficiently large, the complexity of modelling varies with the square of the number of data items involved. If C be the constant factor of complexity, complexity of modelling N data items = $C . N^2$

Complexity of modelling all data items is between

$$C . [\Sigma(s_i + m_i) / n]^2 \quad \text{and} \quad C . [\Sigma(s_i + m_i) / 2]^2 \qquad \text{and}$$

Complexity of modelling shared data items only is between

$$C . [\Sigma(s_i) / n]^2 \quad \text{and} \quad C . [\Sigma(s_i) / 2]^2$$

If the proportion of the shared items and total items ie $[\Sigma(s_i)/ \Sigma(s_i + m_i)]$ is 1:10, the complexity of modelling with shared items to the complexity of modelling with all the items would be approximately 1:100. Therefore, the integrating application system with the shared data items can be designed and built in 1/100th of the time and resources required for construction of an integrating application with all data items.

This shows that, by modeling only the shared data items, the cost is reduced by the square of the ratio of shared data items and total data items. But so far as integration and interoperation of the underlying applications are concerned, the equivalent results are achieved in terms sharing of functions and data.

7.11 *Major Components Of The Proposed Architecture*

When the proposed architecture is implemented, the integrated system will have the following components (vide Fig 7.1):

1) pre-existing application systems,

2) interfaces between participating application systems and respective export objects,

3) an integrating application system using the export objects.

Application systems will continue as before, except for the changes to be incorporated to accommodate the interfaces with controlling objects. Inter-application interfaces, if existing, will be replaced by interfaces to controlling objects. The new addition is the integrating application system, which will include all objects, controlling underlying applications.

Four major steps are involved in the implementation:

1. Documenting data items exchanged among participating applications,

2. Deciding on what data items need be included in the export schemas of individual applications

3. Object-oriented design using the data elements from export and import schemas and construction of an object oriented application system using the objects derived from export/import schemas - an object-based concurrency control scheme may be required to be designed depending on available facilities,

4. Building up interfaces between the controlling object and the controlled application.

7.12 A Simple Example to Illustrate the Concepts of the Architecture

The proposed architecture has been considered for integrating a number of applications of a bank, where each application involves the administration of a special line of products, using the specialised software that provides the best functions for that line of product. The bank's objective of integrating these applications is to manage customer relationship. This application needs to monitor the credits provided to the customer, and help cross-selling of bank's other products to the existing customer at the windows of appropriate opportunities. The integrating application will gather customer details from the application maintaining Customer Information, while specific details for each product will be gathered from the application that administers that line of product. Based on the demographic information and the financial profile available from the Customer Information Systems, and the statistics gathered from each product application, the integrating application can decide, on the basis of a set of rules, the total and currency-wise limits for the customer. Whenever any individual application tends to surpass the total and currency-wise limits the integrating application can interfere and advise the involved application to revise its transaction.

For example, the relevant bank applications are as follows:

Loans: Home Loan, Investment Loan, Personal Loan, Credit Cards - Visa/ MasterCard/

BankCard

Savings: Term deposits, Bonds, Savings

Delivery: ATM, Admin

Mixed: Cheque, Direct Deposit.

The integrating application needs to compute, for each customer, the currency-wise limits and balances, by summing up the currency-wise limits and balances for each product. The integrating application also needs to compute the allowable currency-wise limits, based on the rules available from the Customer Information System. The example, given below, has been simplified by considering single currency for each application.

The integrating system receives debit and credit requests from ATM, and limit adjustment requests from the administrative application. From the ATM request, the integrating application reads the Bank-Id, the Account-Id, the debit-credit code and the amount. If the Bank-Id shows a different Bank, the transaction is passed on to that bank. If the transaction is of the same bank, the integrating application deciphers the product-application-id from the account number, checks the debit-credit request with the overall limits set for the customer, direct the transaction to the product-application, receives the response from the product-application and formats the response back to the ATM.

The integrating system receives limit adjustment requests from the administrative application, often run by the call centre staff. From the limit adjustment request, the integrating application reads the product-application-id, account-id, and the new limit. The integrating application checks the new limit with other product limits and the total limit and decides to grant/reject the new limit request.

Let us use abbreviated terms as follows:

> $CI\text{-}i$ = The customer CI from the application A-i
>
> $CJ\text{-}j$ = The customer CJ from the application A-j
>
> $LI\text{-}i$ = Limit-i of the customer CI from the application A-i
>
> $LJ\text{-}j$ = Limit-j of the customer CJ from the application A-j
>
> $BI\text{-}i$ = Balance-i of the customer CI from the application A-i
>
> $BJ\text{-}j$ = Balance-j of the customer CJ from the application A-j

Let $CI\text{-}i \equiv CJ\text{-}j \equiv X$, where X is the Customer-Id of the total bank, B-x is the total balance of the customer and L-x is the total limit of the customer.

The integrating application will co-ordinate each of the underlying applications to ensure that LI-i from application A-i does not exceed L-x, set by the integrating application, and the sum of the balances for the customer X ie BI-i + BJ-j .... does not exceed L-x.

The integrating application need not care about the implementation details of each application. But it needs to assert which customer CI of one application is the same real world entity as the customer CJ of another application, and it needs to provide methods to get the balance and limits of that customer from individual applications. The integrating application may classify the application on some other basis like currency or term of loans and monitor the limits and balances for that basis and the total customer. Figure 7.4 shows the data model of the integrating application[97].

Following ideas from the proposed architecture have been illustrated below:

- Export Schema instead of the entire schema,

- Encapsulation to hide the details of the schema not appearing in the Export Schemas,

- Canonical data model of the integrating application.

- Correspondence Assertions between elements of the Export Schemas.

---

[97] Binary Data Modelling conventions have been used here. These conventions have also been shown in Appendix-II.

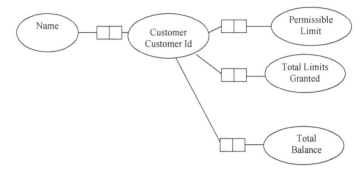

Fig 7.4 Integrating Application

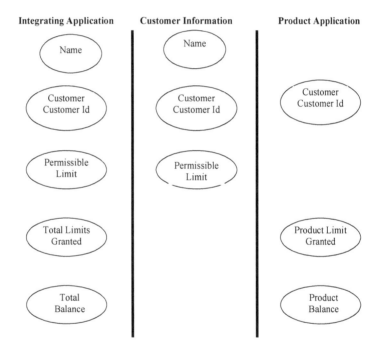

Figure 7.5 Objects of Integrating Applications and Their Counterparts In The Underlying Applications

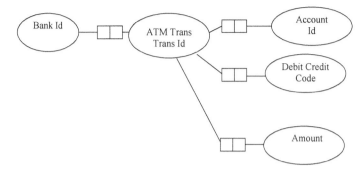

Fig 7.6 ATM transaction to Integrating Application

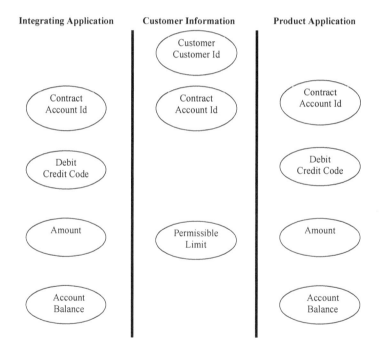

Figure 7.7 ATM Transaction and Its Counterpart In The Underlying Applications

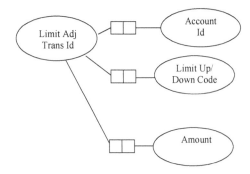

Fig 7.8 Limit Adjustment Transaction to Integrating Application

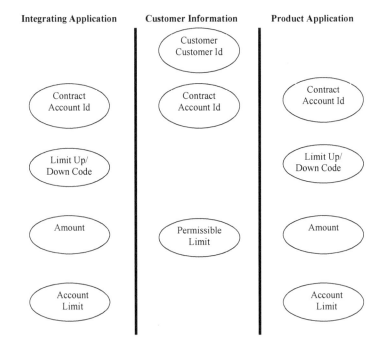

Figure 7.9 Limit Adjustment Transaction and Its Counterpart In The Underlying Applications

Export Schema instead of the entire schema

From each application, an export schema is selected to include the items that are needed to monitor the credits provided to customers. Figure 7.5 shows that the integrating application needs to access *Name* and *Permissible Limit* of the Customer from the Customer Information System, and it needs to get the *Product Limit Granted* and *Product Balance* from each of the Product Applications. However, *Product-Id* and *Loan Contract-Id* are included so that the underlying application can be accessed to get the values for Product Limit Granted and Product Balance. The export schema from each of the product applications has been shown below in tabular form.

HOME LOAN	Customer Id	Product-Id	Loan Contract	Limit Amt	Balance	Curre	Next	Last
		=Home Loan	Id	$.	Amt $.	ncy	Update	Update
Appl A-1	*Customer-1*			*Limit-1*	*Balance-1*		date	date

INVMT. LOAN	Customer Id	Product-Id	Loan Contract	Limit Amt	Balance	Curre	Next	Last
		=Invmt.Loan	Id	$.	Amt $.	ncy	Update	Update
Appl A-2	*Customer-2*			*Limit-2*	*Balance-2*		date	date

PERS. LOAN	Customer Id	Product-Id	Loan Contract	Limit Amt	Balance	Curre	Next	Last
		=Pers Loan	Id	$.	Amt $.	ncy	Update	Update
Appl A-3	*Customer-3*			*Limit-3*	*Balance-3*		date	date

VISA Card	Customer Id	Product-Id	Loan Contract	Limit Amt	Balance	Curre	Next	Last
		=Visa Card	Id	$.	Amt $.	ncy	Update	Update
Appl A-4	*Customer-4*			*Limit-4*	*Balance-4*		date	date

Master Card	Customer Id	Product-Id	Loan Contract	Limit Amt	Balance	Curre	Next	Last
		=Master Card	Id	$.	Amt $.	ncy	Update	Update
Appl A-5	*Customer-5*			*Limit-5*	*Balance-5*		date	date

Term Deposit	Customer Id	Product-Id	Deposit	Limit Amt	Balance	Curre	Next	Last
		=Term Dep	Contract Id	$.	Amt $.	ncy	Update	Update
Appl A-6	*Customer-6*			*Limit-6*	*Balance-6*		date	date

Savings	Customer Id	Product-Id =Savings	Savings Contract Id	Limit Amt $.	Balance Amt $.	Curre ncy	Next Update date	Last Update date
Appl A-7	*Customer-7*			*Limit-7*	*Balance-7*			

DDA	Customer Id	Product-Id =DDA	DDA Contract Id	Limit Amt $.	Balance Amt $.	Curre ncy	Next Update date	Last Update date
Appl A-n	*Customer-n*			*Limit-n*	*Balance-n*			

Encapsulation to hide the details of the schema not required in the Export Schemas

The export schemas do not include all the data items from the underlying applications. For example, the Visa Card details may include the list of merchants who are authorised to provide credits for a particular card, but since the integrating application is not interested in merchant details, this information is private to the Visa Card application and not included in the export schema. As the export schemas are to be built as objects, they can hide implementation details. However, if we have an integrating application, that will restrict the use of Visa card, then these details would be included.

Canonical data model of the integrating application

For the sake of simplicity, we assume that all the objects in the integrating application will use the same data model, ie a canonical data model. This canonical data model is expected to be an object-oriented data model so that the model can capture the semantics of the underlying applications.

Correspondence Assertions between elements of the Export Schemas

The integrating application needs to assert that the customer of one product, say Visa, is the same as that of another product say Term Deposit, and then appraise the total balance/limit of that customer, ie when A-4.Customer-4 = A-6.Customer-6, then the corresponding Visa contract and the corresponding Term Deposit contract belong to the same customer.

The constraints could be set up within each application A-i as follows:

Balance-i must be less than Limit-i, the application A-i monitors controls to ensure that Balance-i never exceeds Limit-i. for a Customer-i.

The integrating application provides a mechanism to specify that the Customer CI for the application A-i is the same real world entity as the Customer CJ of the application A-j as CI-i ≡ CJ-j. It compares CI's figures for balance Balance-i, Limit-i from the application A-i with those of CJ's figures of the balance Balance-j, Limit-j from the application A-j.

From the above example, we find that there is no need to model the details of individual product applications, and they are allowed to operate close to their stand-alone modes. However, checks are imposed by the integrating application to keep the total balance and the total limit granted within permissible limits. The data model for the integrating application is simple, because it needs to include only the export schemas from the underlying applications.

7.13 Data model for the Integrating Application

The central coordinating application, in the proposed architecture, has been proposed to be object-oriented. If a relational data model or ER data model were chosen to implement the integrating application layer, we would have major problems in representing information at different levels of granularity; they are not as expressive as the object oriented data models. Individual applications using incompatible hardware/operating systems/DBMS/ file system combination, may have export and import schemas that cannot be suitably modelled into form of relational tuples. On the other hand, object-oriented data models have been developed to represent complex real world objects more closely; each mini-world entity, however complex, can be represented as one object in the database.

Following considerations have favoured use of controlling objects instead of relational tables:

1. In a relational model, an abstract type in terms of abstract properties cannot be specified, while an abstract type can be specified in object-oriented models.

2. A more general hierarchy of types, ie subtypes and instances cannot be represented in relational models. Relational models need an extended schema language, expressing abstractions like generalisation and aggregation.

3. Relational systems are primarily value-based which means that tuples in a relational database can be distinguished only on the basis of their attribute values. In OOD, instances have their own identities independent of attribute-values, which means two objects/instances can have the same value for any of their features. This reduces the restrictions on modelling.

However, instances from one application cannot be matched with instances of another application on the basis of application specific object-identity; we need to use the value in the same unique identifier used by both applications.

4. Relational systems are unable to represent an entity both independently and in terms of a relationship in which it participates. An object can be accessed directly or as a reference from another object. A relational tuple cannot contain another tuple, it can contain the key-value for another tuple.

5. In relational systems, the database semantics are recorded separately from the data. They must be specified by the designer and consciously applied by the user. In object-oriented systems, consistency can be maintained by specifying assertions; the semantic specifications are checked by executable codes: "the preconditions expresses the properties that must hold whenever the routine is called; the post-condition describes the properties that the routine guarantees when it returns".

Appendix-XIV shows the advantages of using an object-oriented application to integrate the export objects of the participating applications instead of an application using a relational database.

7.14 Non-Traditional Data Structures In Application

In Appendix XIV: Relational vs. Object-Oriented Approaches, we have discussed that a relational solution with the sharable features of the application systems would be inadequate, when heterogeneous databases are incompatible for relational representation, for example graphics, text etc.

Object-oriented data models can represent complex real world objects more closely; texts, graphics, or documents, however complex, can be represented as objects in the database.

Component applications may have some processes with complex objects like documents. Such complex objects need to be in the integrating application, only if more than one application needs to access those complex objects. If, however, the complex objects are privately managed by individual applications, they need not be modelled into the integrating application.

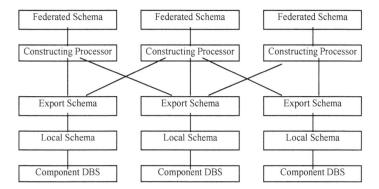

Figure 7.10 Proposed Architecture vis-a-vis Reference Architecture

7.15 Review vis-a-vis Amit Sheth's Reference Architecture

Proposed architecture has been shown in figure 7.8, in terms of the components of the Reference Architecture proposed by Amit Sheth [vide section 4.4.2 of Chapter 4]. The major differences are as follows:

- In Sheth-Larson's architecture, five levels of schemas were introduced to support distribution, heterogeneity and autonomy – Local, Component, Export, Federated and External schemas. In the proposed architecture, only three levels are required. Using the same terminology, these levels are Local-cum-Component, Export, and Federated-cum-External.

- In Sheth-Larson's architecture, translating local schemas into a canonical or common data model develops component schemas. This means the entire local schema of each participating application needs be translated. In the proposed architecture, translation is not necessary for the entire local schema, only the export schema of each participating application needs be translated.

- In the proposed architecture, export schemas can be extracted from the local schemas of component databases, using the native data models of the component databases. Export schemas are then integrated into the federated schema of the integrating application. The federated schema also serves as the external schema, as viewed by the users. As model independent correspondence assertion is used for integration, export schemas can continue in the native data model of component databases.

- The proposed architecture also specifies how semantic links between the elements in the export schemas can be modelled in the integrating application.

7.16 Review vis-a-vis R Muhlberger's Data Demand Model

This has been brought to our attention that R. Muhlberger has introduced a concept, similar to our proposed architecture, in 1995. However, the main ideas of this thesis, in the preliminary form, were first published in 1991, in form of the project work for Masters degree in Computing Sciences. Until recently we were not aware of the Application Data Demand Model, proposed by R. Muhlberger et al[98]. However, we may note the following differences between the Data Demand Model and our proposed architecture:

- The motivation of our proposed architecture is the integration of applications from what the applications share with other applications to keep each informed about the others. We have started from the export schemas to design the integrating schema. Muhlberger, on the other hand, started from an application that demands data from other applications, and only data items required by the application are mapped from underlying applications. This means, if we have another application that demands a different set of data items, that application will be modelled separately. In our solution, the second application will be already covered in the integrating application, if there are no changes in the export schemas.

- While developing a new application, the designer normally looks for the data requirements of the application, and where the application can access the required data. The Application Data Demand model suggests exactly that, and proposes to get the data from the underlying applications, while taking care of the constraints involving those data items in the underlying applications. On the other hand, the motivation of our proposed architecture is the integration of applications, not the requirements of a single application.

- We have provided definitions of shared data items to include the data items, which are required for accessing the shared data items, and also the data items, which are involved in constraints with the shared data items. Data demand model only shows subschema expansion by including constraining data items.

---

[98] Muhlberger R. M. and Orlowska M.E.,(1996), 'A Business Process Driven Multidatabase Integration Methodology', *Database Reengineering and Interoperability*, ISBN030645288, pp 283-295

- Unlike in data demand model, we have shown how the semantic equivalence and relationships between the elements of the export schemas will be asserted and modelled into the integrating application.

- We have explained that to each application, a real world object means a number of its attributes. A different application may be interested in a different set of attributes for the same object. Correspondence between the objects of two different applications are asserted in terms of their common attributes to establish whether these objects are semantically equivalent, related or unrelated.

7.17 Completeness of the Proposed Solution

We consider our solution as effective, only if the schema integration achieved by modelling shared data only is as good as the schema integration by modelling all the data items of the participating databases.

Our definition of shared data items include all data items actually shared plus other data items required for identifying those shared data items from the underlying applications plus those data items that maintain a set of constraints with the shared data items. This means any other data items, if added to the list of shared items, cannot be involved in any constraining relationships with those already existing on the integrating schema. This is because had there be any such relationship, these items would have been included in our iterative process of identifying shared data items. This means the proposed solution is complete, considering that modelling all data items would not provide any more functionality.

Whether one form of integrated schema is better than another, depends on (a) how the values of data items compare with the values maintained by the participating autonomous applications. In the proposed architecture, original applications are allowed to continue to operate in the same way as before the integration. Therefore, the values maintained by the integrated applications would be same as maintained by the participating applications. Additionally, the integrating application will provide windows to other applications.

It is also necessary to check whether or not the constraints or business rules maintained in the individual applications are violated in the integrating application. Our iterative process of selecting the shared data item guarantees that the items in list of shared data items are not involved with any item outside the list. Therefore all constraints maintained by the applications will continue to be maintained. Additionally the constraints involving any of the shared data items will also be maintained by the integrating application.

7.18 Main Contributions of the Proposed Architecture

Application integration by having one global schema requires substantial human intervention to integrate local/individual schemas. By targeting only export schemas from the individual applications instead of the entire schema, the proposed architecture has scaled down the complexity of the integrating schema. Data modelling is made much simpler, because only the elements in the export schemas of participating applications are considered.

We have provided a definition of shared data items to include all data items required to access the export data items, and to include all data items involved in constraints with an item in the list of shared data items. This has helped to identify the objects necessary to be modelled in the integrating application; no other items need be modelled for this.

Identification of semantic links between the elements of involved export schemas has facilitated setting up their relationships in the data/object models. We have considered that the applications view the objects in terms of selected attributes. Based on the domain of values of these selected attributes of the objects of different schemas, they can be considered as semantically equivalent, or semantically related. This equivalence or relationship can be modelled in the integrating application.

Unlike in the centrally integrated applications, functionalities of the original applications are maintained as before integration. This is because the proposed solution allows the applications to continue their original functions.

We have also shown that when the same real world object is modelled in two applications, the instances of one application can be matched with instances of the other application, based on the value of the common attribute that uniquely identifies the object in each application.

7.19 Comparative Analysis With Respect To Other Architectures

Table 7.1, in the following page, shows how the proposed architecture compares with the other architectures. The other architectures, we have compared against are:

- Super Database Architecture [Chapter 4: Section 4.2.1]

- Logically Centralised Schema [Chapter 4: Section 4.2.3]

- Distributed Conceptual Schema [Chapter 4: Section 4.2.4]

- Federated Database Architecture [Chapter 4: Section 4.2.2]

The criteria used for comparison are:

- Number of applications that can be integrated

- Extent of schema integration achieved

- Scope of distributed transaction management

- Type of interfaces between application systems

- Continuing local schemas in the integration architecture

- Complexity of the participating applications

- Use of common or standard user language

- Loosely/tightly coupled schemas for applications

- Inter-operations between local and integrating applications

Number of applications that can be integrated, in any architecture, is mainly restricted by the complexity of the integrated configuration. As more and more applications are added to a set of applications integrated by following the Logically Centralised Schema Architecture, the increase in complexity is huge. This is because, the overall complexity, for large applications, varies almost with the square of the number of data items that need be modelled for the integrating application. While in the proposed architecture, the increase in complexity is very low, because only the export elements from the new schema need be modelled for the integrating application, which again contains only export schemas of the existing applications.

Unlike in the Logically Centralised Schema Architecture, the global schema is not developed in the proposed architecture. However, the schema of the integrating application provides the capability to access the information, as needed, from the underlying application.

Distributed transaction management is one of the main themes of the Superdatabase architecture; this is also covered in the Logically Centralised Schema Architecture, because the transactions, distributed over the sites, affect the logically centralised database. In the

Federated Database architecture, the applications involved are responsible to manage their joint transactions. In the proposed architecture, the distributed transaction management is required only for the transactions that takes place on multiple sites and also affect an object in the integrating application.

In the proposed architecture, the component applications need not interface with one another, each component application interfaces with the central integrating application only. This means, if a new application is added, we need to provide for language-translation between the new application and the integrating application only. No translation is required for the other existing component applications. For the same reasons, the component applications can carry on with different languages, no common or standard user language is required.

In the proposed architecture, the component applications continue with their schemas and functionalities, while in the Logically Centralised Schema Architecture those of the central application replace the functionalities of the component applications.

Since the integrating application in the proposed architecture is object-oriented, it can work with complex type structures, and can mediate between applications dealing in video, text, graphics and scientific objects.

In the proposed architecture, the integrating application is concerned with the export schemas of the component applications, and accesses the underlying application to get the values for the data items in the export-schema. The underlying application may use loosely coupled schemas if necessary. Also, the communication between the integrating application and the component applications are expected to be asynchronous, as some of the component applications may not be always active.

To sum up, while the proposed architecture provides all the required functions of the Logically Centralised Schema Architecture, it eliminates the need for designing a global schema. It retains all current functions of the local applications, while providing the facilities to access other applications via the integrating object-oriented application. The design of object-oriented application, too, is much easier, because only the sharable objects of the local applications are used in the data model of the integrating application. Implementation of the proposed architecture of integration is expected to be transparent to the users of the pre-integration applications. After the implementation, the component applications will continue to provide the services, which they provided before the implementation; plus each application will have an extra window to view some data items from other applications.

In the next chapter, we shall check what needs be done to implement the proposed architecture in one organisation. Various options for building interfaces between controlling objects and controlled databases are discussed. Implementation of the proposed architecture of integration is, to a great extent, transparent to the users of the pre-integration applications, provided the schema of shared data items from each application is identified to build the schema of the integrating application.

Table 7.1 COMPARISON OF THE INTEGRATION ARCHITECTURES

Super Database Architecture	Logically Centralised Schema	Distributed Conceptual Schema	Federated Database Architecture	Proposed Integration Architecture
1) Number of applications that can be integrated				
Integration of site schemas is not considered. Complexity of transaction management and concurrency controls limits the number of applications that can be integrated.	Complexity of the centralised model limits the number of applications that can be integrated. Complexity varies with the square of total number of data items.	Many applications can be integrated, because one central schema and several site schemas are separately modelled. No complex central schema need be modelled.	No limit, but site schemas are not integrated.	Large number of applications can be integrated. Complexity of both site and central schemas are reduced, as only shared data items are modelled.
2) Extent of schema integration achieved				
Schema integration is not attempted	Global schema is developed from site schemas	Each local schema maps to an object; Objects exchange messages with one another.	Schema integration is not attempted	No global schema is developed; Sharable parts of each local schema maps to an object; Objects exchange messages with one another.
3) Scope of distributed transaction management				
Distributed transaction management is the main theme.	Distributed transaction management is taken care of.	Distributed transaction management is not covered.	Distributed transaction management is not covered.	Distributed transaction management is taken care of for sharable features.
4) Type of interfaces between application systems				
via the super database connecting the applications	Interfaces between applications are supervised by global data management.	Interfaces via objects on top of individual applications	Direct interfaces between applications registered as members of the federations	Interfaces via objects on top of individual applications
5) Continuing local schemas in the integration architecture				
As before integration	Global and auxiliary schemas replace the local schemas.	One or more objects added to map each existing local schema	As before integration	One or more objects map export features of local schemas
6) Complexity of the participating applications				
Cannot be extended to complex applications like graphics, text, video etc.	Can be extended to complex applications like graphics, text, video etc.	Can be extended to complex applications like graphics, text, video etc.	Cannot be extended to complex applications like graphics, text, video etc.	Can be extended to complex applications like graphics, text, video etc.
7) Use of common or standard user language				
Not applicable	Required	Not required	Not applicable	Not required
8) Inter-operations between local and integrating applications				
Not applicable	Synchronous and blocking	Asynchronous	Asynchronous	Asynchronous

8. IMPLEMENTING INTEGRATION OF APPLICATIONS

8.1 Introduction

In the last chapter, we have proposed an architecture of integrating disparate applications, by linking the semantically related objects shared in these applications. In this chapter, we have started with disparate applications of a typical organisation, and shown the step-by-step process of integrating these applications, so that they function like one integrated application. We have also considered the management of transactions between the involved applications to ensure that the semantic equivalence and relationship of the involved items are maintained in the inter-operating applications, in terms of both their structure and population, ie schema and data contents.

8.2 The Steps for Implementation

Specifications have been drawn for exploring the feasibility of implementing the proposed architecture [Fig 7.1] for application systems of a financial organisation. There is no need to analyse the applications in full detail, rather it is required to find out what data items /objects are exchanged by the applications, and what other items are involved with these exchanged items either in integrity constraints or as an identifier to these items. The exchanged data items and other involved items are modelled together to design an integrating application. Interfaces are designed between the objects of the integrating application and the underlying application, so that when the integrating application needs to get the value of attributes of its objects, the corresponding equivalent objects of the underlying application are accessed.

Four major steps are involved in the implementation:

1. Documenting data items exchanged among participating applications,

2. Deciding on what data items need be included in the export schemas of individual applications

3. Object-oriented design using the data elements from export and import schemas and construction of an object oriented application system using the objects derived from export/import schemas - an object-based concurrency control scheme may be required to be designed depending on available facilities,

4. Building up interfaces between the controlling object and the controlled database.

8.3 Data Items Exchanged Among Applications

In order to specify the export and import schemas, the current interfaces among the applications need be analysed. The interfaces among the applications could have been implemented in various ways, some of them are automatic, while others are manual. In some cases, the users might act as carriers of information from one application to another - they will access information from one application to input the same into another application. In other cases magnetic tapes could be used for recording data from one application and copying into another application. Inter-region communications or multi-region operations could be used to transfer data items from one application to another. Advanced program to program communication may be established between programs of various applications; also a set of files could be shared among applications in online or batch mode.

The process of identifying export features may provide an opportunity to review what is done on the data files transferred or message queues accessed. All interface data items can be analysed and built into a data model, specifying the attributes of each object as viewed by other objects in the data model.

8.4 Determination of Export Schemas

If we prepare a schema including only those data items exchanged from one application to other applications, we would get a schema, which is a sub-schema of that application. However, we may find that this sub-schema is not independent of the rest of the schema of the application. If a data item in this sub-schema is updated, and there is a constraint involving this data item and a second data item from the rest of the schema, then the second data item needs also be updated in order to satisfy the constraint. However, this sub-schema has to be independent of the rest of the schema of the component application, so that if a data item is added, deleted or modified in the sub-schema, no update should be necessary in the rest of the schema. This sub-schema, therefore, has to include some extra data items instead of including only those being exchanged across the applications; these extra data items are those which are involved in access and/or update of the data items actually exchanged.

If a shared data item has a relationship with a second data item, such that the latter is either a key for accessing the shared data item or is involved in a constraint with the shared data item, then the second data-item has to be included in the model. When this second data-item is included, checks are to be made again for its relationships with any other data-item, if any, which needs be included too. This step will be repeated with every new data-item added until there is no other data-item to be included. Iterative steps of selecting dependent data-items ensure that the sub-schema of shared data-items is independent of the rest of the data-items in the entire schema.

8.5 *Design of Controlling Objects*

The steps in the design of controlling objects are essentially the same as those of object-oriented design of any application. But since only the shared data items need be modelled, data items involved and associated features/functions are much less in number and complexity, than data items involved in the entire application.

Following steps[99] can be applied to information on export and import schemas of each component application:

1. Define information requirements

2. Describe the information as sentences

3. Decompose complex sentences

4. Identify objects, and roles

5. Specify uniqueness constraints

6. Convert sentences to binary sets

7. Add mandatory constraints

8. Add set constraints

9. Analyse subtypes

10. Document, on the information model, business rules relating to the facts as text

11. Refine information model

12. Indicate Client-Supplier relationship between entities in the role-boxes depending on mandatory constraints

13. Derive Ancestor-Descendant relationship between entities depending on subtype-supertype relationship

14. Prepare Object Class Specifications in O-O language like Eiffel or C++

15. Prepare Program Specifications for Integrating Object-Oriented Application

1. Define information requirements

This step consists in functional decomposition of the application domain to elementary units, so that Information Flow Diagram (IFD) can be drawn for each elementary application unit. This step can be restricted to the data elements that are shared with other applications. If an object is not exported to other applications, its implementation could be hidden in the concerned application, and IFDs would not be useful in the design of the integrating application.

If the same conceptual information is present in multiple applications, then this information is shared among these applications and is required to be consistent. This consistency needs be ensured whether or not the same data-name is used to represent the information, and whether or not this is expressed in the same form or type.

2. Describe the information as sentences

Information requirements from the layouts of exchanged information are expressed as primarily simple sentences, which can be translated into graphical models. Sometimes complex sentences may be used at this stage, as they will be decomposed in the next step.

In Appendix-I, the export features of a Credit Card system have been expressed in terms of simple sentences.

The information that a Card can share with other system can be classified into two categories:

1) Information about the Bank's *Contract* of the Card and its selected features,

2) Information about the *Customer(s)* or Identity(s) associated with the Card.

3. Decompose complex sentences

Complex sentences are decomposed into elementary sentences, taking care that no information is lost. For example, the sentence 'Each identity has a name, a postcode and an address' can be decomposed into three sentences as

---

[99] Montgomery I.(1990), *Data Analysis Concepts Binary-Relationship Modelling*, Course Material for M.Sc.(Database), University Of Technology, Sydney, 1990.

Each identity has a name.

Each identity has a postcode.

Each identity has an address.

Decomposition of such sorts, in this exercise, has been carried out in one go and shown in Appendix-I.

4. Identify objects, and roles

The elementary sentences are represented graphically to identify objects, and their relationship and references. Non-binary sentences, if any, have been reviewed and converted to binary sentences by creating intersection entities when required. Deep structures of sentences are also eliminated to make all relationship, attribute or reference facts explicit.

Instead of representing each sentence separately, each sentence is allowed to build up on the model developed by earlier sentences. In this way, all roles played by any individual object are shown at one place, so long they can be conveniently represented.

If the similar conceptual information is present in multiple applications, but expressed in the different form or type, their relationship will be specified in form of correspondence assertions, as follows, after necessary type conversion:

$X_1 \equiv X_2$ means that X_1 and X_2 are equivalent, where X_1 and X_2 will be merged into a single object/class in the schema of the integrating application. For example, if Services of Department-A are identical with Services of Department-B, we may merge them into the single object Services, referred by both Department-A and Department-B.

$X_1 \neq X_2$ means that that X_1 and X_2 are disjoint, where X_1 and X_2 will be generalised into a superclass, where X_1 and X_2 each will include one attribute, which is of different values in X_1 and X_2. For example, Employees of Department-A are disjoint from Employees of Department-B, when the attribute Department is considered, because employees can belong to only one department. However, they can be generalised as Employees of the Organisation, If Department-A and Department-B belong to the same Organisation.

$X_1 \cap X_2 \neq 0$ means that X_1 and X_2 intersect and will have a common subclass for the intersection.

$X_1 \supseteq X_2$ means that X_2 will inherit some properties of X_1, and X_2 can be modelled as the subclass of X_1.

5. Specify uniqueness constraints

Uniqueness Constraints are specified in the graphical model of binary sentences to show which role(s) is unique in the pair of role boxes between each pair of concepts.

6. Convert sentences to binary sets

Sentences with joint uniqueness constraints between two entities are converted to binary sets, by introducing a new joint entity to represent the joint uniqueness. Binary relationship of each involved entity with the new entity eliminates the need to show the roles between them. One such example is the relationship between Transferred-From and Transferred-To Cards; an entity Transfer-Detail has been devised to identify details for a specific transfer to the object Transfer-Detail.

7. Add mandatory constraints

Mandatory constraints are added to show which roles must always be played by an entity, and so it must be recorded in the information base. However, if a primitive entity plays only one role, that role is implicitly mandatory and hence not shown on the model.

8. Add set constraints

Set constraints of the types - subset, equality and exclusion, have been reviewed to check how the relative population of entity instances in different sentences has been controlled. Set constraints have not been shown on the data model to avoid complexity of presentation; they are included in the specification of objects later.

9. Analyse subtypes

Subtype structure of the data model may not be complex. For example, the main participating objects, in a Credit-Card application, are Identity and Contract; Identity has subtypes: Person and Organisation - Organisation has subtypes say Employer Organisation,

Affinity Organisation etc.; Contract has many subtypes eg. Credit Card, Foreign Currency Loan Contract and so on. Other subtypes introduced are to facilitate compile-time type checking in object-oriented implementation; for example all date fields are subtypes of an entity Date, on which all allowable features can be implemented.

10. Document, on the information model, business rules relating to the facts as text

Business rules are documented with reference to the entities in the data model, so that assertion constraints of the objects can be taken from this document. The data model will be taken as the common reference for both the business rules and object class specifications.

11. Refine information model

Following steps are considered to refine information model:

- remodel unstable subtypes,

- add missing membertype subtypes,

- remove membertype facts,

- identify type structures that represent rules.

The information model need be refined for object oriented implementation. Unstable subtypes are removed as otherwise the object with one role is required to be deleted and the same object with another role is required to be added for change of roles. For example, if we had subtypes for Open Contract and Closed Contract, when the status is changed the object of one subtype has to be deleted and created for another subtype - this problem is avoided by having the Account-Status as a feature of the Contract

If we had a large number features applicable to say closed or open contracts, we could have introduced subtypes for Account-Status, ie. Open-Account-Status and Closed-Account-Status, so that the respective features could be assigned to these sub-types of Account-Status.

Appendix-III shows the information model refined for object oriented implementation.

12. Indicate Client-Supplier relationship between entities in the role-boxes depending on mandatory constraints

Client-supplier relationships between the entities, which will now represent classes of objects, are marked in the role-boxes depending on the mandatory constraints of the roles. Appendix-IV shows this relationship.

13. Derive Ancestor-Descendant relationship between entities depending on subtype-supertype relationship

The ancestor-descendant relationship is derived from the subtype-supertype structure, the subtypes inheriting features from supertypes. Appendix-IV shows this relationship.

14. Prepare object class specifications in O-O Language like -Eiffel or C++

The Class Specifications could be written in C++. Though the author finds it convenient to write in the language Eiffel, the language C++ may be chosen considering that application systems using C++ are more popular to the application systems using Eiffel. Appendix-V shows the Class Specifications. Appendix-XI compares the languages Eiffel and C++.

15. Prepare Program Specifications for Integrating Object-Oriented Application

Most of the features expected from objects are included in the class specifications, which encapsulate both codes and data structures. Some of the features for the classes taken together might not be covered in the class specification of individual objects and hence need be included in a separate Program Specification (Appendix VI). In order to visualise the changes in the application systems, a simplified view of the existing interfaces have been shown in Appendix-VII, while Appendix-VIII shows the architecture after the implementation of the proposed architecture.

As the current operating system may not provide adequate mechanism for concurrency control, an object-based concurrency control scheme is discussed next.

8.6 Building Interfaces Between Controlling Objects And Controlled Databases

The design of interfaces between controlling objects and the underlying applications need to consider the business requirements to be fulfilled by the controlling objects. At one extreme end, the controlling objects may not be communicating at all with the underlying applications, they will have default values for all their attributes irrespective of the actual values of the corresponding object in the underlying application. At the other extreme, the controlling objects may be communicating synchronously with the underlying applications, for all their attributes they will access the actual values of the corresponding object in the underlying application. The exact arrangement between these two extremes will be decided by analysing the following issues:

First, business requirements need be evaluated to decide whether we should have asynchronous or synchronous communication between applications and controlling objects. If both the integrating application and the underlying application are concurrently executing programs, and the message is delivered immediately after the request is sent by the application, then the communication is synchronous. Further, if synchronously communicating, the applications can interoperate in a blocking or non-blocking fashion. Blocking means that the requesting application sends a message and waits for the reply before it can do any other task; nonblocking means that the requesting application continues to do other tasks while waiting for a reply.

Second, we need to decide whether the objects in the controlling application will store the value of its attributes, or they only have the meta-data and access methods to get the values of the attributes from the underlying object.

Third, we need to decide whether value-based keys will be used for mapping between the controlling object and the underlying database, or there will be other ways to access the objects in the underlying database.

Fourth, we need to ascertain whether the integrating application is to be run from one site or multiple sites. In the latter case the added complexity is involved for managing concurrency control and recovery, as discussed in the following sections.

8.6.1 Controlling Databases at the Same Site

The simplest case is when all the controlling objects are at the same site, ie under the control of the same operating system. Failure of one object will be handled first by the exception handling mechanism of the language used by the object, and then by the exception handling routines of the operating system. The transactions, however, should be designed as atomic, so that either all sub-transactions within a transaction are committed or all of them aborted.

Site Or Communication Failure

Though the controlling objects are all housed at one site, multiple sites are involved in the entire database: the central site of the object-oriented database is connected to the individual application sites.

If any of the individual sites does not respond to the central site, it could be either a failure of the processor at the site or a failure of the communication link between the central site and the application site. If the communication link between the central site and application site permits (for example, the inter-processor bus between Tandem processors permits such checking), the central site would send a message to itself via the concerned site. If the message is received back the failure is at the site else the failure is in the link. If this type of checking is possible, then the remote application site, too, will send the message to itself to ascertain whether the failure is in the link or in the central node processor.

If both central and remote sites know where the failure is, they can adopt pre-determined strategies depending on replication of data between the database of the underlying application and the central integrating application, and replication among objects in the central application.

If there is no mechanism to differentiate between site failure and communication failure, the controlling object should make itself unavailable in the central site, though other objects will continue to participate in the application.

The most critical case is the failure of the central site. In this case, all applications would be in their stand-alone mode. No updates now can be permitted with that part of the public data, which is either replicated in other applications or is constrained by relationship with data-items held in other application databases. Other data-items, which are constrained in some relationships with these data-items also, cannot be updated. All transactions, that need no messages to be sent to the central site, can be executed without problem. For those transactions, that need be concurred by the central site cannot be executed.

The above discussion shows, following changes are necessary to be made at each application sites for getting integrated as per the proposed architecture:

- finding out which data items are private to the database, which means also to identify the data items that would be shared for queries and items that would be shared for updates,

- implementing a control mechanism that checks, for each update transaction, whether the affected data item is in the public or private domain of the application. If the data item be in the public domain, then the request to update need to be directed to the controlling object, else the data item can be updated by the application, without any approval of the controlling object,

- if a request to update were received from the controlling object, check if the request is for a public data; if not then the transaction should be rejected.

- if two application systems maintain and export the same data, and there are chances that some application can access either of the applications, then all updates to those data items have to be controlled so that all copies of the data-item maintain the same values. However, this is only an improvement after integration; if the applications had been connected to each other directly, this anomaly would have existed.

- a decision need be made whether the controlling object, should have only meta-data, or maintain replicas of some data-items maintained in the application database. If replicas are maintained that improves performance and availability of the objects in the central site object-based application, but adds a task of maintaining consistency between the central and the remote copies.

8.6.2 Controlling Databases at the Remote Sites

When the objects of the controlling application are distributed over sites, CCR ie 'concurrency control and recovery' has to be ensured between the objects of the same application distributed over sites.

The consistency of the distributed object-oriented database of the integrating application can be assured by introducing the concepts of atomicity of transactions. The features of the objects can be so designed that either all or none of the operations in an atomic transaction are carried out. Atomicity encompasses two properties: serializability and recoverability. Serializability means that the effect of concurrent execution of transactions is the same as that when the transactions are executed one after another. Recoverability means the overall effect of an activity is all-or-nothing: the effects of a transaction become permanent when it commits and its effects are discarded if it aborts; a transaction that has not committed or aborted is active. Well-known atomic commitment protocol can be used to ensure the recoverability of distributed transaction.

If replicas be present in the distributed database of controlling objects, the available algorithms[100] for site failures are *Available Copies*, and *Directory-oriented Available Copies*; the available algorithms for communication failures are *Quorum Consensus, Missing Writes* and *Virtual Partitions*.

Available Copies Algorithm uses an enhanced form of the approach: "read-any, write-all-available". *Directory-oriented Available Copies* algorithm uses directories to define the set of sites that stores copies of an item, updates the copies and directories held at these sites.

In the Quorum Consensus algorithm, a non-negative weight is assigned to each site; every site knows the weight of all sites in the network. A quorum is any set of sites with more than half the total weight of all sites. Only if a network component has a quorum of sites, it can process transactions.

The Missing Writes algorithm exploits the trade-off between the "Available Copies" and "Quorum Consensus" approaches. In normal mode, a transaction reads one copy and writes all copies, in failure mode it uses the Quorum Consensus. In the Virtual Partitions algorithm, each site maintains a view, consisting of the sites, it believes it can communicate with. A transaction executes as if the network consisted of the sites in its view, following the "Read-any and Write-all" approach. If the view of the home site changes before the transaction is committed, the transaction will be aborted.

Considering the probabilities of different scenarios[101], Virtual Partition algorithm is recommended because:

- the main purpose of replication, ie. performance improvement, is lost in Quorum Consensus algorithm, where all replicas need be read to find out which one is the latest.

- Missing Writes algorithm makes only minor improvements, which is - quorum consensus is not used unless there is a failure. Improvement in performance depends on the proportion of fault-free time.

As write-quorum is often difficult to achieve, "Voting with ghosts" algorithm can be used as well, so that every failing site is replaced by a ghost or dummy node for write quorum, but read quorum must have all live nodes.

---

[100] Appendix-XI provides strategies for data replication in distributed databases.

8.7 Evaluation of Impacts on the Existing Component Applications

We shall review here what happens to the existing applications after the proposed architecture of object-oriented integration is implemented. We may evaluate the changes, in terms of data management, operational issues and administrative controls of the applications, before and after the changes.

DATA MANAGEMENT

- Physical location of data remains unchanged within the control of existing applications.
- All local data of the applications can be accessed in the same way as in the original component applications, while data from other applications become available through the centralised object-oriented application.
- Application partitioning becomes less visible, as the controlling objects of each application can participate in the same integrating application.

OPERATIONAL ISSUES

- Each of the data items or objects that are shared amongst applications is modelled as an export object in the central integrating application. All aspects of integrity, security, concurrency control and recovery of these export objects are brought under the control of one central integrating application, while the shared data items in the underlying applications are maintained at par with their counterparts ie. the export objects in the central integrating application. This ensures the consistent view of the same data items from different applications.

ADMINISTRATION CONTROL

- Risks in a distributed environment is reduced by eliminating adhoc interfaces between any two data bases, centralised object-oriented application can make assertion controls before any update on the export features of the data base.
- Existing controls of individual applications to minimise risks ie the controls of the Data Base Administration, the Data Dictionary Control, Audit Retention Controls are not lost. The Users in the distributed environment are not expected to find any difference while using local application functions, the access to remote data becomes more transparent.

8.8 Conclusion

We have seen, in this chapter, the step-by-step process of identifying the export schemas of the applications to be integrated, and then linking the semantically related

---

[101] Different scenarios are 1) no failures at all - 85%, 2) only site failures - 8%, 3) only communication failures -

objects from the export schemas into an object-oriented application. We have also considered the management of transactions between the involved applications to ensure that the semantic equivalence and relationship of the involved items are maintained in the inter-operating applications, in terms of both their structure and population, ie schema and data contents. In this context, we have discussed different scenarios of distribution of the component application also periods of inactivity of these applications. Various schemes of transaction management and concurrency control are discussed to suit these scenarios.

Implementation of the proposed architecture of integration is, to a great extent, transparent to the users of the pre-integration applications. This means that the service levels of these applications before and after the implementation would be almost the same. One gain is the extra window in each application to view some data items from other applications. The other major gain is the consistency of the sharable information achieved through the controlling objects, inter-operating in an application system. For the sharable data items, all aspects of integrity, security, concurrency control and recovery are brought under the control of one central application. This ensures the consistent view of the same data item from different applications.

In the next chapter, we shall evaluate how our proposed solution meets the target set in the introduction of this thesis. We shall also identify the areas of further research to make this solution more effective and recommend action plans for I.T. communities and users of I.T. products.

5%, 4) both site and communication failures - 2%.

9. EVALUATION OF THE PROPOSED SOLUTION & CONCLUSION

9.1 Introduction

In this concluding chapter, we shall review how the proposed architecture has helped us in the main goal of this thesis – the integration of applications. We shall check whether our proposed solution is a complete solution, and provides the same functionality as provided by a single application replacing all involved applications. We shall also evaluate the main contributions of our proposed architecture. We shall check how the proposed solution will help reverse engineering of legacy systems. In the last chapter, we have discussed the procedures for implementing the proposed solution for a typical business scenario; here we shall evaluate scalability of implementation. In Chapter 7, we have discussed on configuration changes of the integrated applications; here we shall extend that discussion to consider schema evolution of the involved applications. We shall also evaluate the proposed solution for extreme cases – when the percentages of shared data items are very low and very high. We shall also consider the cases of non-traditional data structures in applications. Finally, we shall evaluate how this solution relates to the industry and how it could change the strategic direction of not only one organisation but also of the information systems community in general.

9.2 How The Proposed Architecture Relates To Our Goals

In the first chapter of this thesis, we identified the problem of application integration as the problem of (a) selecting from each individual application, the minimum number of objects that must be designed into the schema of the integrating application and then (b) linking these objects from different applications together based on their semantic relationship. We have checked that the applications have been developed as isolated though they include objects that are inter-related. The same facts have been represented differently in those isolated applications. Therefore, there is a need to establish the semantic equivalence between objects in spite of technological and syntactical differences in their representation. Similarly, there is a need to establish the semantic difference between objects in spite of similarities in their representation. We have shown how semantic equivalence and difference between objects can be established by correspondence assertion between the objects in terms of correspondence between the attributes of these objects. We have also shown how these correspondence assertions will be modelled into the integrating application, with an example of object-oriented data model for the integrating application.

We have also assessed the complexity involved with establishing semantic equivalence and difference of all the objects in the applications, considered for integration. All proposals targeting one global schema for application integration are too complex to be implemented and require substantial human intervention to resolve the semantic conflicts among the application schemas. Our proposed architecture has shown that we need to select only those objects that matter for integration. These are the objects that the applications need to share with other applications for keeping each informed about the others. The export schema of each application includes the objects that can be shared with other applications. These export schemas can be modelled together to develop an application, which will integrate the component applications.

We have seen that the preferred method of inter-operation among the applications to be integrated is having an application that intermediates among the component applications, instead of either setting up communication between each pair of applications, or combining all component applications into a single application. If communications are set up between each pair of applications, too many translations are needed, and the number of application-to-application translations varies nearly with the square of the number of applications. Combining all applications into one application is very complex and requires substantial human efforts. We have proposed to have one intermediary application, built on the export schemas modelled together, to coordinate with the component applications.

The proposed architecture has shown the ways to identify the data items shared among the applications, and then to assert the relationship among those shared data items belonging to different applications, so that the semantically linked data items are modelled into one object-oriented application. While object-modelling of the shared data items, the other non-shared or private data items can be kept hidden, and need not be considered in the object model of the integrating application.

We consider our solution as effective, only if the schema integration, achieved by modelling shared data items, is as good as the schema integration by modelling all the data items of the participating applications. Whether one form of integrated schema is better than another, depends on (a) how the values of data items in the integrated schema compare with the values maintained by the data items in participating autonomous applications, and (b) whether or not the constraints or business rules, maintained in the component application schemas, are violated after integration.

Our definition of shared data items include all data items required to be shared plus other data items required for identifying those shared data items from the underlying applications plus those data items that maintain a set of constraints with the shared data items. This means any other data items, if included later in the integrating application, cannot be involved in any constraining relationships with those already existing on the integrating schema. Because, if there had been any such relationship, these items would have been already included in the list of shared data items, and modelled in the integrating application. This means, the list of shared data items, as per our definition, is sufficient; any addition to this list would make no improvement in functionality. Therefore, our solution is as good as that achieved by modelling all data items.

The recommendations for object-oriented data modelling of shared data items have been made, because object-oriented models are semantically richer than the models used in the underlying applications. The integrating object-oriented application can often model the functionalities, which are implied in the context of the applications.

9.3 *Completeness of the Proposed Solution*

We consider our solution as complete and effective, only if the schema integration, achieved by modelling shared data only, cannot be improved by adding any extra objects in the integrating application. Following paragraphs explain, why the schema integration cannot be improved by expanding the list of shared data items.

We have proposed the iterative process of selecting all data items visibly shared, plus other data items required for identifying and accessing those shared data items from the underlying applications, plus those data items that are involved in constraints with the shared data items. This process ensures that the export schema of shared data items is independent of the rest of the application. This means that no other data items, if selected from the rest of the application, can be involved in any constraint with those existing on the export schema. Had there be any such constraint, these items would have been already included in our iterative process of identifying shared data items. This means the proposed solution is complete, and modelling any additional data item would not provide any extra functionality.

Whether one form of integrated schema is better than another, depends on how the values of data items in the integrated schema compare with the values maintained by the participating autonomous applications. In the proposed architecture, original applications are allowed to continue to operate in the same way as before the integration. Therefore, the values maintained by the integrated applications would be same as those in the participating applications. Additionally, the integrating application will provide windows to other applications. Only the updates to the objects in the integrating application will be controlled by the integrating application, so that constraints of involved applications are taken care of.

It is also necessary to check whether or not the constraints or business rules maintained in the individual applications are violated in the integrating application. Our iterative process of selecting the shared data item guarantees that the items in list of shared data items are not involved with any item outside the list. Therefore all constraints maintained by the applications will continue to be maintained by them. Additionally the constraints involving any of the shared data items will also be maintained by the integrating application.

9.4 Main Contributions of the Proposed Architecture

The proposed architecture shows how we can create the illusion that the component applications are not disparate; rather they provide services as components of one application. This illusion is created without creating an application that can replace all isolated components or without making direct interfaces between each pair of involved applications. We have rather proposed one central application, acting as intermediary between any two applications. Therefore, the proposed architecture has enabled us to avoid the complex tasks of design and implementation of one global schema, which requires substantial human intervention.

In the proposed architecture, we have used the method of viewing an application as of a set of objects relevant to the processes carried out in the application. We have based the semantics of objects in an application, in terms of types of its attributes and values, and the functions provided by the objects. An application consists of a set of objects, which provide the functionality of the application. Each of these objects represents a real world object, which is simulated in the application. Each object conveys a set of meanings to the application. A different application consists of a different set of objects, which are relevant to the processes carried out in the second application. Two applications may include objects, which are the models of the same or related real world objects. Integration of these two applications consists in linking of the same or related objects of these two applications.

For the proposed architecture, we have provided the definition of shared data items and the iterative process of identifying all shared objects or export objects for each individual application. The schema of the integrating application(s) need to include at least all the objects, which individual applications need to share with other applications. We have expanded the definition of shared data items to include all data items required to access the export data items, and to include all data items involved in constraints with an item in the list of shared data items. We have proposed an iterative process to add elements in the list of shared objects till no other objects need to be added for these two reasons.

We have shown how the data modelling of the export objects from the component applications to be carried out for designing the schema of the integrating application. We have considered that the applications view the objects in terms of selected attributes. Based on the domain of values of these selected attributes of the objects of different schemas, they can be considered as semantically equivalent, or semantically related. We have asserted the semantic relationships among the objects from different applications in terms of equivalence, disjoint, intersection, and inclusion. Based on these relationships, these objects are modelled into the object-oriented schema of the integrating application. We have considered that semantic relationship can exist between objects at different levels of granularity; this means that an object of one application may be related to a lower level object or an attribute of another application.

We have proposed an object-oriented application to be constructed based on the object-oriented schema of the intermediary application. Optionally, we could have other forms of intermediary applications. For example, the intermediary application can be designed to be an Internet based application with XML links to component applications. Again, since we need to consider only the export schemas of the component applications, XML links need to be set only from the export schemas of individual applications to the intermediary applications.

Traditional approaches to integrate applications by considering all data items of all involved applications require substantial human intervention. By targeting only export schemas from the individual applications, the proposed architecture has not only reduced the complexity of the integrating schema, but also simplified data modelling by having only a subset of objects from participating applications.

When applications are integrated with one global schema, functionality of the original applications is not maintained. The proposed solution allows the applications to continue their original functions, therefore functionality before integration are not lost.

9.5 *Reverse Engineering Using The Proposed Architecture*

The proposed architecture can help us get the best of both worlds - continue reaping benefits from existing information resources without any major investments on reverse engineering, assimilate at the same time the benefits of emerging technologies. An undocumented system may be broken into slices of black boxes, where the functionality is known but not the implementation codes. We may then build export objects to interface these black boxes, without caring for their implementation codes; these export objects can then be linked into an integrating object-oriented application.

Reverse engineering is the process of recapturing the essential design, structure, and content of a complex computer system, which has proven useful in running the business. Two major concepts of Reverse Engineering are *logic modelling* and *slicing*. *Logic modelling* leads to the specifications for the sending and receiving of messages, the storing and retrieving of information, and the controlling of business decisions. *Slicing or code isolation* is a method for pulling out from a program the parts concerned with a specified behaviour or interest, such as a particular business rule. Our proposed architecture facilitates using these two concepts of reverse engineering. *Slicing* can be used to partition the existing application into a collection of objects and replace them with modules, which are developed using current technology. The existing application will thus be broken into slices. Some of theses slices may be replaced by new components, while others will continue and have new objects built over them, modelled on their export features. The concept of *logic modelling* can be used in modelling the object-oriented application that will integrate these objects.

9.6 Scalability of the Proposed Architecture

The proposed architecture can be implemented both for small-scale and large-scale integration. The architecture requires selection of the relevant export schema from each involved application, and constructing an integrating application that combines all involved export schemas. The integrating application needs to have interfaces with all component applications. If it is technologically feasible to have an application that can be interfaced with all involved applications, the proposed architecture can be implemented.

Since the proposed solution has made the integrating schema simpler, by targeting only export schemata from the individual applications, the benefit percentage is high if the ratio of objects in the export schema to those in the entire schema is low. If the same ratio of number of export objects to number of all objects is applicable for a large-scale project, the percentage benefit will be the same, but dollar benefits would be higher.

In the chapter 7, we have shown that from each constituent application, we need to select the export schema, which is relevant for its integration with other applications. For large-scale integration, the number of applications would be high and so is the number of export schemas to be integrated into the intermediary application. The integrating application that combines the export schemas of a large number of applications could operate from a single site or multiple sites.

As high interconnectivity and access to many information sources are feasible now, the proposed architecture can be used to integrate diverse systems from a wide geographical area all over world. If data replication is required in distributed databases, we also need to implement suitable algorithms for site and communication failures in a network[102].

9.7 Schema Evolution Of The Component Applications

The configuration of the integrated application may change over time. Some applications may be added, some deleted, and some modified. The integrated application may encompass more sites, or it may be withdrawn from some sites. We have already discussed, in the *section 7.8 Changes in the Configuration of the Integrating Application*, how the changes will be managed in an implementation of the proposed architecture. The schemas of individual applications and the corresponding export schemas may also change over time. For such schema changes, the existing objects, over the export schemas, can be reused and redefined to accommodate the changes.

9.8 Extreme Cases Of The Percentages Of Shared Data Items

Whether or not the proposed solution would be economical in a particular case depends on what percentage of total data items are shared across applications. In Chapter 7, we have discussed two extreme conditions

(a) No data items are shared by one or more individual application(s)

(b) All data items are shared by one or more individual application(s)

If no data items are shared by one application, that application can be excluded from the integration proposal. If in a group of applications, no data is shared by any application, then there is no purpose in integrating those applications. However, if the chances are high that an application, not sharing any object, may later share objects with other applications, then that application may still be interfaced with the integrating application. Moreover, there

---

[102] Data replication in distributed databases has been discussed in Appendix IX, to cover algorithms for site and communication failures in a network.

could be some applications that only receive information from others, but do not share any of its own objects.

If all data items of one application are shared, that application participates in the proposed architecture in a normal way except that all its objects appear in the integrated schema. However, if all objects of all applications appear in the integrated schema, then proposed architecture does not provide any big advantage. Yet, it will be no worse off than other methods of implementing a global schema, rather it would help with the modelling of semantically related objects across applications into the integrated schema.

Considering schema evolution over time, one component application may change the list of its export objects. When integrated for the first time, the ratio of export objects to total objects may be low, and later on this ratio may grow to 100%. The integrating application in the proposed architecture will also evolve in this case as discussed in the previous section.

9.9 Non-Traditional Data Structures In Application

In 'Appendix XIV Relational vs. Object-Oriented Approaches', we have discussed that a relational solution with the sharable features of the application would be inadequate, when heterogeneous databases are incompatible for relational representation, for example graphics, text etc.

If a relational data model were chosen to implement the integrating application layer, we would have major problems in representing information at different levels of granularity. Individual applications using incompatible hardware/operating systems/DBMS/ file system combination, may have export and import schemas that cannot be suitably modelled into form of relational tuples. On the other hand, object-oriented data models have been developed to represent complex real world objects more closely; each mini-world entity, however complex, can be represented as one object in the database.

Even if the data repositories of individual applications are suitable for representation in relational tables, there could be need, in the integrating application, to link elements from two relational tables at different levels of granularity and this cannot be done using relational tables in the integrating application.

9.10 How I.T. Users Can Take Advantage Of The Architecture

Information technology users can adjust their strategies to take advantage of the proposed architecture. Following paragraphs lead to the recommendations for action plans for general users of hardware and software facilities.

Many large organisations have acquired a wide variety of hardware and software facilities for various special-purpose applications. Some might have tried to build in-house skills for each of these technologies. As high costs are encountered in the process, they might consider streamlining their hardware and software platforms. With the proposed architecture, semantically related objects from various applications can be linked, and thus the applications integrated, even though these applications continue to use different hardware and software technologies, which are most appropriate for their business functions. But they need not maintain the in-house skills, nor they need to streamline hardware/software platforms. The organisations have only to ensure that all its application systems communicate with the integrating object-oriented application; the maintenance of individual applications will rest on the respective suppliers - external or in-house; any enhancement to suit specific needs will be incorporated in the object built on top of the application. Thus these organisations will use the most appropriate hardware/software for their business without the need for maintaining skill levels to match those of suppliers of these facilities. Action plans recommended for following this strategy is as follows:

- implement the proposed architecture on few selected systems, say for queries only,

- upgrade the integrating application for updates as well,

- extend this architecture to the rest of the applications,

- replace the individual application systems as needed to keep up with the technology and business needs, while maintaining the interfaces with the central application,

- select the applications whose main functions are coordinating between applications, rather than providing any new functionality and integrate them into the central object-oriented application,

- upgrade the action-plans keeping up with the developments in the business and technology environments.

General users of information technology should acquire the facilities best suitable for their business, while adopting the proposed architecture of integrating both existing and new technologies into their current information system architecture. If all users that rely on information for their operations adopt similar architectures, the ways will be open to integrate applications across the organizational boundaries.

In last thirty years, business world have relied more and more heavily on information systems and made considerable investments. The investment by multiple business groups have contributed to building of information infrastructure, which have benefited the business community in general - some information are available to the business, free of any costs. While maintaining information system, the business does not need to spend on the information that is freely available on the infrastructure. Before we invest in information technology to build application systems to run our business, we need to find out whether we can access that information from other sources. If some other bodies are already maintaining the information we need and cost of accessing that information is less than the cost of maintaining our own information system, it would be prudent to disinvest the information technology and save costs with no or very little effect on the business performance. The proposed architecture could be used to design the application, which integrates the information accessed from the publicly available data from other organisations.

9.11 Users' Expectations from Vendors Of Hardware And Software

As the proposed architecture shows ways to establish semantic links between applications using different technologies and methodologies, the manufacturers need not strive for resolving their differences. Users will be prepared to use heterogeneous software and hardware, so long the vendors can ensure that their products work and do not need skilled users to debug them. For manufacturers of hardware and software facilities, the strategy should be to find the most effective and economical ways to carry out the business functions, irrespective of varieties in technologies, as long as the interfaces can be maintained with a standard set of object-oriented applications.

Some of the areas that appear promising to help develop a reliable integrating object-oriented application are:

- development of continuous fault-tolerant systems, suitable for object-oriented applications,

- development of operating systems, suitable for accessing, transmitting, manipulating and storing instances/objects,

- development of operating systems to facilitate use of algorithms for concurrency control and recovery in replicated databases, so that all these algorithms need not be coded by individual users, and standard object classes or templates are available for use in applications,

- development of facilities to select and use resources within the network to cope with increased heterogeneity of systems, data types and software components as enhanced capabilities of object-oriented systems will create the potential for integrating wide variety of technologies,

- development of schema integration facilities using document type definitions of XML, for example extending DB2 for composing/decomposing contents of XML documents with one or more relational tables.

9.12 *Concluding Summary*

To sum up, in this thesis we have investigated the ways and methods for integrating decentralised information systems and proposed an approach and structure for establishing an integrated application by using the shared information across application systems.

We have started with a chapter of preliminaries and definitions to explain the terms that will be used in the thesis. In the next chapter of introduction, we have checked the motivation for application integration and identified the problem of this thesis as:

1. What objects from individual applications need necessarily be selected into the schema of the integrating intermediary application to provide sufficient application integration,

2. Modelling of these objects from individual applications, so that they can be adequately linked in the integrating application, in spite of their differences in design specifications.

Then we have made a reconnaissance of various issues of application integration to find out what integration of applications means in the real world terms, and why the problem of application integration persists in spite of past attempts and technological advances. In the following chapters, we have reviewed the work done so far to integrate application. We have identified two major conflicts in applications as schema conflicts and data conflicts. Two major ways of integrating applications have been found to be (1) transforming component applications into one application and (2) establishing an integrating application as an intermediary to component applications.

The major contributions of this thesis have been developed in Chapter 7, in which we have proposed an approach to integrate decentralised application systems by identifying a subset of data items of each involved application. These subsets represent the shared information across the applications. In such a way, the integrated application can be achieved by integrating only the selected subsets of the applications. Traditional approaches are to integrate applications by considering all data items of involved application. In the proposed approach, the subsets of the involved applications are expressed as exported objects, which contain the shared information of each involved application for the integrated application. Then the integrated application is achieved by integrating these exported objects using object-oriented techniques.

One global schema for application integration requires substantial human intervention to integrate local/individual schemata; it does not matter what methodology is used. We have scaled down the complexity of the integrating schema, by targeting only export schemata from the individual applications; data modelling is made much simpler.

We have expanded the definition of shared data items to include all data items required to access the export data items, and to include all data items involved in constraints with an item in the list of shared data items. This has helped to identify what objects from individual applications need necessarily be selected into the schema of the integrating intermediary application to provide sufficient application integration,

Identification of semantic links between the elements of involved export schemas has facilitated setting up their relationships in the data/object models. We have considered that the applications view the objects in terms of selected attributes. Based on the domain of values of these selected attributes of the objects of different schemas, they can be considered as semantically equivalent, or semantically related. This equivalence or relationship can be modelled in the integrating application. We have also seen that when the same real world object is modelled in two applications, the instances of one application can be matched with instances of the other application, based on the value of the common attribute that uniquely identifies the object in each application.

Since the proposed solution allows the applications to continue their original functions, functionalities of the original applications are maintained as before integration. This integration approach will facilitate the coexistence of old and new technologies, and help us get the best of both worlds - continue reaping benefits from existing information resources without any major investments on reverse engineering, assimilate at the same time the benefits of emerging technologies. We have also made suggestion about the new roles of general information users to make the best use of this architecture, by letting the application be developed on the technological platform that suits the functionality best. We have also checked how the software and hardware vendors can make the best use of the architecture to complement the new roles of the information systems users. In the next chapter, we shall check what further work need be carried out, both in the industry and the universities, to use the best applications irrespective of the technological heterogeneity, and irrespective of the age and version of the applications.

10. FURTHER WORK

10.1 Introduction

In this chapter, we shall check how the implementation of this architecture can be improved and show the areas, where further research will facilitate interoperation of applications. We have checked in the last chapter that, both the vendors and the users of information technology facilities can take advantage of the proposed architecture. Since only the export schema of each application needs to be interfaced to the integrating application, users, application designers and vendors can choose the best technologies to deliver the application functions; they only need to ensure that the export schema can be linked to the integrating application. The discussion on further work, recommended in this thesis, has been structured as follows:

- Further work for improving performance of the integrated applications in the proposed architecture,

- Research work for enhancing the proposed architecture to take advantage of the new technological developments.

10.2 Further Work For Improving Performance

We can get the most out of the proposed architecture and the recent technological developments by resolving the implementation issues, which may lower the performance level. As original applications continue to function after integration, main issues are in implementation of the integrating application and its interfaces with the component applications. As the integrating application includes one or more objects to represent an application, it is necessary to have efficient interface between the component application and its controlling object in the integrating application. These issues are presented below:

Performance Issues

Component applications, which are directly interfaced before integration, are going to communicate via their controlling objects after integration using the proposed architecture. This means, requests sent from each underlying application would be processed in the object-oriented application. This may introduce delays, depending on the extent, the controlling object needs to interpret the requests from other controlling objects and applications, and generate suitable responses.

However, if all export features of the objects could be pre-compiled, then performance and expressiveness of the objects can be maintained at the same time. This could be achieved by using some tools, which can help provide bridges between application databases and object-oriented databases[103]. Further information about such tools and their methodologies for mapping, translation and data communications need be investigated. The objective is to pre-compile all non-procedural calls, so that they become as efficient as procedural calls.

Fault Tolerance of the Controlling Object-Oriented Application

The failure of the controlling application is critical to the integration; it is desirable to run this as a non-stop fault tolerant system so that failures, at any time, are isolated to individual applications only[104].

Another important consideration is for parallel processing of the objects in the application. If the entire application has a single root object class, the requests from individual applications wait too long, before being addressed. This can be avoided by having multiple-root object classes to facilitate parallel processing. If multiple threads of processing are allowed, all aspects of concurrency control and recovery must be provided to ensure that the results would match the serialized i.e. single-thread execution of the same updates.

Concurrency Control and Recovery (CCR)

Major tasks of concurrency control and recovery are better left to the existing database management systems, considering the substantial research efforts spent on this by respective vendors. Still we need to add concurrency control algorithms in the layer of controlling object-oriented application for

- replication, if any, among the sharable parts of the applications, i.e. when the controlling objects of two different applications include the same real world object, and
- referential integrity of the objects replicated in multiple applications.

We need to identify what CCR tasks can be taken up by the operating system hosting the object-oriented application, and what needs be covered by the controlling application itself. This choice needs to be refined as vendors enhance object-oriented operating systems.

---

[103] Examples of such attempts are products like KEEconnection and ProKappa Data Access Tools from IntelliCorp Inc.

[104] Features of Tandem's Integrity S2 could be investigated for this purpose, though currently it may not support compilers for object-oriented languages like Eiffel.

Option of one controlling object instead of multiple controlling objects

In the proposed architecture, we have shown an object on top of each application. Instead we may consider only one object to control all underlying applications. In the proposed architecture, the integrating object-oriented application can be considered as a single object, which consists of the controlling objects on top of each application. Thus, this single object is modularly developed using individual C_is i.e. the controlling objects of component applications.

Security Of The Participating Applications[105]

Two important issues for an integrated application are security and functionality involving the central integrating application and the underlying applications. The security model must be consistent with the security policy and the functionality must be consistent with the data model. One approach to secure database development begins with a data model. It is extended to include elements and relations from the security policy and becomes a security model. The data model and the security policy represent independent concerns and can conflict with each other.

The logical consistency of the object-oriented database security model, is evaluated from the principles of granularity, dependency, and determinacy.

The granularity principle states that the finest level of granularity for protection purposes should be structures, which correspond to atomic facts. The dependency principle requires that the access class of a fact dominate the access class of any fact it depends upon. The determinacy principle states that factual dependencies should be non-ambiguous.

The inheritance mechanism in an object-oriented database, ie between instances and object-classes, and also between super-classes and sub-classes, need be suitably harnessed to satisfy the principles of granularity, dependency and determinacy.

10.3 *Outstanding Research Areas*

Further research areas identified from this thesis are as follows:

- Using new technologies to link semantically related items,

- Formalising the data aspects of semantic relationship in the proposed architecture,

- Introducing intelligence in the integration architecture

- Introducing XML Extender for OODB and non-OODB applications,

- Vocabulary Standards for XML applications.

10.3.1 *New Technologies To Link Semantically Related Items*

We have checked that recent technological developments have provided us various tools of linking objects across applications. In this thesis, we have mainly considered an object-oriented application as a means of linking the semantically related objects from the export schemas of component applications. However, other options could be effectively used. For example, we could build CORBA-compliant or RMI-compliant objects to interface with the objects in the export schemas of the component applications; the same purpose could be served by using XML, Enterprise Java Beans and/or Message-Oriented-Middleware [MOM][106]. In short, we could use various combinations of new technologies to link objects from export schemas. Further research in applying new technologies will help implementation of links between semantically related objects across applications.

10.3.2 *Data Aspects Of Semantic Relationship*

If we consider an application object to be semantically equivalent to a real world object, we need to consider both schema and data contents. This means we need to know which attributes of an object are relevant and values of those attributes. This thesis has mainly considered the schema aspect of the semantic relationship, though we have considered that adequate transaction management of the objects is necessary to maintain their semantic relationship over time and various update cycles. Instance matching between objects of various applications will lead to identify the same real world object instance in various applications. Further research in the data aspect of semantic relationship is needed.

We have shown how the instances of one application can be matched with instances of another application, based on the value of the common attribute that uniquely identifies the object in both applications. This is when the same real world object is modelled in both applications. Often we would find the same unique identifier has been used in two applications, in other cases the unique identifier in one application can be derived from the unique identifier of the other application. Further research is recommended to link the unique identifiers of the real world objects in various applications.

---

[105] Keefe T.F., and Tsai W.T. (1990), Security Model Consistency in Secure Object-Oriented Systems, *Fifth Annual Computer Security Applications Conference, Tucso, A 2, U.S.A.* (IEEE Computing Society Press, 1990)
[106] IBM's MQ Series product may be chosen for this purpose. MOM provides guaranteed delivery for asynchronous as well synchronous connections. It is used heavily for its message queueing capability.

10.3.3 *Artificial Intelligence in the Proposed Architecture*

The architecture for schema integration by modelling shared data items can be further enhanced, if the O-O application is intelligent enough to resolve the problems of semantic heterogeneity. Two applications may be functioning on different domains with some matching data items. Two applications may be expressing quantities in different units where unit conversion can be carried out. Contexts of two component application systems may influence different assumptions from the same data values. Using two different structural constructs for two applications may represent the same concepts. In Appendix-XIII, we have considered that the architecture for application integration is enhanced, by adding intelligence to the integrating application. This is accomplished by including (1) an object with meta-data of each underlying database to provide knowledge-base of the schema, and (2) an expert object which will use the knowledge-base of all local domains plus a meta-data grammar and a global knowledge-base. The use of such intelligent objects will allow transitions and propagation of schema changes to be carried out with less human involvement and fewer errors caused by ignorance of semantics. Even if human intervention is required, these objects will provide checks to help analysis.

10.3.4 *XML Extender for OODB applications*

When the applications, involved in exchanging data, use DB2 version-7 with XML extender[107], the sending application can compose the collection of relevant tables into XML documents and send to the receiving application. The receiving application can decompose the XML documents into corresponding DB2 tables.

We are looking for an equivalent tool of XML-extender for OODBs. When the applications involved in exchanging data use OODBs, the sending application needs this tool to compose the collection of relevant objects into XML documents and send to the receiving application. The receiving application needs the same tool to decompose the XML documents into corresponding objects in OODB.

Following what is done by stored procedures in DB2 with XML extender, we recommend development of Java codes to compose XML documents from the selected set of objects in a OODB. Another set of Java codes is needed to decompose an XML document and store it in the OODB.

---

[107] IBM Corporation, *DB2 UDB for OS/390 and z/OS V7 XML Extender Administration and Programming*, Document Number SC26-9949-00

Further research is required to find out whether it is possible to write generic Java codes that can work for any types of OODB, and can map any abstract object to XML document and vice-versa.

10.3.5 XML Extender for non-OODB applications

Real life applications may use a DBMS, which is not relational nor object-oriented, some of them may use file systems for data repositories. It will be a complex task to create compatible XML documents which can be composed from the data repositories of the source application, and can also be decomposed to create objects for the destination application. Instead of looking for tools to create XMLs from any type of data repository, we recommend to set up a source OODB to represent the objects from the source repository, and set up another destination OODB to represent the objects from the desination repository. XML extenders for OODBs as proposed in the previous section will be used to exchange data between the source OODB and the destination OODB, while the source OODB will be mapped to the source data repository and the destination OODB will be mapped to the destination data repository. Moreover, if all objects from the source data repository are not interchanged with the destination data repository, we need not map the entire source data repository to the source OODB, we need to map only those objects which are exported from the source data repository, with the source OODB. Similarly, we need to map only those objects which are imported into the destination data repository, with the destination OODB. Further research is necessary to develop the XML-extender for OODBs, this will make use of the architecture proposed in this thesis.

10.3.6 Vocabulary Standards for XML[108] applications

Most major IT suppliers and user groups now have started using XML for information interchange. However, XML does not of itself define how information will be structured, or what it can mean. The user defines the tags and their semantics, giving structure and meaning to the data. XML, like relational databases, provides only a framework for organizing data in a simpler, more flexible, and more powerful way. It shares the same problem of system-to-system interchanges between relational databases. If there be N databases, the number of possible data interchange links can grow as N squared. Even for a small fraction of these interfaces, the resulting complexity will be unmanageable.

---

[108] Robert Worden, *XML E-Business Standards: Promises and Pitfalls*, http://www.xml.com/pub

Through widespread use of XML, we will create a greater data complexity battle - this time across whole industries rather than individual companies. We need to use standard vocabularies for XML across the industry, else widespread confusion is apprehended.

Currently the number of XML-based message standards defined by industry groupings is well over 100, and growing. It is difficult for one industry group to understand all the other standards in enough detail. It is enough work just to update own XML formats to reflect the changing business needs; maintaining thirty or fifty XSLT[109] (the eXtensible Stylesheet Language Transformations) translations as well would be a massive extra workload. To avoid the N-squared trap of incompatible message formats and legacy systems, the individual companies may take control of their own problem. The key consideration is that every business is different. Therefore the individual company needs to build a single technology-independent logical model of all the information needed to drive its business and perform all XML translations via this model. Any data translation between the system and the message format is better done not directly, but in two steps via the logical business model. For each new IT system or XML message format, one needs to define one translation (to the logical business model), rather than N translations to other systems and message formats.

We need further research to set vocabulary standards across the industries, so as to simplify the problems of interfacing with a changing and unpredictable outside world.

10.4 Conclusion

In the last chapter, we have already seen the evaluation of the architecture proposed in this thesis and the concluding summary. In this chapter, we have shown how we can get the best of the emerging technologies using the proposed architecture, by carrying out further research work, recommended in this thesis.

---

[109] G. K. Holman, *What is XSLT?*, http://www.xml.com/pub/a/2000/08/holman/index.html, August 16, 2000

11. INDEX

O

Objects, 20
ODP
  Open Distributed Processing, 51
O-O Federated Database, 76
Operational Issues, 195
Outstanding Research Areas, 213, 214, 215, 216

P

Past attempts of schema integration, 37

R

Real world semantics, 26
Reverse Engineering, 202

S

Schema, 21
Schema Conflict, 100
Schema Transformation, 118

Schematic Discrepancy, 106
Semantic Conflicts, 65
Semantic Equivalence, 21, 27
Semantic Relationship, 21
Shared Data Items, 153
Site Failure, 192
Small Scale Integration, 48
Steps For Implementation, 183
Superdatabase, 42

T

Trader, 54

U

Unifying Semantic Model
  USM, 72

X

XML, 58, 216

Term	Explanation

12. GLOSSARY

Accessing Processor	Software that accepts commands and produces data by executing commands against a database.
ACL	Access Control List
ALUW	Application Logical Unit of Work
API	Application Programming Interface
Application System	A set of programs, objects, databases and files, which together represent a part of the real world.
BPR	Business Process Re-engineering
CAD	Computer Aided Design
CAM	Computer Aided Machines
CASE	Computer Aided Software Engineering
Class of Users	A set of users performing closely related tasks.
Common Data Model (CDM)	A data model to which schemas of different component DBMSs are translated for the purpose of representation in a common format and facilitation of schema integration.
Component Database Administrator (Component DBA)	The administrator of a component DBS (also called local DBA) who, among other things, decides data access rightsof local users as well as (individuals and/or classes) of federation users. It is component DBA's responsibility to manage the local schema, translate it to create the component schemas, and define export schemas.
Component DBMS	A DBMS participating in a multidatabase system. A component DBMS participating in an FDBS is autonomous and allows local operations as well as global operaions that meets its constraints.
Component Schema	A translation of a local schema into an equivalent schema in the common data model.
Constructing Processor	Software that partitions and/or replicates operations produced by a single processor for execution by two or more processors. Also software that merges data produced by two or more processors for consumption by another processor.
CORBA	(OMG's) Common Object Request Broker Architecture
Data Conflicts	Diference in contents or values of data served by different applications
DBMS - Database Management System	Software that manages a collection of structured data. Management includes providing data management services including data access, constraint enforcement, and consistency management,
Database System (DBS)	A database System (DBS) consists of a DBMS that manages one or more databases.

Term	Explanation
DCE	(OSF's) Distributed Computing Environment
DCS	Distributed Conceptual schema
Distributed DBMS	A system that manages multiple databases.
DNS	Domain Name Service
ESIOP	Environment-Specific Inter-ORB Protocol
Export Schema	A subschema of a component schema specifically defined to express the access constraints on a class of federation users to access data represented in the component schema.
External Schema	A subschema or view defined over a federated schema primarily for a pragmatic reason of not having to define too many federated schemas or to tailor a federated schema for smaller groups of federation users than that of a fedrated schema.
FAP	Formats and Protocols
Federated Database System (FDBS)	A system that is created to provide operations on databases managed by autonomous, and possibly heterogeneous DBSs. The software that manages an FDBS is called a federated DBMS (FDBMS).
Federated Schema	An integration of several export schemas created to represent data access requirements and rights of a class or group of federation users.
Federation administrator (federation DBA)	The administrator of a federated schema or the federated databse system who, anong other things, creates and maintains federated and external schemas.
Federation User	A user of an FDBS or an application running over an FDBS.
Filtering Processor	Software that constrains operations that can be applied or data that can be passed to another processor.
GIOP	General Inter-ORB Protocol
Global (or External) Operation	An operation that is not submitted by a local user (e.g., an operation submitted to the component DBS by the FDBMS or another component DBS).
HTML	Hypertext Markup Language
HTTP	Hypertext Transfer Protocol
IDL	Interface Definition Language
JDBC	Java Database Connectivity
LCS	Logically Centralised Schema
Local Schema	A schema of a component DBS in a native data model of the component DBMS.
Local User	A user of a component DBS
MAPI	Massaging Application Programming Interface

Term	Explanation
Middleware	Middleware has been generally described as the run-time system software layered between an application program and the operating system, and between an application program and the network transport layer.
MIPS	Million instructions per second
MOM	Message Oriented Middleware
Multidatabase System (MDBS)	A system that allows operations on multiple databases.
NDS	NetWare Directory Services
Netware	Netware has been generally described as the network operating system. RPCs or RPC-like mechanisms are embedded in the network operating system.
ODBC	Open Database Connectivity
OGIS	The Open Geodata Interoperability Specification (OGIS) provides a framework for software developers to create software that enables their users to access and process geographic data from a variety of sources across a generic computing interface within an open information technology foundation.
OLE	Microsoft's Online Linking and Embedding
OLTP	Online transaction processing
OMG	Object Management Group
OODBMS	Object-Oriented database management system
ORB	Object request broker
OSF	Open Software Foundation
OTM	Object transaction manager
Processor	Software that performs operations on data and commands.
RDBMS	Relational database management system
RPC	Remote procedure call
SAIF	The Spatial Archive and Interchange Format was developed as a means of sharing spatial and spatiotemporal data.
Schema Conflicts	Diference in representation of data served by different applications
Schema Object	A description of a data element in a schema. For example, a schema expressed in the Entity Relationship model has three types of schema objects: entity types, relationship types and attribute definitions. An example of an entity type schema object is an "Employee" entity type.
Schema, subschema, and View	A representation of the structure (syntax), semantics, and constraints on the use of a database (or its portion) in a particular data model. A schema is a collection of schema

Term	Explanation
	objects. a subschema is a collection of subsets of that schema's objexts. a view is any connected portion of a schema. In other words, a schema is a collection of views.
Semantic Relativism	Multiplicity of possible representations of a given real world.
SQL	Structured Query Language
TCP/IP	Transmission Control Protocol /Internet Protocol
TP	Transaction processing
TPM	Transaction processing monitor
Transforming Processor	Software that translates commands from one language or format to another language or format or translates data from one format to another.
UoD (Universe of Discourse)	A part of the real world that will be represented in data models, ie a particular data model will represent facts that are within its universe of discourse, none outside its universe of discourse.
User	An individual or an application usimng a database system.
WWW	World Wide Web
XFN	X/Open Federated Naming Architecture

13. BIBLIOGRAPHY

1. Alzaharani R. M., Qutaishait, M.A, Fiddian N.J. and Gray W.A. (1995), Integrity Merging in an Object-Oriented Federated Database Environment, *Advances In Databases, 13th British National Conference Of Database*, pp 226-248
2. Andrade J.M. et al,.(1996), The TUXEDO System: Software for Constructing and Managing Distributed Business Applications, Addison Wesley Publishing Company, Massachusetts, p 53
3. Barr A., and Feigenbaum E.A. (1981), *The Handbook Of Artificial Intelligence - 1*, Heuristech Press, California, pp 316-319
4. Batini C., Lenzerini M. and Navathe S.B. (1986), A Comparative Analysis of Methodologies for Database Schema Integration, *ACM Computing Surveys*, Vol.18, No 4, pp 323-364
5. Bernstein P.A., Hadzilacos V. (1987), and Goodman N., *Concurrency Control And Recovery In Database Systems*, Addison-Wesley Publishing Co.
6. Bertino E., Negri M., Pellagatti G., & Sbattella L. (1989), Integration Of Heterogeneous Database Applications Through An Object-oriented Interface, *Information Systems*, Vol 14 No.5, pp 407-420
7. Blechar M., et al 1996), AD Technology 2001: Building Infrastructures as Tools Mature, *Strategic Analysis Report (ADM), Gartner Group, R-900-138, Oct25, 1996*
8. Breitbart Y. (1990), Multidatabase Interoperability, *SIGMOD Record*, Vol.19, No.3, September 1990, pp 53-60.
9. Burton B. (1996), Transactions BeyondThe Web, *SDM (Strategic Data Management), Top View, Gartner Group, TV-000-139, 24 May 1996*
10. Burton B.,(1996) Data Disintegration: The Pressure Mounts, *Strategic Analysis Report, R-200-109, Gartner Group, 28th Oct.1996*
11. Carey M.J., et al, Towards Heterogeneous Multimedia Information Systems: The Garlic Approach, *Tech Report, IBM Almaden Research Center, USA*
12. Cattel R.G.G. and Barry D. (1997), *The Object Database Standard 2.0*, Morgan Kaufmann Publishers, USA, 1997
13. Chatterjee A., and Segev A. (1991), Data Manipulation In Heterogeneous Databases, *SIGMOD Record*, Vol.20, No.4, December 1991
14. Chirgwin Richard (1999), *Greater Than The Sum Of Its Parts*, Systems - Enterprise Computing Monthly, July 1999, pp 32-40
15. Cho H., Kim Y.S., Moon S. (1996), *Design and Implementation of an Autonomous Heterogeneous Distributed Database System: DIME*, Document Supply Service, Yonset University, Seol, Korea
16. Cho V., Wuthrich B. (1998), Towards Real Time Discovery from Distributed Information Sources, *Second Pacific Asia Conference On Knowledge Discovery - PAKDD-98*, April 1998, pp376-377
17. Chou H., Shih P. (1994), Managing Object Schemas In A Distributed Database Architecture For Concurrent Engineering, *Journal Of The Chinese Institute Of Engineers*, Vol.17, No.6, pp 871-879.
18. Conrad S., Schmitt I., Turker C, Considering Integrity Constraints During Federated Database Design, *Proceedings of 16th National conference on Advances in Databases, 6th-8th July 1998; pp 119-133*
19. Dan Connolly & Tim Bray, http://www.w3.org/XML/Activity, Extensible Markup Language (XMLTM) Activity, Last modified $Date: 1999/08/05

20.Date C.J.,(1989), An Introduction to Database Systems, *Addison-Wesley/Narosa*
21.Dietz J.,(1994), 'Business Modelling for Business Redesign',*Proceedings of the 27th Hawaii International Conference on system Sciences*, IEEE Computer Science Press, 1994
22.Dogac A., et al (1996), Building Interoperable Databases on Distributed Object Management Platforms, *Communications of ACM*, Sep.1996
23.Dogac A., et al (1996), asuman@srdc.metu.edu.tr, *A Multidatabase System Implementation on CORBA*, 0-8186-7289-7/96 @1996 IEEE, pp 2-11
24.Du W. and Shan M.(1996), Query Processing in Pegasus, *Object Oriented Multibase Systems, A.O.Bukhres and A.K. Elmagarmid ed.*, Prentice Hall, USA, 1996, pp 449-471
25.Evans E., and Rogers D. (1997), Using JAVA Applets and CORBA for Multi-User Distributed Applications, *Internet Computing*, May-June 1997, pp 43-55
26.Extensible Markup Language (XML): Part 2. Linking W3C Working Draft April-06-97
27.Fogelman Jay (1996), The problem with DCE, *Insight IS, Xephon, June1996*
28.Ghosh P. (1996), Integration of Application Systems by Modelling Information Shared among Applications, *Proceedings of the 31st Annual Convention of the Computer Society of India, 30th October to 3rd November, 1996, Bangalore, India*, pp 297-305.
29.Ghosh P. and Feuerlicht G. (2000), Setting up Semantic Links among Disparate Application Systems, *The International Conference on Advances in Infrastructure for Electronic Business Science and Education on the Internet, L'Aquila, Italy,July-Aug2000*
30.Ghosh P. and Feuerlicht G. (1999), Integration Of Applications By Linking Semantically Related Objects Over Internet, *Proceedings of the 34th Annual Convention of the Computer Society of India, 31st October to 6th November, 1999, Mumbai, India*
31.Ghosh P. and Feuerlicht G. (1997), Integration of Application Systems by Modelling Information Shared among Applications, *Proceedings of the Joint 1997 Asia Pacific Software Engineering Conference and International Computer Science Conference, Dec.1997, Hong Kong*
32.Ghosh P., and Feuerlicht G. (1998), Application Integration by Linking Semantically Related Objects Shared across Applications, *Proceedings of the 1998 Australasian Workshop on Software Architectures, 24 Nov. 1998, Melbourne, Australia*
33.Ghosh P., and Feuerlicht G. (1998), Data Replication In Distributed Databases, *Proceedings of the International Symposium on Future Software Technology '98, 28-30 Oct 1998, Hangzhou, China*
34.Ghosh P., and Feuerlicht G. (1998), Disinvestment Of Information Technology, *Proceedings of the International Symposium on Future Software Technology '98, 28-30 Oct 1998, Hangzhou, China*
35. Ghosh P., and Feuerlicht G. (1998), Strategies for Manufacturing Industries to Access Information Maintained by Other Involved Parties, *Proceedings of the International Conference on Information Technology Integration,27-30 Dec 1998, Bangalore, India*
36.Ghosh P., Garg D. and Feuerlicht G. (1997), Integration Of Application Systems: Need Of Schemas In Exchanging Messages And An Intelligent Architecture, *Proceedings of the International Symposium on Future Software Technology '97, 29-31 Oct 1997, Xiamen, China*
37.Ghosh P., Garg D. and Feuerlicht G. (1997), Integration Of Application Systems: Proposed Solution vis-a-vis I.T.Standards And Trends, *Proceedings of the International Symposium on Future Software Technology '97, 29-31 Oct 1997, Xiamen, China*
38.Ghosh P. (2000), Metrics for Success in Client Server Implementation, *The International Conference on Advances in Infrastructure for Electronic Business Science and Education on the Internet, L'Aquila, Italy,31st July- 6th August 2000*
39.Ghosh P., Software Metrics and Object Oriented Systems, *Proceedings of the First Australian Conference on Software Metrics, ACOSM'93, Sydney, Australia*, pp 31-40

40. Harmon P. (1991), What's Happening In Computing?, What's Happening In Expert Systems and A.I.?, *Intelligent Software Strategies*, Vol.7, No.8, August 1991, pp 1-12.

41. Hearst M.A., Levy A.Y., Knoblock C., Minton S., and Cohen W., Information Integration, *IEEE Intell.Syst.(USA), Vol 13, No. 5, Sep-Oct 1998, pp 12-24*

42. Heimbigner D., & McLeod D. (1985), A Federated Architecture For Information Management, *ACM Transactions on Office Information Systems, July 1985*

43. G. K. Holman, *What is XSLT?*, http://www.xml.com/pub/a/2000/08/holman/index.html, August 16, 2000

44. Jacobson G., et al (1988)., *CALIDA*: A Knowledge-based System for Integrating Multiple Heterogeneous Databases, *Proc. Intl. Conf. Data and Knowledge Bases*, Jerusalem, Jun.1988.

45. Johannesson P.(1993), Schema Integration, Schema Translation, And Interoperability In Federated Information Systems, *Doctoral Thesis, Department of Computer and System Sciences, Stockholm Universit*, Printed by Akademitryck AB, Edsbruk

46. Kalinichenko L.A.(1990), Methods And Tools For Equivalent Data Model Mapping Construction, *Proceedings Of International Conference on Extending Database Technology, Venice, Italy, March 26-30, 1990*

47. Karunaratna D.D., Gray W.A., and Fiddian N.J., Establishing a Knowledge Base to Assist Integration of Heterogeneous Databases, *Proceedings Of 16th British National Conference on Advances In Databases,July 6-8, 1998, pp 103-118*

48. Keefe T.F., and Tsai W.T. (1990), Security Model Consistency in Secure Object-Oriented Systems, *Fifth Annual Computer Security Applications Conference*, Tucso, A 2, U.S.A., IEEE Computing Society Press

49. Kent W. (1991), Solving Domain Mismatch and Schema Mismatch Problems with an Object-Oriented Database Programming Language, *Proc. of the 17th VLDB Conference, Barcelona, September 1991*, pp 147-160

50. Kim W. et al, (1993), On Resolving Schematic Heterogeneity in Multibase Systems, *Distributed and Parallel Databases*, Vol.1, No.3, 1993, pp 251-279

51. Kim W., and Seo J. (1991), Classifying Schematic and Data Heterogeneity in Multidatabase Systems, *IEEE Computer, December 1991*, pp 12-18.

52. Light M., Natis Y., Schulte R. (1996), Middleware : The Foundation For Distributed Computing, SMS *(Software Management Strategies) Strategic Analysis Report, Gartner Group, R-200-108, October1996*

53. Litwin W., and Abdellatif, An Overview of the Multi-Database Manipulation Language MDSL, *Proc. IEEE*, Vol.75, No.5, May 1987, pp 621-632

54. Litwin W., Mark L., and Rossopoulos N.(1990), Interoperability of Multiple Autonomous Databases, *ACM Computing Surveys*, Vol.22, No. 3, pp 268-293, September 1990.

55. Liu L. et al (1996), An Adaptive Approach to Query Mediation across Heterogeneous Databases, *Proc. Intl.Conf. Cooperative Information Systems*, IEEE Computer Soc. Press, Los Alamitos, Calif., 1996, pp 144-156

56. Madnick S.(1997), Database in the Internet Age, *Database Programming and Design, January 1997*

57. Mah P.S., and Shin G. (1997), Schema Integration for Heterogeneous Distributed Databases, *Proceedings of the International Symposium on Future Software Technology '97, 29-31 Oct 1997, Xiamen, China*, pp 173-180.

58. Marinos L., Papazoglou M.P., & Norrie M.(1988), Towards the Design of an Integrated Environment for Distributed Databases, *Parallel Processing and Applications*. North-Holland; Elsevier Science Publishers B.V., pp 283-288.

59. Melcher L. (1996), What Will Happen To DCE?, *SMS (Software Management Strategies) Research Note, Gartner Group, M-220-406, 11 June 1996*

60. Meyer B. (1988), *Object-Oriented Software Construction*, U.K., Prentice Hall International Ltd., pp 112-128.

61. Montgomery I.(1990), *Data Analysis Concepts Binary-Relationship Modelling*, Course Material for M.Sc.(Database), University Of Technology, Sydney, 1990.

62. Morgenstern M., Integrating Web and Database Information for Collaboration, Proceedings Seventh IEEE International Workshop on Enabling Technologies,(WET ICE'98) , pp 204-210

63. Morgenthal J.P, Portable Data / Portable Code: XML & Java Technologies, *The Source for Java Technology;* http://java.sun.com/xml/inc;April 1999.

64. Muhlberger R. M. and Orlowska M.E.,(1996), 'A Business Process Driven Multidatabase Integration Methodology', *Database Reengineering and Interoperability*, ISBN030645288, pp 283-295

65. Murphy J. and Grimson J.(1995), The Jupiter System: An Environment for Multidatabase Interoperability, *Information and Software Technology*, Vol 37, 1995, pp 503-513

66. Naiman C.F., and Ouksel A.M. (1995), A Classification Of Semantic Conflicts In Heterogeneous Database Systems, *Journal Of Organizational Computing*, 5(2), 167-193

67. Njssen G.M. and Halpin T.A. (1989), *Conceptual Schema And Relational Database Design*, Prentice Hall Of Australia, 1989

68. Object Management Group & X-Open (1991), *The Common Object Request Broker: Architecture & Specification*, OMG Document Number 91.12.1, Revision 1.1

69. Papakonstantinou et al. (1995), The TSIMMIS Approach to Mediation: Data Models and Languages, *Proc. NGITS workshop*, 1995

70. Papazoglou M.P., & Marinos L., An Object-Oriented Approach To Distributed Data Management, *Journal Of Systems and Software*, Vol.11, No.2, Feb 1990, pp 95-109.

71. Parrington G.D., and Shrivastava S. (1988), Implementing Concurrency Control In Reliable Distributed Object-Oriented Systems, *ECOOP '88, European Conference on Object-Oriented Programming, Oslo, 1988*

72. Perez J.M.(1995), Integration Of Heterogeneous Information Management Systems Using CORBA, *Proceedings of Basque International Workshop on Information Technology:July '95, San Sebastian; Spain*

73. Pires P.F. and Mattoso M.L.Q. (1997), A CORBA Based Architecture for Heterogeneous Information Source Interoperability, *Proceedings 25th Technology of Object-Oriented Languages and Systems:1997, pp 33-49*

74. Poon K (1995), Inside A Trader In Global Trading, *Computer Communications*, Vol.18, No.4, April '95, pp 227-248.

75. Pu C.(1988), Superdatabases for Composition of Heterogeneous Databases, *IEEE 1988 Data Engineering Conference*, pp 548-555.

76. Ram S. (1995), Intelligent Database Design Using The Unifying Semantic Model, *Information & Management*, 29, 191-206

77. Reddy M. (1995), *ORBs & ODBMSs: Two Complimentary Ways To distribute Objects*, Object Magazine, Vol.5, No.3, June 1995, PP 24-30,55

78. Rochester J.B., and Douglas D.P. (1991), Re-engineering Existing Systems, *I/S Analyzer*, Vol 29, No.10, October 1991

79. Rusinkiewicz M. et al (1989), OMNIBASE: Design and Implementation of a Multibase System, *Proc. Annual Symposium on Parallel and Distributed Processing*, Dallas, May 1989

80. Saltor F., Campderrich B., Garcia-Solaco M. (1994), On Architecture For Federated DB Systems, *Deductive & Interoperable Databases: Nov. 1-2, 1994*, Barcelona, pp 8-25

81. Saltor F., Castellanos M.G., and Garcia-Solaco M. (1993), *Overcoming Schematic Discrepancies in Interoperable Databases*, Universitat Politecnica de Catalunya, Pau Gargallo 5, E-08028 Barcelona, {saltor,castellanos,mgarcia}@lsi.upc.es

82. Scheuermann P., et al (1990), Report on the Workshop on Heterogeneous Database Systems held at Northwestern University, *SIGMOD Record*, Vol.19, No.4, Dec.1990

83. Schulte R. (1994), Integrating CORBA and DCE, *SMS (Software Management Strategies) Research Note, Gartner Group, K-401-1467, May 10, 1994*

84. Schulte R.(1994), Middleware: Panacea or Boondoggle?, *SMS (Software Management Strategies) Strategic Analysis Report, Gartner Group, R-401-130, July5, 1994*, pp12-13

85. Sheth, A.P. and Larson, J.A. (1990), Federated Database Systems for Managing Distributed, Heterogeneous, and Autonomous Databases, *ACM Computing Surveys*, Vol. 22, No. 3, pp 183-236, September 1990.

86. Siegel M. and Madnick S.E.(1991), Context Interchange: Sharing the Meaning of Data, *ACM SIGMOD Record*, Vol.20, No.4, pp 77-78.

87. Siegel M. and Madnick S.E.(1991), A Metadata Approach to Resolving Semantic Conflicts, *Proceedings of the 17th VLDB Conference, Barcelona*, pp133-145.

88. Spaccapietra S., and Parent C.(1993), View Integration : A Step Forward In Solving Structural Conflicts, *IEEE Transactions on Data and Knowledge Engineering*

89. Spaccapietra S., and Parent C., Dupont Y. (1992), Model-Independent Assertions for Integration of Heterogeneous Schemas, *Very Large Databases Journal*, 1(1), July 1992

90. Spaccapietra S., Parent C. and Dupont Y. (1991), Automating Heterogeneous Schema Integration, *Technical Report, Ecole Polytechnic Federal*, Lausanne, Switzerland

91. Srinivasan U., and Ngu A.H.H. (1995), Information Re-engineering in Co-operative Clinical Information Systems, *Working Paper, School of Computer Science and Engineering, University of New South Wales*, Australia

92. Srinivasan U., Ngu A.H.H and Gedeon T. (1995), Concept Clustering for Cooperation, *IFIP DS-6 Conference, Atlanta, Georgia, May 1995*

93. Standards Association Of Australia, *Reference Model For Open Distributed Processing*, ISO/IEC JTC1/SC21/WG7 N755

94. Stephenson P.(1991), The Peer Connection, *LAN Magazine*, August 1991, pp 59-63.

95. Tanenbaum A.S.(1989), *Computer Networks*, Second Edition, Prentice-Hall International, Inc., pp 475-490, 540-542.

96. Templeton et al.(1987), Mermaid - A Front End to Distributed Heterogeneous Databases, *Proceedings of the IEEE*, May 1987.

97. Tomasic A. et al (1995), Scaling Heterogeneous Database and the Design of DISCO, *Tech Report, n*2704, INRIA*, France,Nov.1995

98. Tozer J.,.(1993), 'Beyond 'rapid' applications', *Insight IBM, January 1993*

99. Urban S. D., and Wu J. (1991), Resolving Semantic Heterogeneity Through The Explicit Representation Of Data Model Semantics, *SIGMOD Record*, Vol.20, No.4, December 1991

100. West M., and Light M. (1996), Applications via the Internet: Resource or Illusion?, *Application Development & Management Strategies (ADM), Strategic Analysis Report, Gartner Group Inc., R-200-132, 29 April, 1996*

101. Whang W., Navathe S., and Chakrabarty S. (1991), Logic-based Approach for Realizing a Federated Information System, *First International Workshop on Interoperability in Multibase Systems*, ED Y. Kamabayashi et al, pp 92-100, Kyoto, IEEE Computer Society Press

102. Wilson L.B., and Clark R.G.(1988), *Comparative Programming Languages*. U.K.; Addison-Wesley Publishing Company, pp 11-13

103. Worden R, *XML E-Business Standards: Promises and Pitfalls*, http://www.xml.com/pub

104. Wright J.H., A Reference Model For Object-Oriented Distributed Systems, *British Telecom Technology Journal*, Vol-6, No-3, July 1988, pp 66-75.

105. Xephon (1996), Candle Moves Into MQ Management, *Insight IS*, May 1996

APPENDIX - I

EXPORT FEATURES OF CREDIT CARD SYSTEM
EXPRESSED IN SIMPLE SENTENCES

The information that a Card can share with other system[110] can be classified into two categories:

1) Information about selected features of the Bank's contract of the Card,

2) Information about the Cusomer(s) or Identity(s) associated with the Card.

1) Information About the Card

. A Bank's Credit-card contract is identified by and must be related to a Card.

. The contract can be de-assigned from one Card and assigned to another Card. The former has the Card-No of the latter. During the process of transfer a Transfer-Details is created.

. The contract can be closed, but the Card has to be made inactive at the same time.

. A Card, inactive for a specified period can be purged or destroyed.

. A Card is identified by a unique Card-No, which also serves as the common reference for the Identity using the card ie the Cardholder and the Identity granting Credit, ie the Merchant selling goods/services to the Cardholder.

. A Card has a Product-Code, which has one of the values available in the list Of credit-card product codes ie

Bankcard - Standard	Bankcard - Staff
Visa - Classic	Visa - Classic Staff
Visa - Gold	Visa - Business
Visa - Affinity (Group 1).........	Visa - Affinity (Group n)
Mastercard - Standard	Mastercard - Staff

. A Card has a Warning-Code, valid values are nil or something.

. A Card has a Block-Code, valid values are space or something.

. A Card has a Alt-Block-Code, valid values are space or something.

. A Card has an Account-Status, valid values are open, closed or transferred.

. A Card has a Date-Card-Opened.

. A Card has a Date-Card-Closed.

---

[110]   Note. Information shared with systems other than Customer Prospect System are ignored for this analysis, but can be
      modelled in a similar manner.

APPENDIX - I

. A Card has an Account-Balance.

. A Card has an Arrears-Amount.

. A Card has an Instalment-Amount.

. A Card has an Administrating-Branch.

. A Card has an Credit-Limit.

. A Card has an Interest-Rate-Within-Limit.

. A Card has a Debit-Interest-This-Year.

. A Card has a Date-Of-Last-Transaction.

. A Card has a Date-Of-Last-Customer-Transaction.

. A Card has a Total-Number-Of-Cardholders.

. A Card has a Date-Of-Card-Expiry.

. A Card has a Debit-Interest-Last-Year.

. A Card has an Last-Credit-Limit.

. A Card has an Last-Credit-Limit-Date.

. A Card has a Highest-Balance-So-Far.

. A Card has a List-Of-Delinquency-History.

1.1) Information About Transfer-Details

. Transfer-Details has the Card-No-Transferred-From.

. Transfer-Details has the Card-No-Transferred-To.

. Transfer-Details has the Date-Card-Transferred.

. Transfer-Details has the Time-Card-Transferred.

2) Information About Customer(s)

. A Card must be owned by an identity - Primary Cardholder.

. The Primary Cardholder can be replaced by another identity, which will be the current Primary Cardholder.

. A Cardholder can have one or more identities to share the card - Secondary Cardholders.

. Primary Cardholder may have a relationship with the Secondary Cardholder.

. The relationship between Primary Cardholder and Secondary Cardholder could be Spouse, Child, Employee.

. A Cardholder could be a Person or an Organization.

. A Cardholder could be a Person, representing an Organisation

. A Personal Cardholder may have an Employer

APPENDIX - I

. A Personal Cardholder has a Date-Of-Birth

. A Personal Cardholder may have a Home-Phone-No

. A Personal Cardholder may have a Work-Phone-No

. A Personal Cardholder may have a Work-Phone-No

. A Personal Cardholder may have a Signatory-Or-Not-Status

. A Personal Cardholder may have a Resident-Or-Not-Status

. A Personal Cardholder could belong to an Affinity Group

. A Personal Cardholder could have a Tax File Number

. A Personal Cardholder could have one or more other contracts with the Bank

. Each of the "Other Contracts" of Cardholder is of a Type - i.e one of the Product Type offered by the Bank

. Each of the "Other Contracts" of Cardholder has a Contract Identification Number [111]

. A Customer has an Address

. An Address has a Address-Line-1.

. An Address may have a Address-Line-2.

. An Address may have a City-Name.

. An Address may have a State-Name.

. An Address has a Postcode.

. An Address has an Effective-From-Date.[112]

---

[111] Note. Each of the Identities or Customers associated with the Card has an Identity Number allotted and maintained by Customer ProspectSystem (CPS).

[112] If an Address is changed New Address is sent to CPS, A New Address information could be received from CPS. If the Effective-From-Date of the New-Address is more recent than Current-Address, then Current-Address is replaced by New-Address, else Current Address information is sent to CPS.

APPENDIX - II

Conventions Used In Drawing Conceptual Schemas

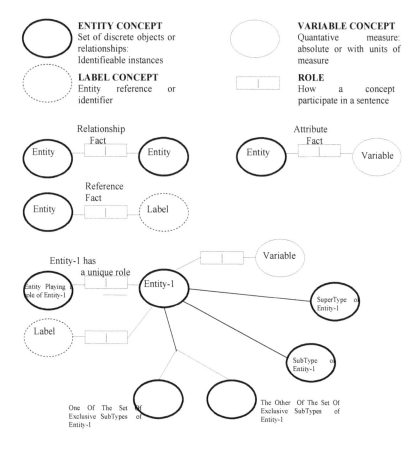

APPENDIX - III

Information Model For Integration Of Two Systems

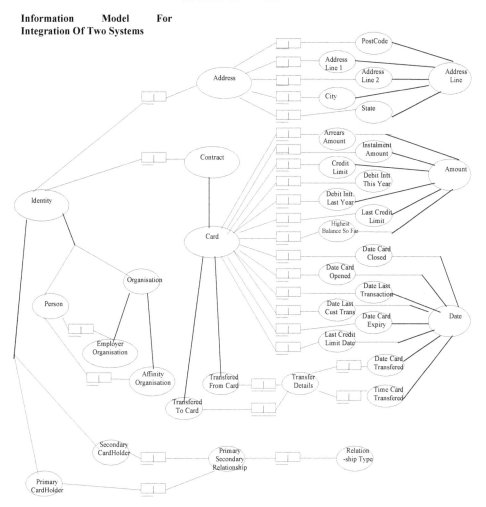

APPENDIX - IV

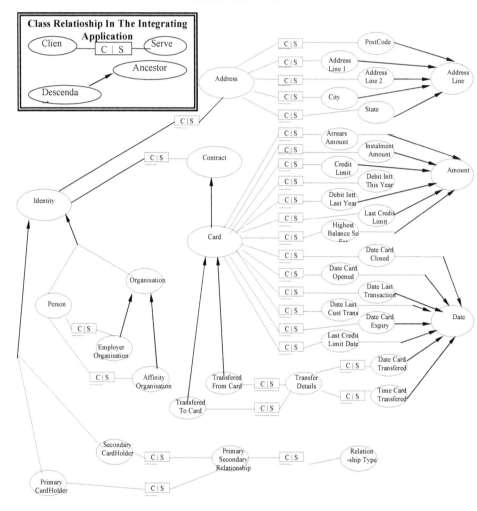

APPENDIX – V

CLASS SPECIFICATION OF OBJECTS IN C++

Class Specifications of controlling objects in the integrating object-oriented application are provided below. The syntax has not been checked and the application has not been coded.

```
class    Contract    {
public:
        // export features of contract
        Contract (int ProductCode, int ContractId,
        Int IdentityId, Identity* InvolvedIdentity);
        ~Contract() };


class    Card : public Contract {
public:
        // export features of Card
        Card (  int ProductCode,    int CardNo,    int IdentityId,
                char WarningCode, char BlockCode,
                char BlockCode, char AltBlockCode,
                char AccountStatus, date DateCardOpened,
                date DateCardClosed, amount AccountBalance,
                amount ArrearsAmount, amount InstalmentAmount,
                branch AdminBranch, amount CreditLimit,
                rate InterestRateWithinLimit,
                amount DebitInterestThisYear,
                date DateOfLastTransaction,
                date DateOfLastCustomerTransaction,
                int TotalNoOfCardholders,
                date DateOfCardExpiry,
                amount DebitInterestLastYear,
                amount LastCreditLimit,
                date LastCreditLimitDate,
                amount HighestBalanceSoFar,
                delqlist DelinquencyHistory,
                transfer TransferDetails);                    };
```

APPENDIX - V

int getProductCode()   {return ProductCode}

void setProductCode()

// Code here to get and set various features of Card

//...

Card: :Card (int ProductCode,   int CardNo,   int IdentityId,

                            char WarningCode, char BlockCode,

                            char BlockCode, char AltBlockCode,

                            char AccountStatus, date DateCardOpened,

                            date DateCardClosed, amount AccountBalance,

                            amount ArrearsAmount, amount InstalmentAmount,

                            branch AdminBranch, amount CreditLimit,

                            rate InterestRateWithinLimit,

                            amount DebitInterestThisYear,

                            date DateOfLastTransaction,

                            date DateOfLastCustomerTransaction,

                            int TotalNoOfCardholders,

                            date DateOfCardExpiry,

                            amount DebitInterestLastYear,

                            amount LastCreditLimit,

                            date LastCreditLimitDate,

                            amount HighestBalanceSoFar,

                            delqlist DelinquencyHistory,

                            transfer TransferDetails)

// Common Export Information For Any Contract

:Contract (int ProductCode,   int CardNo,   int IdentityId),

// Information Special For Credit-Card

WarningCode (WarningCode), BlockCode (BlockCode),

BlockCode (BlockCode), AltBlockCode (AltBlockCode),

AcountStatus (AccountStatus), DateCardOpened (DateCardOpened),

DateCardClosed (DateCardClosed), AccntBalance (AccountBalance),

ArrearsAmount (ArrearsAmount), InstlmtAmount (InstalmentAmount),

AdminBranch (AdminBranch), CreditLimit (CreditLimit),

InterestRateWithinLimit (InterestRateWithinLimit),

DebitInterestThisYear (DebitInterestThisYear),

DateOfLastTransaction (DateOfLastTransaction),

DateOfLastCustomerTransaction (DateOfLastCustomerTransaction),

TotalNoOfCardholders (TotalNoOfCardholders),

DateOfCardExpiry (DateOfCardExpiry),

DebitInterestLastYear (DebitInterestLastYear),

LastCreditLimit (LastCreditLimit),

LastCreditLimitDate (LastCreditLimitDate),

HighestBalanceSoFar (HighestBalanceSoFar),

DelinquencyHistory (DelinquencyHistory),

TransferDetails (TransferDetails)

```
        {
// Assertion Check Improvised For C++ Before Construction
        ValidityCheck (/* List Of Checks e.g. Product Code */);
        return crd;
        };


Card :: getProductCode()
{
//use extern function to get the value from controlled database
//using CardNo as the key
};
Card :: setProductCode()
{
//use extern function to set the value in controlled database
//using CardNo as the key
};
//.........................................................
// Code here to get from and write to the controlled database,     // the values of all features


class    Identity {
public:
        // export features of Identity
        Identity (int IdentityId, Address IdentityAddress,
                        name IdentityName, phone IdentityPhone);
```

APPENDIX - V

~Identity() };

class   Organisation   :public Identity {

public:

    // export features of Organisation is same as Identity

    Organisation : Identity (int IdentityId,

            Address IdentityAddress, name IdentityName,

            phone IdentityPhone);

    ~Organisation() };

class   Person :public Identity {

public:

    // export features of Person are as follows

    Person: Identity (int IdentityId, Address IdentityAddress

                name IdentityName, phone IdentityPhone),

        (Organisation* OrganisationAffinityGroup,

        Organisation* OrganisationEmployedBy,

        date DateOfBirth,

        phone WorkPhoneNo,

        char SignatoryOrNotStatus,

        char ResidentOrNotStatus,

        int TaxFileNumber,

        Contract* ContractRef[10]);

    ~Person() };

class   PrimaryCardHolder   :public Person {

public:

    // export features of PrimaryCardHolder are as follows

    PrimaryCardHolder : Person (int IdentityId,

            Address IdentityAddress

            name IdentityName, phone IdentityPhone,

            Organisation* OrganisationAffinityGroup,

            Organisation* OrganisationEmployedBy,

            date DateOfBirth,

APPENDIX - V

      phone WorkPhoneNo,

      char SignatoryOrNotStatus,

      char ResidentOrNotStatus,

      int TaxFileNumber,

      Contract* ContractRef[10]),

      (PrimaSecondaryRelation* SecondaryCards[4],

      Card* CardOwned);

      ~PrimaryCardHolder() };

class   SecondaryCardHolder :public Person {

public:

      // export features of SecondaryCardHolder are as follows

      SecondaryCardHolder : Person (int IdentityId,

          Address IdentityAddress

          name IdentityName, phone IdentityPhone,

          Organisation* OrganisationAffinityGroup,

          Organisation* OrganisationEmployedBy,

          date DateOfBirth,

          phone WorkPhoneNo,

          char SignatoryOrNotStatus,

          char ResidentOrNotStatus,

          int TaxFileNumber,

          Contract* ContractRef[10]),

          (PrimaSecondaryRelation* PrimaryCards);

      ~SecondaryCardHolder() };

class   PrimaSecondaryRelation   {

public:

      // export features of PrimaSecondaryRelation are as follows

      PrimaryCardHolder* PrimaryCardAttached,

      SecondaryCardHolder* SecondaryCardAttached,

      Char RelationshipType) /* Spouse Child Parent Employ Etc */

      ~PrimaSecondaryRelation() };

APPENDIX - V

```
class Address    {
public:
        // export features of Address
        Address (AddressLine Addressline1, AddressLine Addressline2,
             AddressLine CityName, AddressLine StateName,
                PostCode* PCodeOfAddress,
                    date DateEffectiveFrom,
                Identity* AddressOfIdentity[5]);
        ~Address()  };


class Addressline       {
public:
        //export features of AddressLine
        extern char name_string[30]};


class name       {
public:
        //export features of name
        extern char name_string[30]};


class date       {
        int day, month, year;
public:
        void set(int, int, int);
        void get(int*, int*, int*);
        void validDate(); /* Assertion For Valid Dates */
};


class time       {
        int hours, minutes, seconds;
public:
        void set(int, int, int);
        void get(int*, int*, int*);
```

APPENDIX - V

```
        void validTime(); /* Assertion For Valid Time */
};


class amount    {
public:
        // export features of amount
        amount (int dollar, int cents);
        ~amount()  };


class rate      {
public:
        // export features of rate
        amount (int percentageIntegers, int percentageFraction);
        ~rate()  };


class branch
public:
        //export features of branch
        extern char name_string[30]};


class transfer    {
public:
        // export features of transfer
        transfer (Card* TransferFrom, Card* TransferTo,
                        date DateCardTransferred, time TimeTransferred);
        ~transfer()  };


class delqlist    {
public:
        // export features of delqlist
        delqlist (char  delinquencyType,
                        date DateDelinquent);
        ~delqlist()  };
```

APPENDIX - VI

PROGRAM SPECIFICATION FOR
INTEGRATING OBJECT-ORIENTED APPLICATION SYSTEM

Objects participating in the integrating application system have been specified in terms of C++ class declaration in Appendix-II. Main participants in the application are Identity objects and Contract objects. Card objects, Kapiti objects and other contract objects are sub-types of Contract.

A Contract object sends messages to Identity objects under the following conditions:
. When a Contract object (say a Card object) updates any of its features known to the Customer Prospect System. List of these export features are specified in the class specification of Card object. On receipt of such a message, the related Identity object updates its replica of the concerned contract with effect from the date specified and informs the Contract object about the action taken.
. When a Contract object is deleted. On receipt of such a message, the related Identity object marks the concerned contract of the identity as deleted with effect from the date specified and informs the Contract object about the action taken.

When a new Contract object is created, it has to find an existing Identity object to be associated with or request for creation of a new Identity object to be owner of the contract. While creating a new Contract object, information of another contract, current or closed, if any, with the Bank will be gathered. If the Product-type and Contract-Identification-No of another contract is available, a message will be sent to the Contract object with the same Contract- Identification-No to get the Identity-No of the involved identity. Once the involved identity is identified in the Customer Prospect database, the message will be sent to the corresponding Identity object with information about all sharable feature of the object added, so that Identity object can create a replica of the Contract object, to be associated with the Identity Object and inform the Contract object about the action taken.

If no information is available about any old or existing contract of the identity,opening a new conytact, but Tax-File-No is available, existing Identity objects will be scanned for the same Tax-File-No. If such an Identity is found, the message will be sent to it with information about all sharable feature of the object added, so that Identity object can create a replica of the Contract object, to be associated with the Identity Object.

If no information is available about another contract or Tax File No, the contract object will be created with a dummy Identity-No assigned to it. Request for a Identity-No will be sent to the officer, in charge of the Customer Prospect System, in form of periodic reports or electronic mail. The officer will match the available

APPENDIX - VI

details of the owner of the new contract with the corresponding information of the Customer Prospect Database, to locate any existing Identity-No. If no such Identity is available in the Customer Prospect database, a new Identity object will be created and associated with the replica of the Contract object. The Identity-No of the new Identity object will be notified to the requesting Contract Object. The concerned Bank officer may optionally use an expert system for matching the available details with its information base to expedite the task.

An Identity object will send a message to its associated Contract objects, when any sharable information information of the Identity is changed by another Contract object or by an officer responsible for administration of the Identity object. On receipt of such messages, the Contract object will check its controlled database, to ascertain whether the received information has a an effective-from date later than that in the database. If so it will update the database, else it will send the up-to-date information to the Identity.

Current interface between the Credit Card system and Customer Prospect system is via the overnight batch processing. If the similar interface is only required to be achieved in the integrating application, the messages will not be triggered as and when the events occur, they will be stored in a queue of messages. A Clock object will ask the Contract object application system and the Identity object application system to send their messages at specified times during the day.

APPENDIX - VII

Simplified View Of The Existing Interfcaes

Between Credit-Card & Customer Prospect Systems

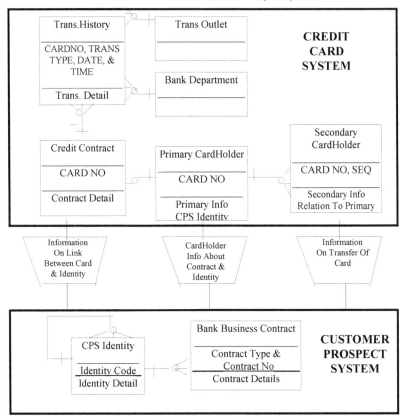

APPENDIX - VIII

Architecture Of Object-Oriented Integration Of Three Systems

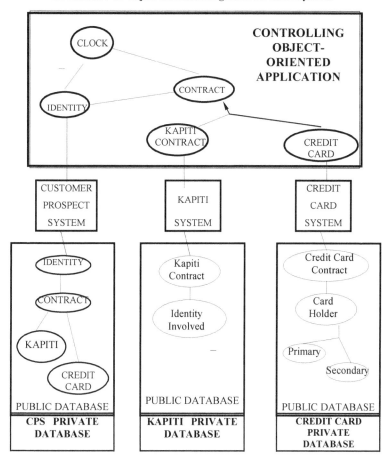

APPENDIX - IX

Data Replication in Distributed Databases

1. Overview

A replicated database is a distributed database in which many distinct stored copies or replicas of some data items are stored at many distinct sites. Replication is desirable for the following reasons:

- Performance - Applications can operate on local copies instead of having to communicate with remote sites.

- Availability - A given replicated object remains available for processing as long as at least one copy remains available.

- Distribution Of Workload - Processing of queries can be optimized, by having concurrent queries at different nodes and collating the results from various nodes.

The major disadvantage of replication is that when a given replicated object is updated, all copies of that object must be updated. Research is still on to keep the replication transparent to users, ie to achieve Replication Independence which should allow replicas to be created and destroyed dynamically at any time in response to changing requirements, without invalidating any of the user programs or activities.

This report has the following major objectives:

(1) to identify the update propagation problems in a replicated database,

(2) to review the state-of-the-art techniques designed to ensure data integrity in face of site and communication failures,

(3) to review the commercially available products in terms of their capability to address the problems identified in (1),

----

(4) to recommend strategies for implementing replicated databases.

2.   Problems Associated With Replication

The complexities of problems in a distributed replicated database can be simplified into following categories and their combinations:

- One copy vs multiple copies - A replicated database should behave like a one-copy database to users. In a one-copy database, users expect the interleaved execution of their transactions to be equivalent to a serial execution of these transaction. The replicated data will be transparent to the users, only if the interleaved execution of their transaction on a replicated database is equivalent to a serial execution of those transactions on a one-copy database.

- Single site vs multiple sites - In a single site, all operations on the database is known to the operating system at the site. When operations are requested from a remote site, there could be three reasons for the two sites being unaware of the actual happenings:
  ◊ the site responsible for carrying out the operations may not receive the request,
  ◊ the site responsible for the operations may not be able to comply because of its own failure
  ◊ the remote site may not receive the acknowledgement even after the operations are carried out.

- Distributed files vs distributed database - Referential integrity is not a concern in a distributed file system. When a replicated object is a part of a graph of references, each update on the object may involve updates on the entire graph of references. Update on one of the replicas, may fail the assertion constraints for other replicas.

- Recovery and Concurrency Control - In a replicated distributed system, a single transaction involve updates on replicas at multiple sites. To ensure that a given transaction remains atomic, the set of sites involved must either commit in unison or roll back in unison.

3.   Algorithms For Replica Processing

State-of-the-art algorithms for replica processing can be classified into two groups depending on the problems addressed by them: Site Failures and Communication Failures.

Problems of site failures are addressed in the following Bernstein[113] algorithms:

- Available Copies - This algorithm enforce special protocols to ensure correctness with the approach: "read-any, write-all-available".

---

[113] Bernstein P.A., Hadzilacos V., and Goodman N., <u>Concurrency Control And Recovery In Database Systems</u>, Addison-Wesley Publishing Co., 1987

- Directory-oriented Available Copies - This algorithm uses directories to define the set of sites that currently stores the copies of an item, updates the copies and directories held at sites.

Problems of communication failures are addressed in the following algorithms:

- Quorum Consensus - In this algorithm, a non-negative weight is assigned to each sites; every site knows the weight of all sites in the network. A quorum is any set of sites with more than half the total weight of all sites. Only if a network component have a quorum of sites, it can process transactions.

- Missing Writes - This algorithm exploits the trade-off between the "Available Copies" and "Quorum Consensus" approaches. In normal mode, a transaction reads one copy and writes all copies, in failure mode it uses "Quorum Consus"

- Virtual Partitions - In this algorithm, each site maintains a *view*, consisting of the sites, it believes it can communicate. A transaction executes as if the network consisted of the sites in its view, following "Read-any and Write-all" approach. If the view of the home sites changes before the transaction is committed, it will be aborted.

3.1 Failure Definitions

A distributed system consists of processing sites, communicating to one another via direct communication links, or indirectly via a chain of links.

When a site experiences a system failure, processing stops abruptly and the contents of volatile storage are destroyed. When the site recovers from a failure, it first executes its local recovery procedures which brings the site to a consistent state so that it can resume normal processing. Thus a site is always either working correctly or not working at all - it never performs incorrect actions. A partial failure is a situation where only some sites are operational, but uncertain about the state of the other sites.

A communication failure occurs when a site is unable to communicate with one another, eventhough neither is down. If the two sites communicate, the messages are delivered uncorrupted. The basic type of communication failures is network partitions. In general, a network partition divides the operational sites into two or more components, where every two sites within a component can communicate with each other, but sites in different components cannot. As broken links are repaired, communication is re-established by merging the sites in partitioned components.

Another type of communication failure is connected with the choice of timeout period, ie when the time to receive an acknowledgement hapens to be bigger than the timeout period. This is called timing anomalies, or timeout failures.

Both site failures and communication failures manifest themselves as the inability of one site to exchange messages with another. Usually failures are detected by using timeouts. Site A sends a message to site B and waits for a reply within a pre-determined period of time T called the timeout period. If a reply arrives, clearly A and B can communicate. If T elapses and A has not yet received a reply, A concludes that it cannot communicate with B, ie either 1) B is down, or 2) A and B belong to different network partitions, or 3) timing anomalies exist.

Failures in replicated databases complicates failure handling, especially in case of communication failures. A site may try to read or write its copies without being able to synchronise against Reads and Writes on copies of the same data item at other sites.

3.2   Atomicity of Failures and Recoveries

A copy x_A of a data item x at site A is available to site B if A correctly executes each Read and Write on x_A issued by B, and B receives acknowledgement of that execution.

Copy x_A may be unavailable to B for one of the following reasons:

- the comunication network correctly delivers to A Reads and Writes on x_A issued by B, but A is unable to execute them, either because A is down or A has suffered a failure of the storage medium that contains x_A, ie there is a site failure;

- A does not receive Reads and Writes on x_A issued by B, or A receives and executes them, but B does not receive A's acknowledgement of such executions, ie there is a communication failure.

A copy x_A is available (or unavailable) if it is available (or not available) to every site other than A. A failed copy x_A can be recovered by using different algorithms.

Failure and recovery events should be atomic. That is, all transactions should have a consistent view when copies fail and recover. A transaction learns about a failure when it tries to read or write a unavailable copy. Similarly, it knows that a copy could not have failed yet if it successfully accesses that copy. Fault-tolerant algorithms must not only control the order in which transactions read and write copies, but the decision whether or not to issue a Write on a copy.

To create a new copy of x, or to recover a formerly failed copy of x, say x_B, the algorithm must store an initial value in x_B. Any transaction that ordinarily writes into x can initialize x_B. Whenever it writes into other copies of x, it writes into x_B too. Rather than waiting for such a transaction to appear, the algorithm can force the initialization of x_B by running a special transaction, called a *copier*. The copier simply reads an existing copy of the data item that is up-to-date and writes that value into its new copy. In both cases, the algorithm must ensure that no transaction reads x_B until it has been initialized.

The algorithm must also make x_B known to all transactions that update x, so that they will write into x_B whenever they write into other copies of x. This requires some synchronization in order the recovery events to be atomic in all respects to all interested transactions.

----

4.   Site Failure Tolerant Algorithms

These algorithms handle site failures but not communi- cations failures, ie they assume that every other site is either down or operational, and that all operational sites can communicate with each other. Therefore, each operational site can determine independently which sites are down, simply by attempting to communicate with them. If a site does not respond to a message within the timeout period, then it must be down.

4.1   Available Copies Algorithm

Available Copies Algorithm uses an enhanced form of the approach: "read-any, write-all-available". The scheduler uses strict two phase locking ie after transaction Ti has read or written a copy of x_A, no other transaction can access x_A in a conflicting mode until after Ti has committed or aborted.

When a transaction Ti issues a Read(x), the transaction manager (TM) at Ti's home site will select some copy x_A of x and submit Read(x_A) to the site A. If x_A is initialized i.e updated by a transaction that has committed, the scheduler (SCH) and database manager (DM) at site A will return the value read. The site A may delay or reject Read(x_A) depending on the status of initialization of x_A. If site A is down, or x_A is not initialized, then Ti's TM will time out; it then either could abort Ti, or submit Read(x_B) to another site B. If no copy of x can be read, then Ti must abort.

When Ti issues a Write(x) operation, its TM sends Write(x_A) operations to every site A where a copy of x is supposed to be stored. If A is down, Write(x_A) will not be received and nor be acknowledged; so Ti's TM will time out.

If A is operational, Write(x_A) will be handled. If x_A has been initialized, then Write(x_A) is processed and a response returned indicating whether it was duly processed or rejected. If x_A has not been initialized, site A could either use Write(x_A) to initialize xA,, or it may ignore Write(xA), as if site A is down as far as x_A is concerned.

After sending Writes to all of x's copies, Ti's TM waits for responses. It may receive rejections from some sites, positive responses from others (meaning the Write has been accepted and performed), and no responses from some others (those that have failed or that have not initialized their copies of x). Writes for which no responses are received are called <u>missing writes</u>. If any rejection is received or if all Writes to x's copies are missing, then Write(x) is rejected and Ti must abort. Otherwise, Write(x) is successful.

Transaction Ti's <u>validation protocol</u> starts after Ti's Reads and Writes on copies have been acknowledged or timed out. At that time Ti knows all its missing writes as well as the copies it has actually accessed, ie read or written. The validation protocol consists of two steps:

1. <u>missing writes validation</u>, during which Ti ensures that all copies it tried to, but could not write, are still unavailable,

2. <u>access validation</u>, during which Ti ensures that all copies it read or wrote are still available.

Missing writes validation is performed before access validation.

To validate missing writes, Ti sends , for each copy x_A that Ti found unavailable, a message UNAVAILABLE(X_A) to site A. A will acknowledge such a message only if it has, in the mean time, initialized x_A (ie processed a Write x_A). The assumption is that there are no communication failures, which implies if Ti has not received any acknowlegdement, no such acknowledgement was sent and, therefore, that all copies Ti could not write are still unavailable.

If the missing writes validation step succeeds, then Ti proceeds with access validation. Ti sends a message AVAILABLE(x_A) to site A, for each copy x_A that Ti read or wrote. A acknowledges this message if x_A is still available at the time A receives the message. If all AVAILABLE messages are acknowledged, then access validation step succeeds and Ti is allowed to commit. Otherwise Ti must abort.

The validation protocol requires a significant amount of communication and is therefore expensive. All UNAVAILABLE messages from Ti to some particular site combined into one message. Similarly AVAILABLE messages and acknowledgements can be combined. Still we need two steps (ie missing writes validation and access validation), each requiring two rounds of exchanges - the UNAVAILABLE/AVAILABLE messages and acknowledgements.

If there is no site failure, the missing writes validation protocol is avoided. Moreover, access validation can be combined with atomic commitment, ie the VOTE-REQ message can be used as an implicit AVAILABLE message, a YES response from a site can be used as an implicit acknowledgement for AVAILABLE.

4.2   Directory-Oriented Available Copies Algorithm
This algorithm uses directories to define the set of sites that stores copies of an item, updates the copies and directories held at sites.

For each data item x there is a directory d(x) listing the set of x's copies. A directory may be replicated, that is, it may be implemented as a set of directory copies, stored at different sites - let the directory for x at site U be denoted dU(x), which contains a list of the copies of x and a list of directory copies of that site U believes are available. Concurrent access to the directory copies is controlled by the same scheduler that controls access to data item copies. The only difference is that ordinary transactions can only read directories; directories are updated by two special transactions, Include (or IN) for creating, and Exclude (or EX) for destroying data item copies.

When a site A containing x recovers from failure, or when A wants to create a new copy of x, DBS runs a transaction IN(x_A). IN(x_A) brings the value of x_A up-to-date by finding and reading a directory copy dU(x), locating an available copy of x (say x_B) and copying x_B's value into x_A.

When a DBS tries to access data at a site and observes the failure, it believes on the basis of directories it has read, that certain copies are stored at the failed site. For each such copy, it runs an EX transaction. $EX(x_A)$ declares x_A to be unavailable by removing x_A from each available copy of $d(x)$.

To process Read(x) on behalf of a user transaction, DBS reads a copy of $d(x)$ say $dU(x)$. If it tries to read a directory copy that is unavailable, then it ignores the attempt and tries other copies until it finds one available copy.

After performing all its operation, transaction Ti must carry out its <u>validation protocol</u>. The possibility of missing writes is eliminated by the fact that the set of available copies for x is listed in $d(x)$ and, unless all these copies are actually written Ti will abort. Thus only <u>access validation</u> is needed in this algorithm. Moreover, in the directory-oriented algorithm, access validation can be done by merely checking that the directory copies that Ti read still contain the data item copies Ti accessed. Thus, if directory copies are stored at all sites, access validation requires no communication at all.

Since every execution of the algorithm observe creations and failures in the same order, it can be proved that the execution is one copy serializable.

5. Communication Failure Tolerant Algorithms

Whenever the network is partitioned, transactions in different components may have conflicting accesses on different copies of the same data item. Since sites in different components cannot communicate, they cannot synchronize transactions that execute in different components. Therefore, nearly all algorithms for handling communication failures focus on preventing transactions that access the same data item from executing in different components.

5.1 Quorum Consensus Algorithms

In the quorum consensus algorithm, a non-negative weight is assigned to each copy x_A of a data item x. A read threshold RT and a write threshold WT are defined for x, such that both 2.WT and (RT + WT) are greater than the total weight of all copies of x. A read (or write) quorum of x is any set of copies of x with a weight at least RT or WT. These rules ensure that each write quorum of x has at least one copy in common with every read quorum and every write quorum of x, ie the intersections between any two sets is not an empty set.

Every site has a transaction manager responsible for translating Reads and Writes on data items into Reads and Writes on copies. A transaction manager translates each Write(x) into a set of Writes on each copy of some write quorum of x. It translates each Read(x) into a set of Reads on each copy of some read quorum of x,

APPENDIX - IX

----

and it returns to the transaction the most up-to-date copy that it read. The most up-to-date copy should have the highest version number, which initially is 0.

When the transaction manager processes Write(x), it determines the maximum version number of any copy it is about to write, adds one to it , and tags all copies that it writes with that version number.

This algorithm requires reading all of the copies in the write quorum before writing any of them. This can be done by having Write(x_A) return its version number. Then the transaction manager can send the new value and new version number piggybacked on the first round of messages of atomic commitment protocol. Even if some copies are down and therefore unavailable to Reads and Writes, as long as there are enough copies around to get a read quorum and a write quorum, transactions can still continue to execute. Every pair of conflicting operations will always be synchronized by some scheduler, namely, one that controls access to a copy in the intersection of their quorums.

The quorum consensus algorithm works with any scheduler that produces seializable executions. If a transaction Tj reads a copy of data item x, it reads from the last tansaction before it, Ti, that wrote any copy of x. This is because Ti wrote a write quorum of x, Tj read a read quorum of x, and every read and write quorum has a non-empty intersection. Since Ti is the last transaction that wrote x before Tj read it, Ti placed a bigger version number on all of the copies of x it wrote than the version number written by any transaction that preceeded it. This ensures that Tj will read the value written by Ti, and not by some earlier transaction.

An advantage of this algorithm is that recoveries of copies require no special treatment. A copy of x that was down and therefore missed some Writes will not have the largest version number in any read quorum of which it is a member. Thus, after it recovers, it will not be read until it has been written at least once.

Some of the disadvantages of the quorum consensus algorithm are as follows:

1. A transaction must access multiple copies of each data item it wants to read so it can build a read quorum. Thus, appli- cations that have much more query type transactions than updates, will not perform well under this algorithm.

2. A large number of copies is needed to tolerate a given number of site failures. To tolerate one failure, three copies are needed, for two failures 5 copies are needed and so forth.

3. All copies of each data item must be known in advance. A known copy of x can recover, but a new copy of x cannot be created because it could alter the definition of x's quorums. In principle, this definition can be changed dynamically, but this requires special synchronization.

An interesting variation on voting is <u>voting with ghosts</u> (/Van Renesse Tanenbaum '88/). In most applications, reads are much more common than writes, so RT is typically a small number and WT is nearly equal to number of replications. This choice means that if few nodes are down, it may be impossible to obtain a write quorum at all. Voting with ghosts solves this problem by creating a dummy server, with no storage, for

----

each real server that is down. A ghost is not permitted in a read quorum, as it does not have any files to be read; but it may join a write quorum, in which case it just throws away the file written to it. A write only succeeds if at least one server is real. When a failed server is rebooted, it must obtain a read quorum to locate the most recent version, which it then copies to itself before starting normal operation. The algorithm has the same basic voting scheme, namely, RT and WT are so chosen that acquiring a write quorum and a read quorum at the same time is impossible. The only difference is that dead machines are allowed in write quorum, subject to the condition that when they come back up they immediately obtain the current version before going into service. As dead nodes are not allowed in a read quorum, intersection of a read quorum with another read or write quorum cannot include any dead node; but intersection of two write quorums could be a dead node though a write of a replicated data is seldom possible without a read preceeding it.

A generalisation of quorum consensus algorithm is described in /Herlihy '90[114]/ based on /Herlihy '86/. The basic containers for data are called objects. Each object has a type, which defines a set of possible states and a set of primitive operations that provide the only means to create and manipulate objects of that type. For example, a File might provide Read and Write operations, and a first-in-first-out (FIFO) Queue might provide Enque and Deque operations. Each of the objects's operations has a set of quorums, which are sets of sites whose cooperation is needed to execute that operation. A quorum assignment associates each operation with its set of quorums. An operation's quorums determine its availability, and the constraints governing an object's quorum assignments determine the range of availability properties realizable by replication. An analysis of the object's type specification yields a set of constraints on quorum assignment necessary and sufficient to ensure the correctness of the replicated implementation. Quorum consensus replication systematically exploits type-specific properties of data to support better availability and concurrency than conventional algorithms in which operations are classified only as Reads and Writes.

A replicated object is implemented by two kinds of modules: repositories and front-ends. Repositories provide long-term storage for the object's state, while front ends carry out operations for users. Different objects may have different sets of repositories. Because front-ends can be replicated to an arbitrary extent, perhaps placing one at each user's site, the availability of a replicated object is dominated by the vailability of its repositories. Internally, a repository's state is represented as a log, which is a sequence of entries, where an entry is the timestamped record of an operation. In practice, logs can usually be replaced by more compact data structures. An user executes an operation by sending an invocation to a front-end. The front-end merges the logs from an initial quorum of repositories to construct a view. It chooses a response consistent with the view,

----

[114] Herilihy M.P., Concurrency And Availability As Dual Properties Of Replicated Atomic Data, Journal Of the A.C.M., Vol-37, No-2, April 1990, pp257-278

appends the new entry to the view, and writes out the updated view to a final quorum of repositories. A quorum for an operation is any set of repositories that includes both an initial and a final quorum. Front-ends, executing concurrent operations, synchronize through short-term locks at repositories.

By introducing some degree of flexibility in defining object specific quorums, this algorithm mitigates the disadvantages of the basic quorum consensus algorithm.

5.2 The Missing Writes Algorithm

Quorum consensus algorithms are resilient to communication failures at the expense of increased cost of reads and degree of replication. This makes sense if communication failures are frequent. During periods of reliable operations, however, quorum consensus costs are too high.

The missing write algorithm combines read-one/write-all-copies approach with quorum consensus by making transactions sensitive to communication failures. Each transaction executes in one of two modes: normal mode, in which it reads any copy and writes all copies, or failure mode, in which it uses a quorum consensus algorithm. A transaction must use failure modes if it is aware of missing writes, ie that a copy x_A does not contain updates that have been applied to other copies of x.

Every transaction which become aware of missing writes for x should either abort or switch to failure mode, ie quorum consensus type of Reads and Writes. If Ti is aware of missing writes for x before its start, it will run in a failure mode. If Ti has started in normal mode and become aware of missing writes for x during its run, the database system should abort it and restart in a failure mode. Alternatively, the database system can try to upgrade to failure mode on the fly by making sure Ti reads/writes a read/write quorum of x.

A transaction Tj, which tries to write on copy x_A, but receives no acknowledgement, is straight-forward aware of missing writes for x_A. A transaction Tj, which tries to read a copy x_A which is down, is also straight-forward aware of missing writes for x_A. In both cases, Tj should propagate this knowledge to all subsequent transactions in order to comply to one-copy serializability requirements.

If Tj tries to read a copy x_A which has failed and recovered before any transaction has tried to update x, Tj should read an up-to-date copy of x.

The missing writes propagation consists of the following actions: When Tj becomes aware of missing writes on x_A through unsuccessful attempt to access this copy, it attaches a list L containing in this case of x_A to every copy x_B that it accesses. By definition, Tj should now access the read/write quorum for x. If Tj has discovered that another copy of x, say x_D is down, it adds it to the list. It also tags the list to indicate whether it read (or possibly read and wrote) x_B.

When subsequent transaction Ti accesses any x_B in a mode that conflicts with the list's tag, it becomes aware of those missing writes. For that purpose, the database manager should acknowledge Ti's access to x_B by

----

returning the copy of the list. Ti can now propagate the list, along with other such lists it received, to all copies that it accesses.

After recovering from failure, the database system at site A has two tasks:

1. It must bring each newly recovered copy x_A up-to-date. For that purpose, it starts a copier transaction which reads a quorum of copies of x and updates them using the most up-to-date value that it read, using version numbers.

2. It should delete x_A from the lists of missing writes on all x copies, so that transactions accessing those copies need not incur the overhead of quorum consensus algorithm. It can do that by sending messages to all sites that have a copy of x to remove xA from their lists.

There is a problem that while these messages are being processed, x_A may fail again and miss some Writes, prompting new entries x_A in the list of missing writes. The deletion messages should not invalidate these new entries. To avoid such errors, the list should contain the version number of the failed copy x_A. Thanks to the first task, the newly failed x_A will have a bigger version number than that of the previously failed x_A. As these messages would contain the older version number, they will not be allowed to invalidate the new x_A entries in the lists of missing writes.

5.3 Virtual Partition Algorithm

The main justification for data replication is to have a copy of x at every site where the user would need it, thus reducing the probability of remote access to x and the costs thereof. The previous algorithms need access multiple sites to form a quorum for each operation, contrary to what data replication is all about. The virtual partition algorithm is designed so that a transaction never has to access more than one copy to read a data item.

In the virtual partition algorithm, each copy of x has a non-negative weight and version number, each data item x has read and write thresholds, and read and write quorums are defined in the same way as in the quorum consensus algorithms, but serve a different purpose.

Each site maintains a list of sites which it "believes" it can communicate, ie site's view of the network. As site and communication failures occur, this view changes. The basic idea is that if the view at the time a transaction starts differ from the view at the time it is ready to commit, that tran- saction aborts. Moreover, whenever a site A's view changes, all active transactions whose home site is A must abort. They can all then be restarted and try to run within A's new view.

A transaction executes as if the network consists of sites that are in its home site's view. To process any Read(x) or Write(x), there must be a read/write quorum which is easily calculated from the view list and

----

the information about where copies of x exist which is kept at every site. In case of a quorum consensus, the transaction reads the nearest copy of x, but writes on all copies of x within its view.

Site A becomes aware of its view inconsistency when a transaction with home site A tries to access a site B belonging to A's view but fails to do so. Another possibility is that A is not in the view of B and B rejects the access.

In both cases, a special <u>View Update</u> transaction is issued by A's database system in order to adjust the views of all the sites from the old to the new view and to bring all up-to-date copies of all data items for which there is a read quorum in the new view.

As View Update transaction may be started simultaneously by two or more sites, a special view formation protocol is used. Associated with each view is an unique view identifier

VID = (c,s), where s is the site identifier and c is a counter stored at s and incremented each time s tries to create a new view. After generating a new VID, site A initiates a two phase protocol to establish the new view:

1. A sends a JOIN-VIEW message to each site in its new view and waits for acknowledgements. This message contains A's new VID.

On receiving the message, site B compares the new VID of A with its current VID and, if the latter is less thean the former, it sends a positive acknowledgement to A; otherwise it may respond negatively or not at all.

2. After receiving acknowledgements, A can proceed in one of two ways:

a) it may abort the creation of the new view if it has not received acknowledgements from all sites within it and then restart the protocol with higher VID;

b) it may ignore any rejected invitations, restructure the new view including only the positively responded sites, and send a VIEW-FORMED message attaching the new view list to it.

Each site that receives that message adopts the new view and the new VID (received in the previous message) as its current view and VID. It need not acknowledge the receipt of the message.

When a new view is created, all copies of data items for which there is a read quorum in the new view must be brought up- to-date. This is because in the new view, any such copy might be read. The task of updating such copies is carried out by the new view initiator site A. Version numbers can be used to determine the most fresh copy. This procedure need not be performed for copies that A can tell are up-to-date, ie copies of x at sites belonging to the previous view provided they have the highest version number. When it is not the case, for example a new site G is included in the view and x_G has the highest version number, all other copies of x have to be updated. All update operations are carried out like ordinary distributed transactions in order to preserve the serializability of the executions.

The virtual partition algorithm guarantees one-copy serializability by ensuring that all transactions see failures and recoveries in the same order. Each transaction executes entirely within a single view and commits only if this view has not been changed. All sites within the view list have the same view. The write-all approach within a view ensures that all sites containing copies of x will be visited and, if one of them is down, the home site aborts all its active transactions and initiates a view formation protocol.

In this algorithm, the set of copies of each data item is fixed, as in the quorum consensus algorithms, in order to preserve the quorum attributes. Adding new copies requires special synchronization.

When a site B recovers, it must bring each newly recovered copy x_B up-to-date and make itself part of some view, respectively update its own view. It can do that by initiating view formation protocols, increasing its VID until all or most of the sites in its pre-failure view agree to join the new view.

During the execution of a view formation protocol, reads at operational sites can be served, but writes should be postponed until the new view is formed, as they have to be executed for all copies within the view. A read request after such a delayed write request should also be postponed. In case of frequent failures, the overhead of view formation may considerably slow down the performance, taking into account also the abortion of all active transactions at the site which becomes aware of view discrepancies.

6. Commercially Available Products

Commercially available products for distributed database systems are:

SQL*NET (Oracle), Ingres/star (Ingres), ENCOMPASS (Tandem), SQL-SERVER (Sybase), SQL-7 (Microsoft, Ingres, Sybase). None of these systems support fault tolerant algorithms for processing replicated distributed data.

In order to guarantee consistency of replicated data items, Distributed Ingres follows the primary copy method ie each data object is associated with a known primary site, also called master site, to which all updates in the system for that data object are first directed. Different data objects may have different primary sites; updates can be executed only if the primary copy of a data object is available. Update requests are sent to non-primary copies either before or on the commitment of the update transaction. Its main drawback is its vulnerability to failures of primary copy sites.

The TANDEM NonStop SQL does not employ the replication process in its distributed database processing. It provides Browse Access, Stable Access, and Repeatable Access to concurrent users at three data consistency levels.

The LOCUS Distributed File System, though not a database management system, allows replicas of files at different nodes. The system allows file modifications at only one copy of the filegroup (the primary pack). The modifications can originate from any using site, but must use the primary site as the storage site. This approach eliminates the possibility of conflicting updates to a file, but limits the availability as the primary pack must be

----

in the user's partition for a file to be modified. When a pack is suspected to be inconsistent, the system brings it up to date by propagating the files that have changed, determined by one of the two mechanisms:

. a low overhead kernel protocol that handles only a limited number of changes,

. a more general application process that reconcile the entire filesystem.

7.   Recommended Strategy For Replication

We have seen, so far, how site and communication failures affect the functioning of a replicated distributed data base system, apprised the limitations of commercial products and reviewed the algorithms devised to maintain continuity of operations in spite of failures. Now, we like to derive here a set of recommendations for implementing replicated distributed database to meet different scenarios of failures.

Scenario 1: No Failures At All

A database transaction should read any copy, read all copies.

Scenario 2: Only Site Failures

A database transaction should read one copy, write all available copies. Failing site, in its recovery procedure, should update its replica, by copying from a live one. But there is no foolproof way to determine, wheter a site/ a group of sites have failed or they are live but in different partitions. So we cannot apply the algorithms devised only for site failures.

Scenario 3: Only Communication Failures

In this case, nodes are divided into two or more partitions. A database transaction should read one copy of the biggest up-to-date partition, and write all copies of the same partition. Other partitions should know that they are minor partitions with respect to a data-item, hence should make that data-item unavailable to a transaction. This means, another partition can process the transactions accessing data-items, in which that partitions holds majority of replicas. Here again, we cannot ensure that whether a site has failed or partitioned.

Scenario 4: Both Site And Communication Failures

In this case, database transactions, that need to access only the biggest up-to-date partition, can be processed. The algorithms for communication failures alone should work, while a failing site has to recover its local data-items as well as replicated data-items.

From the analysis of four scenario, we find that a site failure can be dealt as a communication failure, because a failing site does not communicate; local recovery is the only additional task that a failing site must complete before it is treated as a partitioned site.

From the algorithms for communication failures, we recommend Virtual Partition algorithm because,

. the main purpose of replication is lost in Quorum Consensus algorithm, where all replicas need be read to find out which one is the latest,

----

. Missing Writes algorithm makes only a minor improvement, quorum consensus is not used unless there is a failure. Improvement in performance depends on the proportion of fault-free time.

As write-quorum is difficult to achieve, we also like to have Voting-With-Ghosts algorithm, so that every failing site is replaced by ghost node or dummy node for write quorum, but read- quorum must have all live nodes. No ghost node would be in the intersection of a read quorum with another read or write quorum, but two write quorums may intersect on ghost nodes. But the probability of having a transaction, with a write without a read is very low; so we can improve the availability of the database, when several nodes are down, though atleast one is live.

Implication Of Cache

The local caches for different sites may keep copies of replicated data items. But this should impose no special constraints; when write of a data item is committed, each available site should write that data item and/or refresh the cache copy, if any. Whether to write this item on stable storage or not that can be decided by the site algorithm. While recovering from a failure, the failed site will copy the replicated data item from one of the up-to-date sites; but the checkpointing and logging procedures used for local data should be applied on replicated data as well, to take care of situations when all nodes are down, or the only node having the most up-to-date copy of a data item is down.

Implication Of Schema Change

Data base schema is expected to be replicated at all sites. Any change in the schema needs to be propagated to all sites, because use of local data in a partition may be affected by the changes in schema, or a partition may have read or write quorum for a data item without being aware of the changes in the schema. Therefore a schema change should lock all data items that could be affected, till the transactions for schema-change are completed; also unless all the sites are available, a schema change cannot be allowed.

Implications Of Referential Integrity

In case of communication failures, update of replicas in one partition, may lead to loss of referential integrity in other partition. Suppose entities A and B have one-to-many relationship, which is manadatory at both ends. If a replica of A exists in one partition that does not have any instance of B, referential integrity for that partition is lost for A. An algorithm should ensure that a transaction that may affect referential integrity, should run when all nodes are available.

8. Conclusion

For a fault-tolerant replicated distributed database, we recommend the implementation of the VIRTUAL PARTITION together with the VOTING WITH GHOSTS algorithm. This choice leads to less expensive failure-free operations, while cost of recovery is not increased. Moreover, substitution of dummy nodes for each failed node, increases the probability of having a write-quorum in a partition and thus increase the continuity of operations.

Choice of maintaining data in cache and stable storage is recommended to be similar to other non-replicated data items.

Updates of replicas can be implemented as nested transactions, where the parent transaction may commit, even if some child transactions abort, because of non-availability of some sites.

Any change in replicated database schema can be allowed only when all sites are operational, with no communication failure in the network. The transactions that can affect referential integrity can be allowed, only when all copies of the instances, participating in the relationship, are available.

9. Bibliography

1) Alsberg P.A., and Day J.D., A Principle For Resilient Sharing Of Distributed Resources, Proceedings of the 2nd Annual Conference of Software Engineering, IEEE Press, Washington D.C., 1976, pp 627-644.
2) Berri C., Bernstein P.A., and Goodman N., A Model Of Concurrency In Nested Transaction Systems, Journal Of ACM, Vol 36, No 2, April 1989, pp 230-269
3) Bernstein P.A., and Goodman N., Concurrency Control In Distributed Database Systems, ACM Computing Survey, Vol 13, No 2, June 1981, pp 185-221
4) Bernstein P.A., and Goodman N., The Failure And Recovery Problem For Replicated Databases, Proceedings of the 2nd Annual Symposium on Principles Of Distributed Computing, ACM, N.Y., Aug'83, pp 114-122
5) Bernstein P.A., and Goodman N., An Algorithm For Concurrency Control And Recovery In Replicated Distributed Databases, ACM Transactions on Database Systems, Vol 9, No 4, December 1984, pp 596-615
6) Bernstein P.A., Goodman N., and Lai M.Y., Two-part Proof Schema For Database Concurrency Control , Proceedings of the 5th Berkeley Workshop on Distributed Data Management And Computer Networks, Berkeley, CA, Feb.1981, pp 71-84
7) Bernstein P.A., Hadzilacos V., and Goodman N., Concurrency Control And Recovery In Database Systems, Addison-Wesley Publishing Co., 1987
8) Chan A., Fox S., Lin W.T., Nori A., and Ries D., The Implementation Of An Integrated Concurrency Control and Recovery Scheme, Proceedings of the SIGMOD Conference: International Conference On Management Of Data, N.Y., June 1982, pp184-191
9) Cooper E.C., Circus: A Replicated Procedure Call Facility, Proceedings of the 4th Symposium on Reliability in Distributed Software and Database Systems, IEEE Press, washington D.C., Oct 1984, pp 11-24
10) Date C.J., Twelve Rules For A Distributed Database, Computerworld, June 8, 1987

APPENDIX - X

OBJECT-ORIENTED DATABASES (OODBs)

Table Of Contents

1. An OODB Has To Be A Database

An object-oriented database management system must first of all provide all the features and functionality that we expect from a modern database management system. As features vary from one DBMS to another, we may classify them as

. features that are considered essential

. features that are frequently present

. features that are sometimes present.

1.1 Essential features

Model and Language - A DBMS has a non-trivial model and language, ie the DBMS understands some structure on the data (the data model) it contains, and provides a language for manipulating structured data.

Relationships - A DBMS can represnt relationships between entities, the relationships can be named, and the language can query those relationships. Relationships may be expressed as physical links (ie pointers) or logical links (i.e value based identification).

Permanence - A DBMS provides a persistent and stable store. Persistency means that data are accessible after the end of the process that creates them. Stability means that data have some resiliency in the face of process failure, system failure and media failure. Most DBMSs have recovery mechanisms to cope with the process and system failures, generally by writing information about changes to a secondary storage and using this information to make corrections in case of a failure. Media failures are dealt with by duplicating storage devices or backing up information on tapes.

APPENDIX - X

Sharing - A DBMS permits data to be shared, ie multiple users can use the database simultaneously, although not the same data item at once. Conventional DBMSs have a concurrency-control mechanism that prevents users from executing inconsistent actions on the database, usually by locking data items when they are read or written. It generally provides atomicity of transactions, ie a group of related operations gets executed in an all-or-nothing manner.

Arbitrary Size - The address space of a DBMS is not constrained by limitations in the physical processor. Thus, the size of a database should not be limited by the amount of main memory, or by the address range of virtual memory.

1.2   Frequent features

Integrity Constraints - A DBMS can help to ensure the consistency of its data by enforcing integrity constraints, which are statements that must always be true for data items in the database. Examples are domains for fields in records, uniqueness of identification keys, and referential integrity constraints, which ensures that the reference in one data item must lead to another data item. Some DBMSs provide triggers to initiate actions, when constraints are violated.

Authorisation - Most DBMSs support ownership of data by particular users, and provide the owner with a mechanism to permit selective access to data by other users.

Querying - Especially in relational DBMSs, there is a facility to express the desired query or update on the database without requiring the query writer to provide the details of working out the answer.

The query language generally exists in two versions: one for queries embedded in the program the other for adhoc queries by the users. The query language needs to be generic, ie applicable to any data item.

Separate Schema - Most DBMSs maintain a central schema, a catalog of the types defined in the database and names of objects declared to be of those types. Different programs and users share this meta- information. The schema of a database is often itself represented as data in the database, and is hence accessible through the query mechanism for regular data. There is no notion of 'compile time' after which type definitions and variable declarations are fixed, as new type deinitions and their instances can be added at any time.

Views - This feature allows definition of virtual data, which are not stored explicitly, but are computed from the stored data. Views are also used to provide selective access to data, to present data to suit users' requirements, and to provide a stable interface to part of the database even though the logical structure may change.

Database Administration - A special interface is often available for the database administrator to perform data-managent functions like re-organising, statistic monitoring, auditing, archiving etc.

APPENDIX - X

1.3   Less Frequent features
<u>Report and Form Management</u> - Many database vendors include or sell as an option a facility to generate forms and reports from high- level specifications.

<u>Data Dictionary</u> - A data dictionary is an extension of the database schema, to provide documentation, information on timeliness and reliability of data, procedures to validate data on entry, procedures to format data on output, information of database applications outside the DBMS e.g. non-DBMS application programs.

<u>Distribution</u> - The latest commercial offerings support databases distributed over multiple computers or sites, to improve availability and performance by keeping data at sites where they are used most.

2   Basic Object-Oriented Concepts For An OODB
An object defines a protocol through which users of the object may interact. The object can have a state that is stored in an encapsulated piece of memory. This hiding of an object's stored state is crucial feature of an object-oriented language. Unlike previous memory-oriented languages, the object- oriented languages do not define types as templates for memory structures.

An object has a state that is expressed by the results of functions ie messages or operations. The values of these functions are other objects. This means,, if one object x refers to another object y, then there exists a function f, such that $f(x) = y$.

Object-oriented languages provides for abstract data types that encapsulate implementation. The abstract data-type approach defines the interface by a set of strongly typed operation (also called messages) signatures. It also requires that each type defines a representation that is allocated for each of its instances. This representation is used to store the state of the object. Only the methods implementing operations for the objects are allowed to access the representation; thus the representation can be changed by recoding only the methods, without affecting the rest of the system.

Object-oriented data models are also characterised by the ability to make references through an object identity. For this capability   something about the object is required to remain invariant across all possible modifications of the object's values. Identity allows us to express the notion of shared structure. We can distinguish between the idea of referring to two things that are alike and that of referring to two things that are in fact the same.

A set of permissible object references may be larger than the set object identifiers. While there is one-to-one correspondence between identifiers and objects, there may be many-to-one mapping from references to identifiers. In many current databases, it is possible to delete data items (ie records). In the object-oriented case, if an object x is deleted, other objects might have stored the identity of x, which may lead to dangling references. To avoid this, it is preferable to adopt the semantics of garbage-collected languages, such that the objects are not deleted, but, instead references to objects are destroyed. When all references to an object have been removed, the system reclaims the storage occupied by that object.

APPENDIX - X

References that make use of an object's identity directly are much like pointers in conventional programming languages. Since all accesses to an object x is through the messages defined on its type, computing association between x and a set of other objects must be done by a method. This method can make use of a stored identity or a value based expression, as in a query language. In this way, object- oriented databases provide a framework for unifying value-based and identity-based access Unlike primary keys of relational database, object identifiers are unique across the database, not just for a relation. Also, if primary keys of a RDB convey some information about the application- world, their values may change, while object-identifiers are invariant.

A frequent feature of object-oriented models is a typing scheme that includes some form of inheritance ie type definitions can be incrementally modified by adding subtype definitions that modify the original type. The combination of the supertype definitions and the subtype modifications produces a completely defined new type.

3   Requirements of An Object-Oriented Database

An object-oriented databse must, at least, satisfy the following requirements:

- It must provide database functionality, ie include all the essential features listed in section 1.1
- It must support object identity
- It must provide encapsulation, which should be the basis for defining abstract data types
- It must support objects with complex state; the state of an object may refer to other objects, which in turn may have incoming references from elsewhere.

In addition to the minimum functionalities listed above, object-oriented databases should provide the following features to exploit the benefits of object-oriented techniques:

- ensure persistence of objects from a distinguished root object in the database,
- provide static type checking of methods, to ensure that, at run-time, the immediate type of a variable is always a sub-type of a declared type,
- support grouping of objects by a specification hierarchy of types, an implementation hierarchy of methods, and a classification hierarchy of explicit collection of objects,
- support polymorphism through dispatching ie the actual method executed at run-time for a message expression is dependent on the type of receiver of the message,
- support built-in types for aggregate objects, such as sets, lists and arrays
- provide a structured name space for persistent variables,
- support a query language that is of high level and is amenable to optimisation,
- support named relationships

- provide for accessing versions of an object's state, and for assembling configurations of consistent versions of objects.

4   Review of Special Features Of OODBs
Considering that features such as identity and encapsulation distinguish object-oriented DBMSs, in this section, we like to discuss how these features makes an OODBMS different from other established DBMSs.

Relational databases present a view of the persistent data space to the programmer consisting consisting of primitive values of integers, reals and strings and requiring that all aggregate objects be represented as tuples or sets of tuples over these primitive values. This view of data may be convenient for data processing applications that are primarily concerned with producing reports. It is a hindrance, however, for system programs that are roughly as complex as an operating system or a compiler. They need data structures like stacks, queues and streams of bytes. An object- oriented database allows programmers to create abstractions that match the data structures that are needed for complex applications.

The relational data model is value-based, while O-O data models are identity-based. A value-based system expresses the relationship between two objects by embedding the same value in two or more related objects. An identity-based model can relate two or more objects independently of their embedded values.

Though O-O data models are identity-based like some earlier network models (e.g. CODASYL), the notion of typing and extensibility makes O-O data models considerably different. They add abstraction based on encapsulation of methods and incremental modification mechanism in form of inheritance.

Although object-oriented systems can provide references based on identity, identity is not the sole basis for relationships in the model. As computing association between two objects is done by methods defined in the objects, the methods can make use of value-based expression as well. Thus O-O databases provide a framework for unifying value-based and identity-based access.

APPENDIX - XI

Object-Oriented Languages: Eiffel Vs C++

1   Criteria for Evaluation

Concept of objects is a major departure from conventional understanding of programming languages. First, our languages have different look, language constructs and mechanisms. Second, our programming methodologies must adapt to different disciplines of building applications. Third, we need new models that can help us to describe and analyse the systems we build.

We are a long way from having standard criteria, because the object models supported by different languages emphasize different properties of object; the problem of language integration to reuse the systems developed in other languages, and development of a common object-oriented interface language is only being researched, as in this project.

Under these circumstances, we restrict our criteria for evaluation to following major topics:

1.1   Requirements of object-oriented programming languages
Criteria of evaluation, based on object-oriented features are:

- disciplined data structure access

- encapsulation

- classes

- inheritance

- multiple and repeated inheritance

- automatic memory management

- polymorphism and dynamic binding

1.2   Traditional programming considerations
Our criteria for traditional programming considerations are:

APPENDIX - XI

- Language Design

- Language Features

- Domains Of Application.

1.3   Requirements for evolution of development methodologies
Our criteria for evaluation   have been extended to findings of recent research on object management, software management, user environments, acquaintance problem, evolution problem, global behaviour problem, presentation problem, defence problem and temporal problem.

2   Comparison Based On Requirements of Object-Oriented Languages

2.1   Disciplined Data Structure Access
Disciplined data structure access is a form of information hiding to constrain all accesses to a data structure only through the standard interface.

In Eiffel, only the *export features*, as declared in the definition of the *class* of the object, are accessible. If the export feature is a procedure, no information is passed out but changes to data structure is allowed. If it is a function, information about a part of the data structure is made available, but no change can be made to the structure.

C++ provides similar constructs for *class* by which all use of data structures and internal housekeeping are channeled through specific interfaces of *member functions*, declared as *public*. But this restriction is violated in following cases:

- Most C++ programs use 'header files', which describe shared data structures. Any file needing the data structure will gain access to them through an 'include' directive (handled by built-in C preprocessor) of the form

  #include <stream.h>

  #include <error.h>

where suffix.h are header files in Unix environment. Files containing functions, data definitions, macros (referred to as suffix.c files) can also be similarly included.

- A user can bypass the interface provided by a header file by inserting extern declarations into .c files.

- Macros manipulate strings and know little about C++[115] syntax and nothing about C++ types and scope rules. Only the expanded form of a macro is seen by the compiler, so an error in a macro will be reported when the macro is expanded, not when it is defined. But such definitions are permissible.

---

[115]   Stroutstrup B., The C++ Programming Language, Addison-Wesley Publishing Company, USA 1986, p113 p129.

APPENDIX - XI

- The protection of private data relies on restrictions of the use of class member names. It can therefore be circumvented by address manipulation. A function can be called to take its address, the pointer obtained by taking the address of a function can then be used to call the function.

- Normally class member names are distinguished from other names by using a *scope resolution operator* :: .
  For example

  class x {
      int m;
  public:
      int readm()   { return x::m; }
      void setm(int m) { x::m = m; }
  };

  In *x::setm()* the argument name m hides the member m, so that the member could only be referred to using its qualified name, x::m. But, C++ allows declaration of global names by using no prefix before scope resolution operator ::. for example, *::setm()* is a global name and can be used by any class.

- C++ allows a function to be declared as a *friend* of a class, private part of which then is accessible by the function.

2.2   Encapsulation

Encapsulation ie provision to define the modules that encapsulate a structure description, with the routines that manipulate data, is available in both Eiffel and C++. An Eiffel *class* is a module that may consist of static components (data) and dynamic components (procedures and functions). *Class* and *struct* of C++ provides the similar concept of encapsulation, where *struct* is a class with all members public.

C++ has some specialised features to have self-sufficient objects, so that one may view every object as carrying along at run-time the operations applicable to it. Instances of "structure types" may contain among their fields, references (pointers) to functions. For example, a structure type of REAL_STACK may be defined by the type definition

```
typedef struct {
    int last;
    float impl[MAXSIZE];
    void(*pop)();
    void(*push)();
    float(*top)();
    BOOL(*empty)();
    } REAL_STACK;
```

If a_stack is a variable of this type and C_pop is a popping function, one may assign to the pop component of a_stack a reference to this function, as follows:

a_stack.pop = C_pop

It implies that every instance of every class physically contains reference to all routines that may be applied to it.

2.3   Classes

Classes provide the concept of identifying every non-simple type as a module and every high-level module as a type. A program that provide types that closely match the concepts of the application is typically easier to understand and easier to modify than a program that does not. A well chosen set of user-defined types makes a program more concise; it also enables the compiler to detect illegal uses of objects that otherwise would not be detected until the program is tested.

Class declarations in Eiffel and C++ share some common characteristics but also have a number of differences.

Both languages define the class interface unambiguously - by export list in Eiffel and public member functions in C++. Information hiding is achieved explicitly in C++ with declaring member functions as protected or private, an implicitly in Eiffel by not including secret features in the export list. There is, however, an Eiffel syntax for selective export of a feature to a particular class only.

In C++, member functions are declared as function prototypes in the class body and as implementations outside the body, which raises questions of scope for both compilers and maintenance programmers. the compact form of declaring all features within the class body in Eiffel seems more readable and maintainable.

The initialisation of a new object attributes is done by default in Eiffel, but explicitly in C++ through the constructor member function. More sophisticated initialisations in Eiffel are achieved through user-defined procedures.

The main difference between Eiffel and C++ classes is the introduction of assertions in Eiffel. The rationale behind assertions is that an abstract data type is not just defined by set of operations on a data structure, but also by the formal properties of these operations. Eiffel enables and encourages programmers to express formal properties of classes by writing assertions which may appear in the following ways:

- routine preconditions express conditions that must be satisfied whenever a routine is called. For example, accessing an integer array by index requires that the index is not outside the size of the array. Preconditions are introduced by the reserved word *require.*

- routine postconditions, introduced by the reserved word *ensure*, express conditions that are guaranteed to be true on routine return if the preconditions have been satisfied on routine entry.

- class invariants must be satisfied by objects of the class after their creation and after any call to a routine of the class. They represent general consistency constraints that are imposed on all routines of the class.

Syntactically, assertions are boolean expressions. Assertions should play an important role in object-oriented languages as resultant modules (classes) are truly extensible and reusable only if they are correct.

Eiffel system can be executed in check assertion mode during module design and testing. To provide such a facilty in a C++ class, a new member function needs to be introduced.

The notion of routine pre/post-conditions and invariants is not explicitly supported in C++ , perhaps, because this language, as its parent C, is targeted to experienced programmers who know when such functions are required. Nevertheless, assertions are important techniques to ensure correctness and therefore should be included in the language.

```
+---------------------------------------------------------------+
|  class WORKER export                                          |
|      hasWorked, findPay, display                              |
|  inherit                                                      |
|      PERSON rename Create as personCreate, display as         |
|                      personDisplay                            |
|              redefine display                                 |
|  feature                                                      |
|      payRate, hours, gross, tax, net :REAL;                   |
|      Create is                                                |
|          do                                                   |
|                personCreate; -- renamed Create of ancestor|
|                ........     -- get name, sex, payrate    |
|                .........      -- for this worker           |
|            end; -- Create                                     |
|      .........                                                |
|      .........                                                |
|      display is     -- display is redefined here             |
|          do                                                   |
|                ..........         -- additional routine    |
|              personDisplay      -- renamed routine       |
|                ..........         -- additional routine    |
|            end -- display                                     |
|  end  -- class WORKER                                         |
|                                                               |
|                  Figure XIV-1                                 |
+---------------------------------------------------------------+
```

2.4   Inheritance

Inheritance facilitates definition of a class as an extension or restriction of another and contributes to reusability and extendibility of software products.

Implementation of inheritance in Eiffel is illustrated in Figure XIV-1. In this example, descendant class WORKER inherits all the features available in the ancestor class PERSON, which is a more general class. Class WORKER has renamed an inherited routine 'display' as 'personDisplay' to use the code as part of a new expanded routine; it has also redefined the routine 'display' as it requires to use the same name for its expanded routine.

The ancestor class could be also a *deferred class*, ie with atleast one *deferred feature*. Objects cannot be created from a deferred class as all features are not defined. The actual definition of the deferred routines are supplied by the child class; redfinition is not necessary for deferred features.

In C++, the concept of inheritance in implemented by using derived classes as illustrated in the extract of code below:

```
class worker : public person {
    // ...
};
```

Here, class 'person' is made a *public base class* of class 'worker', which means any public member of class 'person' is also a public member of class 'worker'.

C++ also provides for declaring *private base class* by simply leaving out the word public, e.g.:

```
class worker : person {
    // ...
};
```

This means that member functions of the class 'worker' can use the public members of 'person' as before, but these members are not accessible to users of class 'worker'.

More controlled restrictions on access to inherited features have been implemented in Eiffel through export list; a descendant class can selectively export its own or inherited features.

In C++, it is possible to use the *friend* mechanism to grant access to either specific functions or every function of a class. For example:

```
class person {
friend void  worker:: print();
    //
};
```

would solve the problem for worker::print(), and

```
class person {
friend class worker;
    //
};
```

would make every member of class 'person' accessible to every function of class 'worker'. However, a cleaner solution is achieved by introducing a derived class to use only the public members of its base class. For example:

```
void worker::print()
{
    person::print();  // print person information
```

    // ...   // print worker information

    }

This is similar to use of rename feature in the Eiffel example.

2.5   Multiple And Repeated Inheritance

Multiple and repeated inheritance, which allows one class to inherit more than one classes and the same class more than once, facilitates reuse of codes for the classes, which are subtypes to more than one supertypes.

In Eiffel, a class may inherit from more than one parent, and the child then can use features from both parents.

For example:

    class STORABLE_LIST_OF_POINTS export

        retrieve, store,

        start, forth, offright, item, put_right, ...

    inherit

        STORABLE;

        LINKED_LIST[POINT]

    end -- class STORABLE_LIST_OF_POINTS

All the features are inherited by this class, so a client class can now declare an object to be of type STORABLE_LIST_OF_POINTS, manipulate points on the list during a session, then store the list at the end of a session.

The earlier version of C++ did not provide for multiple inheritance; this has been introduced in version-2.

Eiffel has also implemented repeated inheritance which facilitates combining descendant classes of same parents.

For example, consider a parent class DRIVER with two descendant classes FRANCE_DRIVER and US DRIVER. The latter classes can be combined to define a class FRENCH_US_DRIVER as follows:

    class FRENCH_US_DRIVER export

        age, birthday, french_address, us_address,.....

    inherit

        FRANCE_DRIVER

        rename   address as french_address,....

        US_DRIVER

        rename   address as us_address,....

The features age and birthday have not been renamed along any of the inheritance paths and provision is made to have two addresses one at France, the other at US.

This feature has not been examined for C++, as multiple inheritance and rename feature were not available in version-1.

2.6 Automatic Memory Management
Automatic memory management is a feature to deallocate space for unused objects without programmer intervention.

Eiffel provides for automatic garbage collection. "A garbage collector is usually organised in two phases: a *mark phase* which, starting from the roots, traverses the active part of the structure, marking all live objects it encounters; and a *sweep phase* that traverses the whole structure literally, putting all unmarked elements into the list of available cells and unmarking all objects. Here too an extra field is required (for marking purposes), but space overhead is negligible, as one bit suffices per object."[116]

C++ does not provide for automatic garbage collection. A programmer has an option to write constructor and destructor routines for creation and deallocation of objects. When a class has a constructor, it is called whenever an object of that class is created. When a class has a destructor, it is called whenever an object of that class is destroyed. For example:

class classdef {

    table members;

    // ....

    classdef(int size); // constructor same name as class

    -classdef();   // destructor name is -classname

};

Care needs be exercised, if tables are created using *new*, as they must be destroyed by using *delete*. There is no equivalent feature enabling a destructor to decide if its object was created using *new*, nor is there a feature enabling it to decide whether it was invoked by *delete* or by an object going out of scope. The user can store the relevant information somewhere for the destructor to read, or have to ensure that objects of that class are only allocated appropriately.

2.7 Polymorphism and Dynamic Binding
Polymorphism and dynamic binding allows program entities to refer to objects of more than one class at runtime and to have different realisations in different classes.

Eiffel enforces static type checking at compile time, to ensure that all operations will work at run time, but it allows to dynamically change the type of a name, but only to a descendant class. For example: POLYGON is an ancestor of other three classes for the objects p,r,s,t where

---

[116] Meyer B., Object-Oriented Software Construction, Prentice Hall International (UK) Ltd., 1988, p366

----

p:POLYGON; r:RECTANGLE; s:SQUARE; t:TRIANGLE;

When the form of object is known, one can create an object s and assign it to the existing POLYGON name, using assignment in the form: p := s

The type of object p has now been dynamically defined to be different from its static type, and the features from class SQUARE will be used.

C++ provides the facility of dynamic binding through the concept of *virtual functions*, which overcome the problems with the type-field solution by allowing the programmer to declare functions in a base class that can be redefined in each derived class.

For example:

```
struct employee {
    employee* next;
    char*    name;
    short    department;
    // ...
    virtual void print();
};
```

The keyword *virtual* indicates that the function print() can have diffeent versions for different derived classes and that it is the task of the compiler to find the appropriate one for each call of print(). But only constraint is that, a virtual function must be defined for the class in which it is first declared. Suppose, we have to print employees of different derived classes in one list and print patterns are different for each derived class, it is possible to adjust the print lines depending on the type or class of employees.

3   Features of Traditional Programming That Will Continue
3.1   Language Design Issues

Expressive Power of Eiffel is reflected in the concept of objects, real world objects are dealt with appropriate computer representations which may be called internal objects, belonging to some classes. Though C++ has implemented the concept of classes, a class is not defined as a compact unit. A class declaration shows only the headers of the routines, member functions are declared elsewhere; Analogy could be drawn to a case where Data Divisions of all Cobol programmes are kept together and all Procedure Divisions kept together somewhere else. This separation of headers and member functions has reduced the expressive power of C++.

Simplicity and orthogonality are well balanced in Eiffel for the convenience of programmers, even users can code programs. C++ is orthogonal ie almost any combinations of syntaxes could be mixed, but it is not simple

----

as it inherited lot of complexities from the parent language C, particularly those with pointer manipulation and operator combinations.

Implementation of C++ is succesful with regard to object code efficiency and size of compiler. C++ and its standard libraries are designed for portability. C++ can be implemented on most systems that support C. C libraries can be used from a C++ program, and most tools that support programming in C can be used with C++.

The Eiffel compiler uses C as intermediate language, making Eiffel potentially portable to any environment supporting C. The first implementations run on Unix systems (System V, BSD, Xenix). The compilation speed and object code efficiency of Eiffel are apparently lower, but Eiffel has a smart compiler, it compiles only those modules that need to be recompiled. Eiffel looks at the system, and works out the dependencies between classes in the system and finds out which modules use the modified definition of a class and hence are to be compiled.

Error detection and correction is better achieved in Eiffel than in C++, which has weakness mainly for pointer variables and it is difficult to check, at compile time, the variables they refer. Eiffel is a strongly typed language; all the features and only those features, defined for a class can be used by that class. Eiffel compiler checks that all the feature calls in the system are legal; if a system compiles, Eiffel will be able to do all the operations defined in the code.

Correctness and standards are ensured by the language design of Eiffel so that a program satisfies the specification, this assurance mainly stems from the ability of classes to represent the real world objects. It also provides documentation tools e.g.

short class - gives an external view of class;

flat class - gives a listing of internal details of a class

ancestors class - gives a list of all ancestors of a class.

History of development of C++ suggests that there was no deliberate attempt to enforce standards. " There never was a C++ paper design; design, documentation, and implementation went on simultaneously. Naturally, the C++ front end was written in C++. There never was a C++ project either, or a C++ design committee. Throughout, C++ evolved, and continues to evolve, to cope with problems encountered by users, and through discussion between the author and his friends and colleagues." (Stroutstrup)

3.2 Language Features

APPENDIX - XI

Eiffel program shows a compact unit of a class, whereas a C++ class is coded in more than one places. All the member functions of C++ program could be distributed freely with member functions of other classes, the presence of scope resolution operator :: can only relate them together.

Basic Types- Eiffel has four simple types INTEGER, REAL, CHARACTER, BOOLEAN. There is also a class STRING, which is like an array of characters; this is not a basic type. Any number of abstract types can be used, provided a class is defined for it.

Fundamental types in C++ are char, short int, int, long int, unsigned, float and double. The void type specifies an empty set of values. There is a conceptually infinite number of derived types constructed from the fundamental types.

Complexities of derived types of C++ show that Eiffel is much simpler language to use so far as data types are concerned.

Type Checking- Eiffel is strongly typed language; if a system is compiled, no type incompatibility can occur at runtime. Type checking in C++, like its ancestor C, is rather laxed and vary from compiler to compiler. Some concerns are:

- Pointer assignment is not checked so that, for example, a pointer-to-integer may be assigned to a pointer-to-float.
- In an expression such as   P -> ...   in which P is to be a pointer to a field of structure, there is no check on type of P.
- Arguments to functions are not checked.
- The union mechanism is advertised as being a way to circumvent type checking.

In most C installation the software *lint* is used to detect violation of type checking. Unfortunately, the details of the checking lint performs are not documented.

Declaration and Scope Rules-

Eiffel does not allow any global variable. Scope of the variables for a class is restricted to the class. Local variables are local to one feature of a class. Communications between two objects are carried out via strictly defined interfaces of export lists. A client object can access an export feature of a supplier object s by qualifying the feature name as s.feature name.

C++ has three kinds of scope: local, file and class.

Local- A name declared in a block is local to that block.

Names of formal arguments for a function are treated as if they were declared in the outermost block of that function.

File- A name declared outside any block or class can be

----

used in the file in which it is declared after the point of declaration.

Class- The name of a class member is local to its class and can only be used in a member function of that class, after a . (dot) operator applied to an object of its class, or after a -> operator applied to a pointer to an object of its class.

A data member of a class may be *static*; function members may not. There is only one copy of a static member shared by all objects of the class in a program.

Scope is clearly defined in Eiffel, where all program modules are classes. The *Root class* in Eiffel does not have its exact counterpart in the *main program*, which can access any global variable within the scope of file.

Expressions

The operator precedence charts of Eiffel and C++ clearly show how complex C++ is compared to Eiffel. Moreover, use of side-effects in expression is prevalent in C++; it includes operators such as "++" which increments its argument and then returns it, encouraging the programmer to code statements e.g.:

A[J++] = B[K++]

inside a loop to copy vector B into A. Here the assignment statement both copies an element of an array and increments the indices J and K.

Arrays in C++ follow a convention of having zero as the last element, which can easily introduce errors; for example

char v4[] = {'a', 'b', 'c', 'd' };

Here v4 is a vector of four (not five) characters; it is not terminated by zero, as all library routines require.

One similar case of programmer confusion is

int *x[] means x is an array of pointers to integers, but

int(*x)[] means x is a pointer to an array of integers

C++ has a mechanism for *operator overloading*, by which a programmer can define a meaning for operators when applied to objects of a specific class. Several different function declarations can also be specified for a single name; the correct function is selected by comparing the types of the actual argument with the formal argument type.

Assertion and Exception Handling- C++ does not provide adequate facility for assertion but for some library macros. Eiffel provides for checking pre-condition of a feature in form of *require* and post-conditions in form of *ensure*. Similarly, C++ does not provide any built-in feature to handle exceptions. In Eiffel, exceptions are generated when an assertion is found at run-time to be violated, or when the hardware or operating system signals an abnormal condition. The *rescue/retry* mechanism guarantees that a routine may only terminate by either executing its body to its normal termination or signalling a failure to its caller.

Parallel Processing- Neither Eiffel nor C++ provides for parallel processing at this stage. From the general low level approach of C++, it is apparent that suitable primitives could be written, though 'a special linguistic feature for compiling an indivisible test-and-set operation' may be necessary.

Eiffel has been tested with more than one root classes. "...an effort is under way to provide Eiffel with support for concurrent computation on the basis of the Eiffel exception mechanism; the language's composition facilities (classes, genericity, inheritance) are used to offer support for various high-level modules such as rendez-vous, monitors etc." (B.Meyer)

Domains Of Application

Object-oriented programming is yet to be introduced in large scale. From the level of implementation, it appears Eiffel would be more suitable for Business Data Processing and Scientific Programming.

"One of the original aims of C was to replace assembly coding for systems programming tasks. When C++ was designed, care was taken not to compromise gains in this area. .....C++ possesses features that are intended for manipulating hardware facilities in a direct and efficient way without regard for safety or ease of comprehension." [B. Stroustrup] With facilities to handle registers and manipulate bits, C++ has an edge over EIFFEL in Programming For Operating Systems and System Utilities. C has been extensively used for Business Data Processing and Scientific Programming, despite all complexities in the language; C++ should suit these areas much better than C does. By combining conventional imperatives and object- oriented features, C++ can offer the programmers the best of both worlds.

4   Requirements for Evolution Of Development Methodologies
Object management- With the evolution of object-oriented processing, an object-oriented programming language will be required to provide run-time support for the objects in terms of

- Persistence - automatic saving of objects between sessions, through either virtual memories or object-oriented databases (OODB) [Extension to Eiffel class STORABLE]
- Concurrency - multiple concurrent threads; communications and concurrency control through message passing or OODB
- Distribution - global object-naming, and remote message passing or method invocation
- Security - access rights or permission to invoke objects' operations.

Depending on the intended application domains, these kinds of functions can be provided either by the operating systems or object-oriented databases. These issues indicate that we need to address an integration problem of bringing object-oriented databases (OODB) closer to object-oriented programming languages (OOPL). Neither Eiffel nor C++ is ready for this, we may require both low level approach of C++ and high-level discipline of Eiffel to address these issues selectively.

Software management

As software is being developed in OOPL, it is required to keep track on the dependencies between classes and objects and their realizations. In a distributed environment, we must also manage the distribution of evolving software. A tool to manage repository of software would be necessary, and OOPLs would require to play complementary roles for repository management. C++, Eiffel or some other language need to address this issue.

User environments

Evolution of object-oriented enviroments may pose the need to present the objects for direct manipulation by users. Depending on the type and location of objects, there could be need to have expert systems to present and manipulate complex types of objects. OOPLs may need to model these expert systems as classes that can handle these presentation and manipulation. It is too early to assess whether Eiffel or C++ could be developed for these needs of user environments.

Acquaintance problem

For an object to be effective in a network environment, it may have to communicate with other totally unknown objects. This problem is related to the binding problem in programming, with consideration to limited visibility about the features of other objects. Again neither C++ or Eiffel can be evaluated for this at this stage.

Evolution problem

When new classes evolve by inheriting features from other classes, it is possible to put the features that inherently incompatible. Some metrics may be needed to screen out the incompatible features. Eiffel might have answers to these problem by using the assertions of invariants, pre- and post- condition checking. C++ has no constructs for these issues.

Global behaviour problem - There could be need to constrain behaviour of objects in response to some global problems, like an actor must conform to script of the play, or a charged particle must react to forces of a magnetic field. This could be related to specification and verification of constraints like pre- and post-condition checking in Eiffel.

Defence problem - If objects can react to each other, there could be need to protect objects from intrusion of other objects. This is related to security and access control. In Eiffel terms, only selected classes might be permitted to Forget an object, also the Export list could be altered depending on the client objects.

Temporal problem - We may need to introduce the notion of time for the objects acting in real time, e.g. robots. In Eiffel or C++ classes could be defined for real time, which can send messages to access features of an object depending on timing or synchronization of events.

5   Summary Of Evaluation

Based on the evaluation of the languages with respect to requirements for OOP, traditional requirement for programmers' convenience and capabilities to cope with future object- oriented environments, we may summarise the strong points of each language as follows:-

Strong Points Of Eiffel

i) *Correctness* is ensured, because classes are small, routines are small and interfaces are clearly defined. Definition of C++ classes is not compact; it is possible that routines from header files as well as from the subroutine calls from main program will produce results, not anticipated from class details.

ii) *Robustness* is ensured from pre- and post-conditions of routines and invariants of the classes.

iii) *Extendibility and reusability* is better achieved in Eiffel, as multiple and repeated and multiple inheritance are established features of the language. C++ does not support genericity; in Eiffel generic classes can be built, this can take type of the object as parameter, so the same code can be used for variety of classes.

iv) *Compatibility* is ensured by Eiffel compiler as all classes are compatible subject to the list of export features of supplier class and the list of all features of client class.

v) *Expressive Power* is reflected better in Eiffel's concept of objects, real world objects are dealt with appropriate computer representations ie internal objects.

vi) *Programmer's convenience* - Language constructs for expressions, precedence of operators, program control are simple to use. Error checking at compile-time eliminates most possibilities of run-time error, and better mechanism for assertion and exception handling is provided. C++ programs, on the other hand require special skills about the hardware environment and pointer manipulation, and hence are difficult to be maintained.

vii) *Garbage collection* - Eiffel provides for automatic memory management. In C++, constructor and destructor routines are to be written by programmer to reclaim space of an unused object.

Strong Points Of C++

i) *Portability* - Systems developed in Eiffel are portable only in Unix environment (System V, BSD, Xenix). C++ is used on a large number of architectures including ATT 3B, DEC, VAX, IBM370, Motorola 6800 running versions of Unix.

ii) *Compatibility to C* - C++ has provided compatibility to C, which is already in wide use. Therefore, it is possible to access the existing C software codes, and library routines.

APPENDIX - XI

----

iii) *Instruction sets from conventional language* - C++ combines conventional imperative and object-oriented features, to give programmers the best of both worlds.

iv) *Operating Systems System Utilities* - C++ was designed to be a 'close-to-the-machine' language, so that all important aspects of the machines are handled simply and efficiently in a way that is reasonably obvious to the programmer. C++ can be conveniently used for system programming.

6 Conclusion
Eiffel and C++ are powerful object-oriented languages with bright and ensured future, although for different reasons.

Eiffel is designed as an object-oriented language. Eiffel provides a rich library of well-designed classes and is implemented through C preprocessor. This will ensure its wide acceptance as object-oriented design/programming language for large commercial systems.

But considering the aspect of language integration, so that we continue to do all good things we are able to do now, C++ is required to play an important role in the transition period. C++ can bank on the wide community of C users, mostly experienced software specialists, which will be attracted by the object- oriented features provided by C++ and its interface to C - not only C programs can run in C++ environments, but through friend notion and other syntax features C programs can be quite easily incorporated into complex software systems.

Both languages are interesting to work with and may co-exist without much competition - one being an object-oriented extension of a conventional language, and the other setting de facto standards in object-oriented design and programming.

The organisation, under study, has the facilities for C++ already. The recommendation is, therefore, to continue usage of C and C++ so as to access the rich library of C language via C++ till they are redeveloped in a better language like Eiffel.

7 Bibliography
1) Feuer A.R., and Gehoni N.H., A Comparison Of The Programming Languages C and Pascal, ACM Computing Survey, Vol .14, No.1, March 1982
2) Koenig A., C++: Objects, Values, and Assignment, Journal Of Object Oriented Programming, July - August 1989
3) Marcotty M., and Ledgard H.F., Programming Language Landscape, SRA, 1986
4) Meyer B, Object Oriented Software Construction, Prentice Hall, 1988
5) Sethi R., Programming Languages - Concepts and Constructs, Addison Wesley 1989
6) Wichmann B.A., A Comparison Of Pascal and Ada, The Computer Journal, vol 25, No 2, 1982
7) Wilson L.B., and Clark R.G., Comparative Programming Languages, Addison Wesley 1988

EXCHANGE OF DATA & MESSAGES BETWEEN LOGICALLY SEPARATE SOFTWARE TIERS

LOGICALLY SEPARATE SOFTWARE TIERS
When the software components are modularised and they have clearly defined interfaces, these components are considered to be in separate logical tiers; usually the software runs in a separate process or address space, with no visible sharing of data and control. Software that is in a separate tier might run on the same computer, but could be moved to a separate computer, if desired, without redesigning the components. Functions of the component application systems can be considered to be one of the three general types: (1) data management, (2) application logic, and (3) presentation. A logically separate tier can include one or more of the three component functions, either in full or in part. Depending how these three functions are split across the network, five basic types[Fig XV.2] of co-operative processing are possible, which are *Distributed Presentation, Remote Presentation, Distributed Function, Remote Data Management, Distributed Database*[117].

Modularity of logical software tiers depends on the existence of a stable interface, often considered as a contract, between the components that makes it possible for changing one component without affecting the other.

Logically separate software tiers can make it easier to:

• Have new software program modules work with programs from an earlier generation

• Develop/ maintain software components independently of other components

• Splitting of software into physically separate tiers can help balance the workload and tune the applications.

If the interfaces between layers are generalised and publicly documented, logically separate software tiers can offer the following additional benefits:

• Get software components from different developers to work together without custom tailoring.

• Substitute one product for another, for example unplug one DBMS and replace it with another.

Logically separate software tiers can enhance the flexibility, durability, extensibility and cost-effectiveness of an application, but usually consume more CPU cycles than an equivalent monolithic system would need because of the overhead of the interface layers. Logically separate software tiers may be either *two-tier* or *three-tier* and may interoperate by either *data shipping* or *message shipping*.

---

[117] Schulte R. (1994), Middleware: Panacea or Boondoggle?, SMS *(Software Management Strategies) Strategic Analysis Report, Gartner Group, R-401-130, July5, 1994*

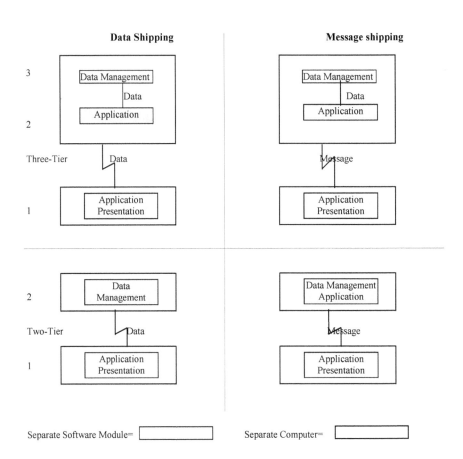

Fig XII.1 Data Shipping & Message Shipping: Two-tier and Three-tier

Two-Tier and Three-Tier Data Shipping

Most client/server applications are two-tier and ship data. The first tier consists of presentation logic and application logic, residing in the same process space. The DBMS or the file system constitutes the second logical tier. In a typical DBMS configuration, SQL is used to define the interface between the tiers [Fig XV.1].

Since SQL dialect used in the DBMS tier is often vendor-specific, the flexibility of the two-tier computing is limited. A change in DBMS or even a change in the application database design may not be easily accommodated.

Flexibility can be increased by inserting another software tier between the application and the back-end DBMS - a Data Access Tier or DAT[118]. The purpose of the data access tier is to buffer the application from the database DML, the location of the database and/or the structure of that particular application data model. The application sees only a consistent API, usually SQL-based and probably based on some version of the ODBC API. A DAT may make it possible to change the data manager (for example, from VSAM to Sybase), the server platform (for example, moving the database from MVS to Unix), and the application database design (e.g. adding columns and tables), without changing the client application anyway. A DAT approach is usually called a three-tier approach. In some forms of three-tier data shipping, the DAT is capable of transferring data asynchronously.

A three-tier data-passing application is usually deployed on two hardware tiers, but occasionally is configured across three hardware tiers. Three tier data shipping provides more power and flexibility than two-tier data shipping.

Two-Tier and Three-Tier Message Shipping
Like data shipping, message shipping can be designed using two, three or more tiers [Fig XII.1]. In a typical two-tier message passing model, the first tier includes presentation services, presentation-related application logic and some business logic. The second tier includes the application logic that deals with the data manager and some additional business logic. Two-tier message shipping is most commonly implemented using DBMS stored procedures. It supports the *distributed function* model and is therefore more network-efficient than two-tier data shipping, which uses the *remote data management* model.

In three-tier message-shipping, the three segments of application logic reside in logically separate tiers. The interface between each of the three tiers is clearly defined and does not rely on visible intra-process sharing of data or control. This makes it possible for the first tier to run on the desktop, while the application business function runs on a separate system (e.g., a Unix sever) and the DBMS runs on a third system (e.g., an MVS host). In practice, however, three-tier message shipping applications generally run on two hardware tiers to minimise network traffic.

The primary advantage of the three-tier message model over the two-tier model is that the three-tier model can make it possible to independently modify or replace the business logic (application function), the database or

---

[118] Light M., Natis Y., Schulte R. (1996), Middleware : The Foundation For Distributed Computing, SMS *(Software Management Strategies) Strategic Analysis Report, Gartner Group, R-200-108, October1996*
Schulte R. (1994), Middleware: Panacea or Boondoggle?, SMS *(Software Management Strategies) Strategic Analysis Report, Gartner Group, R-401-130, July5, 1994*

the front-end user presentation component without having to change the other components. A typical two-tier model is less flexible, so changes in one segment imply changes in other segments.

A three-tier message shipping application could be built using any form of program-to-program link, including a low-level conversational mechanism (e.g. APPC, CPI-C, or sockets), an RPC, a TP monitor, an electronic mail bus, an object request broker, message passing middleware or message queuing middleware. All distributed function mechanisms do not deliver the same benefits to a message shipping architecture. For example, RPCs are better suited for synchronous, inter-application communication, because both parties to the communication must agree in advance on the exact message format. By contrast, message-based systems, EDI systems and object-request brokers allow more flexibility at compile time and/or run-time, and therefore have some advantages for inter-application messaging. Message queuing systems and other deferred delivery mechanisms add another dimension of flexibility.

Three-tier approaches impose more overhead than two-tier approaches. In the case of three-tier data shipping, another layer of data catalogues need be maintained, and extra levels of data reformatting and conversion may need be carried out. In the case of three-tier message shipping, additional RPCs or messages may need be prepared, packed, sent, received, unpacked and interpreted, compared to the same operation running in a two-tier architecture. In most cases, two-tier and three-tier approaches will use the same two-tier hardware configuration and may even have the same amount of network traffic, but the extra interfaces between the layers of a three-tier design involves more overhead within the same computer. This overhead can cause significant impact on response times, throughput and consumption of system resources. Most real-world applications are conversational in nature; data must be retrieved from a database and shown to the user in the course of performing a task. In three-tier computing, this give-and-take interaction has to be implemented via the communications between the tiers. Depending on the conversational nature of the application, cross-tier communications may need be activated several times, in the course of a single unit of work, thereby increasing the overhead of communication. In response to this issue, TP applications may be designed to appear conversational to the end-users, while being non-conversational with the underlying database. Also, response time may be improved by transferring a part of the task from real-time (synchronous) processing to asynchronous processing, by putting messages on a queue for execution at a later time.

These sorts of work-arounds and dropping hardware prices are expected to make three-tier computing advantageous in next few years.

In three-tier message-shipping, the three segments of application logic reside in logically separate tiers. The interface between each of the three tiers is clearly defined and does not

----

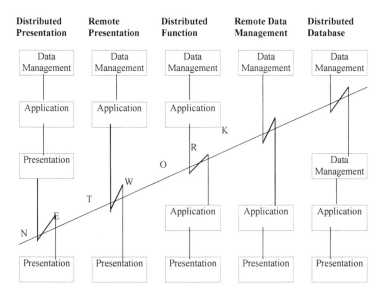

Fig XII.2 Five Basic Styles Of Co-Operative Processing[119]

rely on visible intra-process sharing of data or control. This makes it possible for the first tier to run on the desktop, while the application business function runs on a separate system (e.g., a Unix sever) and the DBMS runs on a third system (e.g., an MVS host). In practice, however, three-tier message shipping applications generally run on two hardware tiers to minimise network traffic.

The primary advantage of the three-tier message model over the two-tier model is that the three-tier model can make it possible to independently modify or replace the business logic (application function), the database or the front-end user presentation component without having to change the other components. A typical two-tier model is less flexible, so changes in one segment imply changes in other segments.

A three-tier message shipping application could be built using any form of program-to-program link, including a low-level conversational mechanism (e.g. APPC, CPI-C, or sockets), an RPC, a TP monitor, an electronic mail bus, an object request broker, message passing middleware or message queuing middleware. All distributed function mechanisms do not deliver the same benefits to a message shipping architecture. For example, RPCs are better suited as to synchronous, inter-application communication, because both parties to the communication must agree in advance on the exact message format. By contrast, message-based systems,

---

[119] Schulte R., Middleware: Panacea or Boondoggle?, SMS (Software Management Strategies) Strategic Analysis Report, Gartner Group, R-401-130, July5, 1994

EDI systems and object-request brokers allow more flexibility at compile time and/or run-time, and therefore have some advantages for inter-application messaging. Message queuing systems and other deferred delivery mechanisms add further flexibility.

Three-tier approaches impose more overhead than two-tier approaches. In the case of three-tier data shipping, another layer of data catalogs need be maintained, and extra levels of data reformatting and conversion may need be carried out. In the case of three-tier message shipping, additional RPCs or messages may need be prepared, packed, sent, received, unpacked and interpreted, compared to the same operation running in a two-tier architecture. In most cases, two-tier and three-tier approaches will use the same two-tier hardware configuration and may even have the same amount of network traffic, but the extra interfaces between the layers of a three-tier design involves more overhead within the same computer. This overhead can cause significant impact on response times, throughput and consumption of system resources. Most real-world applications are conversational in nature; data must be retrieved from a database and shown to the user in the course of performing a task. In three-tier computing, this give-and-take interaction has to be implemented via the communications between the tiers. Depending on the conversational nature of the application, cross-tier communications may need be activated several times, in the course of a single unit of work, thereby increasing the overhead of communication. In response to this issue, TP applications may be designed to appear conversational to the end-users, while being non-conversational with the underlying database. Also, response time may be improved by transferring a part of the task from real-time (synchronous) processing to asynchronous processing, by putting messages on a queue for execution at a later time. These sorts of work-arounds and dropping hardware prices are expected to make three-tier computing advantageous in next few years.

Message Shipping vs. Data Shipping
Data shipping is attractive for the following reasons:

- Data shipping follows the traditional methods of application design and database management, and hence it is more easily understood. By contrast, message shipping requires a different design practice and imposes a strict discipline on the development of applications. Data shipping allows various aspects of application logic to be intermingled and data be dependent on the context of the application, while a full three-tier message-shipping approach requires careful planning. In a messaging system, designers and application programmers need to divide the various aspects of the application so as to be comfortable with the mechanics of an RPC (call/return), messaging (send/receive) or other paradigm.

- Data shipping can make full use of many of today's powerful tools, such as Power Builder, including their ability to generate SQL statements. By contrast, some message-shipping approaches may require more layers of middleware and/or additional reliance on third generation languages.

- For routine, small to medium-sized applications, initial development will generally be faster and easier with data shipping than message shipping approaches. The choice of tools for either approach can make a huge difference.

- If data shipping is used to link new applications with existing databases, such as a new PC application reading from an MVS DB2 database, the existing MVS applications do not have to be modified. By contrast, messaging approaches require a new MVS application or, the MVS application needs be modified before it can be reused within an invasive encapsulation.

On the other hand, message shipping is attractive for the following reasons:

- When messages cross the network, they will use the *distributed function* architecture rather than the *remote data management* form of communication implied by data shipping. This brings the familiar benefits of fewer and shorter messages, lower network overhead and potentially faster response times.

- Messaging makes it possible to leverage the investment in existing mainframe applications by encapsulating them. New, distributed (Unix or PC) applications can execute the business logic and integrity checks encoded within the old applications without having to replicate the logic in the new application.

- Messages give the developer complete flexibility regarding what runs in each application. For example, the data-related application code can interact with VSAM, IMS, SQL, real-time data feeds and other resources. By contrast, the data server component in a data shipping model may be unable to map into these resources fully and efficiently.

- Last and most importantly, message shipping is better than data shipping at insulating components from each other. SQL, or other data-centric communication methods, cannot isolate the application logic fully from changes in the data side. Even within the environment of a single relational DBMS, a view mechanism will be unable to shield the application program fully from the changes that are likely to be made to the application data model over time.

With a message shipping approach, not only the data model can change, but the DBMS can be replaced by another DBMS or data source without changing the presentation or application code. Also, the front end can be replaced without modifying the application code or DBMS. Moreover, the function server or the business logic application code can be reused by many applications or replaced over time without disrupting the presentation or data management pieces. This implies a lower overall cost for maintenance and enhancements, although the initial development expenses will be higher in some cases.

Message shipping complicates the simple applications but it simplifies complex applications. Three-tier message shipping is therefore best suited to applications with:

- Many programs, especially if mixing different languages and tools,

---

- Multiple data sources and/or heterogeneous DBMSs,

- An expected application life beyond three years,

- High volume and/or complex design,

- Anticipated ongoing modifications and additions,

- Inter-application communication, especially if asynchronous.

Message shipping is expected to be increasingly popular for client/server production applications and sophisticated forms of decision support. Because it requires a significant change in application design, however, growth in its use will be slow.

NEED OF INFORMATION ABOUT THE SCHEMA IN MESSAGE PASSING
In the preceding paragraphs we have seen that, in two-tier or three-tier message passing, *distributed function* style of cooperative processing [Fig XII.2] is to be followed, which means the application logic is split into different tiers, and since the same application sends the message from one tier and receives in the other tier, the knowledge about the schema is with the application. Therefore, we cannot say the messages are exchanged without the need for any schema.

The *distributed function* style [Fig XII.2] of cooperative processing can be implemented either (1) between each pair of the component applications, or (2) between a central integrating application and each component application, so that in (1) messages are exchanged between the component applications or in (2) between a central integrating application and each component application. But, in order to decipher what is contained in a message, one needs to set up a message dictionary, which in turn needs the knowledge about the meta-data of the involved systems. In either case, the involved application needs to know, where to send the message in order to elicit a response that can be sent to the original requestor. Having a schema in the integrating application will be of advantage, as the schema will have the information about all information shared by the underlying databases and how these information items can be mapped into the integrating schema.

APPENDIX - XIII

INTELLIGENCE IN THE INTEGRATING APPLICATION

AN INTELLIGENT OBJECT IN THE INTEGRATING APPLICATION

The architecture for schema integration by modelling shared data items can be further enhanced, if the O-O application is intelligent enough to resolve the problems of semantic heterogeneity e.g. two applications may be functioning on different domains with some matching data items, two applications may be expressing quantities in different units where unit conversion can be carried out, contexts of two component application systems may influence different assumptions from the same data values, and the same concepts may be represented by using two different structural constructs for two applications. Figure XVI.1 shows inclusion of intelligent objects in the architecture. Each of these knowledge bases KB_i would store the knowledge of metadata of local databases in the form of semantic network, similar to those used for understanding natural languages. In its simplest form, a knowledge base will consist of a list of simple sentences, which express the relation between different data items. The meta-data-grammar will contain rules for syntactic and semantic analysis of these sentences. This grammar would be much simpler than those required for understanding natural languages, because it is restricted to the domains of the participating databases. Knowledge bases of local domains will include representational concepts, naming conventions, value domain restrictions and constraints.

The use of such intelligent objects will allow transitions and propagation of schema changes to be carried out with less human involvement and fewer errors caused by ignorance of the semantics. even if human analysis and intervention is required, these objects will provide necessary checks to help analysis.

Inclusion Of New Applications

Once the integration architecture has been established with some applications, other applications - both old and new ones - need to be integrated into it. Inclusion of a new application means adding a new object in the integrating object-oriented application to represent the corresponding application.

A new application is a new object that uses the features of the existing objects and optionally may introduce some new objects and features. If the writer/designer of the new application knows the objects and features, which are used in the central application and can be used in the new application, then only the new objects need be introduced. We do not need any intelligent object here, because the writer/designer is intelligent and has knowledge about the existing objects.

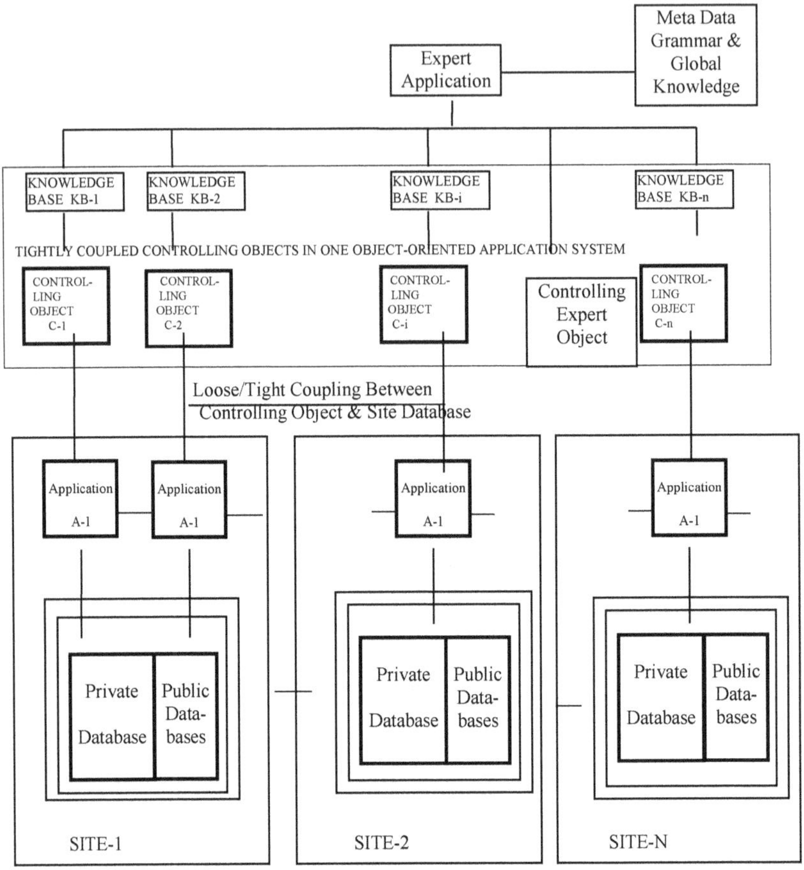

Figure XIII.1 An Intelligent Architecture

N.B. There could be several applications on the same database. The application concerned will determine what parts of the database are private and what parts are public. for the sake of simplicity, rigid boundaries are shown between public and private parts.

APPENDIX - XIII

In most occasions, the writer/integrator of the new application may not know the relevant objects and features of the central O-O application, because the information may be too much and too diverse to be grasped. In such cases, we may consider that the writer knows only the new application while an expert can introduce the new application to the existing objects. The intelligent object will fill in the role of this expert. It will use a dictionary, which will have a list of these objects and features. It will also have a grammar called meta-data-grammar, that will specify the rules how the objects and features of the dictionary can be used.

Recording Semantics In The Dictionary

The semantics of an application system may be recorded in such a fashion, that another application may interpret these semantics. In the simplest form to note the semantics, we need to record, for each data item, its relationships with other data items - a set of rows of information, each row containing a data-name it is related to and the relationship with it. Relationship could follow the syntax followed in the original design e.g. ISA, IS-PART-OF, HAS etc.

The next refinement is necessary to remove ambiguity in the relationship syntax e.g. HAS is ambiguous - John has a book, has a house, has a wife, has a car, has a visa-card and so on. We need to disambiguate these relationship by providing more meaningful expressions, say:

John is owner-occupier of a house at 1, ABC St, Sydney,

John is married to his wife, a living lady known as Lisa,

John possesses a book - "I'm OK", which he may read

John maintains an account with visa card no xxxx-xxxx-?

The next step is to analyse these sentences in terms of the meaning of the verbs used, case relationship of the data item with the verb, and that of other data items related through the same verb. The goal is to find out the rules, how the objects and the features are related to each other, which will be captured in the meta-data grammar.

When the rules of the meta-data grammar, are available, we are in a position to prepare the dictionary. If we have in our dictionary the terms like Noun, Pronoun, Verb etc, we will note with each word its type; we may have class names too, if they are introduced in the grammar. the grammar should also specify the way these words can participate, as in a sentence they may participate in Subject-Verb-Object order, where only a type of words can become the subject, another type can become the verb and so on. Once we decide a set of grammar rules, that are valid for all the domains of the applications concerned, we are in a position to apply them on the objects of the applications.

For each database, we aim to build a knowledge-base to show:

- a list of classes/objects available for query/update

- how an object is identified in the database, does any or more attributes have unique names

- relationship of each export data item with other data items in the same or different databases.

Objects with metadata of a local database will serve as the knowledgebase of the local application, while an object with the knowledgebase of all local databases will serve as the global knowledgebase.

CONCLUSION

We have considered an architecture which uses shared objects to integrate application systems. This architecture bids fair to get the best of the both worlds - it protects the investment in existing application systems, while it draws the benefits of leading edge technologies to have fast and efficient systems. This architecture for application integration is enhanced, by adding intelligence to the integrating application by including (1) an object with meta-data of each underlying database to provide knowledge-base of the schema, and (2) an expert object which will use the knowledge-base of all local domains plus a meta-data grammar and a global knowledge-base.

The use of such intelligent objects will allow transitions and propagation of schema changes to be carried out with less human involvement and fewer errors caused by ignorance of semantics. Even if human intervention is required, these objects will provide checks to help analysis.

In the next chapter, we shall check what needs be done to implement the proposed architecture in one organisation. Various options for building interfaces between controlling objects and controlled databases, and an object-based concurrency control scheme are discussed. Implementation of the proposed architecture of integration is, to a great extent, transparent to the users of the pre-integration applications. This means that the service levels of these applications before and after the implementation would be almost the same. One gain is the extra window in each application to view some data items from other applications.

APPENDIX - XIV

Relational vs. Object-Oriented Approaches

INTRODUCTION

In this section, we like to check whether the central coordinating application needs be object-oriented. If a relational data model was chosen to implement the integrating application layer, we would have major problems in representing information at different levels of granularity. Individual applications using incompatible hardware/operating systems/DBMS/ file system combination, may have export and import schemas that cannot be suitably modelled into form of relational tuples. On the other hand, object-oriented datamodels have been developed to represent complex real world objects more closely; each mini-world entity, however complex, can be represented as one object in the database.

Following considerations have favoured use of the object-oriented data model for the integrating application instead of the relational data model:

1. In a relational model, an abstract type in terms of abstract properties cannot be specified, while an abstract type can be specified in object-oriented models.

2. A more general hierarchy of types, i.e. sub-types and instances cannot be represented in relational models. Relational models need an extended schema language, expressing abstractions like generalisation and aggregation.

3. Relational systems are primarily value-based, which means that tuples in a relational database can be distinguished only on the basis of their attribute values. In OOD, instances have their own identities independent of attribute-values, which means two objects instances can have the same value for any of their features. This reduces the restrictions on modelling.

4. Relational systems are unable to represent an entity both independently and in terms of a relationship in which it participates. An object can be accessed directly or as a reference from another object. A relational tuple cannot contain another tuple; it can contain the key-value for another tuple.

5. In relational systems, some of the database semantics are recorded separately from the data. These are the cases, which cannot be expressed by usual DBMS definitions. They must be specified by the designer and consciously applied by the users or database administrators. In object-oriented systems, consistency can be maintained by specifying assertions; the semantic specifications are checked by executable codes. For example, in a language like Eiffel, the preconditions expresses the properties that must hold whenever the routine is called, and the post-condition describes the properties that the routine guarantees when it returns.

ADVANTAGES OF O-O DATA MODELLING CONCEPTS

If an object-oriented application is used to integrate the export objects for the participating applications, following advantages can be gained:

1. Uniform design method can be used at all levels of granularity.

2. Nested objects of arbitrary complexity can be represented.

3. With codes encapsulated in objects, information about implementation can be hidden.

4. Object-oriented techniques facilitates design of distributed databases by features of data abstraction and data localisation.

5. Layers of abstraction may be used to develop a hierarchy of data - the topmost layer representing the most general view and lower layers representing more complex and specialised views.

6. Mismatch between the data manipulation language (DML) of the database, and the general-purpose programming language mismatch can be avoided.

7. Operational mapping can be used to avoid structural mapping.

Uniform Design Method At All Levels Of Granularity

If the data items of the underlying applications are viewed as objects, a common design methodology can be applied to these objects at any level of granularity. Unlike in relational databases, an object can have another object as its component. If the reference to another object is provided via a foreign key in a relational table, type checking cannot be provided for it.

Representing Nested Objects Of Arbitrary Complexity

O-O data modelling techniques support modelling of complex objects - nested objects of arbitrary complexity; relationship can be defined between these objects and classes of objects can be organised into an inheritance hierarchy; an entity can be modelled as a single object of arbitrary granularity and not as multiple tuples in multiple relations. Therefore, properties of objects need not assume simple data values, rather they can be objects of arbitrary complexity.

Information Hiding With Code Encapsulated In Objects

An object can either be primitive or non-primitive. A primitive object is a non-decomposable atomic value, such as a string or integer. A non-primitive object consists of a collection of attributes, which support the modelling of real world entities and not only their structures. The state of an object is accessible only through its message interface which controls the behaviour of objects. The behaviour of an object is encapsulated in methods which comprise the code that manipulates or returns the state of an object.

Data Abstraction And Data Localisation

Object-oriented techniques facilitates design of distributed databases by features of data abstraction and data localisation. Data abstraction suggests the suppression of the irrelevant details in favour of emphasizing and representing more appropriate details. Data localisation suggests modelling of each entity as independently as possible, subsequently all properties can be synthesized to produce the overall design.

Layers Of Abstraction To Develop Hierarchy Of Data

Object-oriented data modelling techniques provide for the concept of data abstraction where layers of abstraction may be used to develop a hierarchy of data - the topmost layer representing the most general view and lower layers representing more complex and specialised views.

Five forms of abstraction and inter-object relationships are useful in building data hierarchies in distributed heterogeneous environments, namely:

1. classification or typing
2. aggregation or type composition
3. generalisation or sub-typing
4. association or membership, and
5. relativism or representing an n-ary relation as an entity.

Classification establishes an *instance-of* relationship between a generic object-type in a schema and an object in the database content.

Aggregation establishes an *is-part-of* relationship between the component objects and the whole or aggregation object.

Generalisation establishes an *is-a* relationships between category objects and the generic object having common properties of the category objects. Category objects are regarded as specialisation or sub-types of the generic objects, which is regarded as the super-type.

Association represents the *member-of* relationship between a member and its corresponding set. Association selects a subset of object instances of a pre-specified class of similar objects.

Relativism is the principle of considering an object both independently and in terms of any relationship in which it participates. The relationship between objects can be considered as an object in its own right.

The above modelling techniques of composition/decomposition, association/membership, and generalisation/specialisation can take advantage of property inheritance and are highly useful in integration of schemas in heterogeneous databases.

Alleviation Of Impedance Mismatch

While integrating a number of applications using different database management systems, there could be impedance mismatch between the data manipulation language (DML) of the database, and the general-purpose programming language in which the integrating application is written. There are two aspects of this mismatch.

One is the difference in programming paradigms; for example, between a declarative DML such as SQL, and an imperative programming language such as PL/I. The other aspect is the mismatch of the type systems. A loss of information occurs at the interface, if the programming language is unable to represent the types or classes represented in the DBMS. Object-oriented database management systems (OODBMSs) and object-oriented programming languages (OOPLs) solve the impedance mismatch problem by making making more of data-types of a general-purpose programming language persistent, or by adding database types, such as lists and relations, to the type system of the general-purpose programming language. Benefits of adding computational completeness, in this way, to the data manipulation language are:

- Type checking can be performed in the integrating object-oriented application, instead of getting type checking done across the language boundaries,

- Constraints can be expressed in terms of the data model of the integrating object-oriented application, and are not required to be enforced in the procedures written in the application programming language.

- Efficiency and speed of execution are improved as no trade-off between compilation and interpretation can be considered.

- The combination of structured query language and general-purpose procedural language disappears in favour of a uniform programming interface at the disposal of the user/ application programmer.

Operational Mapping Through O-O Interface
When the applications to be integrated include not only the traditional file systems and DBMSs but also graphical and textual databases, as in the areas of office automation and computer integrated manufacturing (CIM), the integration problems are particularly difficult. In these systems the semantics of data is often deeply dependent on the way in which programs manipulate the data and schema does not exist. Traditional approaches of "Structural Mapping"[120], based on the definition of correspondence between data elements of the systems to be integrated are inadequate in such areas. Instead, using the "Operational Mapping" approach, correspondence between operations at different levels can be defined. Since objects are externally known in terms of operations instead of data representations, an object can be defined to map the operations of each local database, while these objects can participate in the integrating application system.

---

[120] Kalinichenko L.A.(1990), Methods And Tools For Equivalent Data Model Mapping Construction, *Proceedings Of International Conference on Extending Database Technology, Venice, Italy, March 26-30, 1990*

APPENDIX - XV

The Proposed Architecture vis-à-vis A Reference Model

A Reference Model For Object-Oriented Distributed System

After the component applications are integrated, the integrated system will act like a distributed system, whose objects are spread over the network. We like to consider here a reference model for distributed systems. British Telecom Research Laboratory (BTRL) has developed a reference model - the Distributed System Model (DSM) to address the various concerns of a distributed object-oriented system[121]. Objectives of the distributed object-oriented system coincide with those of an integrated systems distributed over a network, in terms of:

- a common reference which could also be used for design and development of new systems, and integration of the existing systems,

- facilitation for reusing software, and this could be used to continue using features of the existing application systems,

- decoupling of system and software design from implementation technology, in order to facilitate interworking between systems and software provided by different manufacturers - this will facilitate integration inspite of technology used.

When a number of disparate applications are integrated, objects from these disparate applications interact with one another. These interactions can be viewed in terms of a few dimensions. The following dimensions of distributed systems have been considered in this model, each of these dimensions can be considered separately and as well as in combination with other dimensions in an architectural framework:

. Object Interaction   . Object Definition.   . Communications   . Local Storage

. Local Processing   . Management   . Physical Structure   . Temporal.

Object Interaction - Interaction between objects are via strictly defined interfaces or export features of the objects

Object Definition - Definition of objects are provided in terms of data models, so that each entity can be expressed in terms of class specifications of a object-oriented language

----

[121] Wright J.H., A Reference Model For Object-Oriented Distributed Systems, *British Telecom Technology Journal*, Vol-6, No-3, July 1988, pp 66-75.

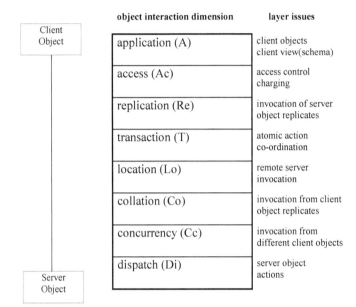

Figure XV.2 Object Interaction Dimension

Communications - Communications between objects at different sites, are in a homogeneous network, though there are various layers of communication between local database systems and the objects in the integrating application

Local Storage - Mapping between the logical storage of distributed application and physical storages of sites are provided by keeping objects with meta-data in the integrating application, which extracts data from local storages to instantiate objects.

Local Processing - Local processing resources can be invoked by the objects in the integrating application for all its logical processing.

Management - The objects being managed can be abstracted towards the entities responsible for management. The lower levels of this abstraction will be similar to the OSI management framework, whereas the higher levels of abstraction will conform to the enterprise model of management for the application.

Physical Structure - The system is represented as a hierarchy of physical nodes where each node may be further subdivided into smaller nodes. Nodes can be modelled as virtual machines at the next higher level of abstraction.

Temporal - This dimension is concerned with the system life cycle and the life cycles of objects within it. In some cases, it may be necessary for some objects to be able to establish relationships (bindings) with other objects in a dynamic fashion; in other cases these bindings may be established during system design or configuration and may persist for the lifetime of the system.

Object Interaction Dimension -

Interactions among objects of inter-operating applications can be viewed in terms of selected dimensions. In the object interaction dimension (OID) model [Fig XVIII.2], interacting objects are assumed to conform to a client-server relationship in the distributed system, with no direct interaction between peer objects. The client object appears in the application layer of the OID, whereas the server object functions in the dispatch layer of the OID. This is in contrast to the OSI model, where both client and server would be application entities.

Access Control Layer - Access Control Manager uses Schema Server to know of the existence of server objects, Access Control Server to control the rights to perform operations on server objects, and Charging Server for charging for access to the server object.

Replication Collation Layers - Invocation and management of replicated objects is handled, at the client end of the binding, by the replication layer (Re-layer) which provides for one-to-many invocations. Collation facilities are needed at the server end of the binding to handle many-to-one invocations.

Transaction Layer - This layer, in conjunction with concurrency, commitment and recovery (CCR) management handles the co-ordination of individual operations. Its functions may be summarised as follows:

- providing facilities for users to construct transactions (atomic actions) from individual operations,
- coordinating the commitment of nested transaction,
- ensuring the correctness of transactions in a partitioned system
- detecting and resolving conflicts between transactions.

Location Layer - The function of the location layer (Lo-layer) is to provide locational transparency for the invocation of objects on remote nodes in the distributed system. The Lo- layer entities map the invocations and responses between the Tr- and Co-layers onto the services provided by the communication entities, enhancing those services where necessary.

Concurrency Control Layer - This layer controls concurrent invocations of the server object by different client objects. Operations which would normally cause conflicting modifications to bound data are serialised so as to

----

appear independent. This serialisation is controlled by reference to concurrency predicates which express static concurrency constraints and by locks applied by clients which define dynamic concurrency.

Dispatch Layer - This lowest layer of the object interaction dimension is responsible for:

- dispatching processes in response to invocation requests,
- synchronising interactions between objects with processes in the server and client objects,
- invoking actions on server objects,
- taking the object in and out of service.

The Di-layer effectively implements the functional definition or program-codes for each operation on the object.

The *distributed object support environment [DOSE]* combines the object interaction, communications, local processing, local storage and management dimensions to provide a set of access and management services for objects in distributed systems. There are two main types of actions which may be performed on objects - generic or object specific.. The generic actions are common to most objects, while object specific actions are invoked as parameters of the generic INVOKE action.

The reference model, described above, models the definition and implementation of objects in distributed systems. The Object Definition Environment (ODE) and the Distributed Object Support Environment (DOSE) of the model specify the infrastructure to support the activities of system development and distributed operating system services. The important differences between DOSE and the traditional concept of operating system are - traditional operating system presents the user with a single perspective of the system in terms of services and resources, while DOSE has a perspective for each object in the system so that the system appears as a group of objects each of which has a set of generic and object-specific operations which can be performed on it. Thus every object has its own mini operating system. Each user may have different perception of the system depending upon the objects it has in its schema.

The reference model could be used as a framework for defining the architecture of a distributed system, for example of a set of application systems to be integrated by linking semantically related objects. The integrating application could be first designed to model object-definitions and object-interactions only, assuming other dimensions of communication, storage, replication, collation, and transaction management to be transparent; the other complications can be gradually introduced by removing the transparency assumptions one by one.

Review Of The Proposed Architecture In Terms Of Object Interaction Dimensions
The integrating object-based application can be reviewed in terms of the object interaction dimensions discussed in the section 2.4.1. An object in this application can play the role of either a server or a client depending on whether it supplies information or it requests it.

Access control can be implemented by restrictions on both the server and the client objects. The services available from a server object is declared as its export features. Only those client objects, which are authorised to use these services, will have the features to invoke these services.

Replication and collation control will be incorporated in the methods of the client and the server respectively. If a client invokes more than one server, its method will incorporate the algorithm to merge the threads of invocation. Similarly, if a server responds to more than one client, it has to provide the assertion methods to maintain consistency; for example, Eiffel language provides for invariants, pre-condition and post-condition checking.

Transaction management ie atomic action co-ordination will ensure that a method either performs all related updates or no effect of the transaction is visible.

An atomic action possesses the properties of serializability, failure atomicity and permanence of effects. Using the synchronisation facilities provided by the underlying operating system, a type or class can be constructed to provide specific concurrency control technique. Other user-defined types can inherit this concurrency control facility by making use of the type-inheritance mechanism available in object-oriented programming languages.

Depending on whether or not the controlling O-O application spans more than one site, and also whether or not replicas are used for some objects, the algorithm for concurrency control and recovery need be suitably designed.

OPERATIONS IN THE SYSTEM, INTEGRATED AS PROPOSED

The integrating application system will interact with multiple underlying applications and in this process execute data manipulation commands of the respective databases. Some of the tasks relevant to the operation of distributed DBMSs are also relevant here; these tasks are: (1) Queries Involving Multiple Applications/Databases, (2) Command Translation, (3) Optimisation in Query Processing, (4) Transaction Management Across Applications[122].

The integrating application is proposed to be object-oriented, with a tightly coupled view of the export schemas from the underlying applications. It is expected to reconcile naming and data structure conflicts among applications, and provide location, distribution and replication transparencies. However, it need not provide a multi-database language[123] to access data from multiple component database systems; it will send queries to the export objects, which, in turn, will query the underlying applications and provide answers to those queries.

There is a need to translate the commands expressed in the language used in the controlling object so that these can be executed in the underlying application using its native data model. However, this translation is required only between the integrating application and underlying applications, not between any pair of underlying applications.

Heterogeneity and autonomy of the databases of the underlying applications introduce additional complexities. The same operation may be optimised differently and may involve different costs of performance in different underlying databases. Again, as the cost is likely to depend on other loads on the underlying database, and these loads are not known to the integrating application, the cost of performing an operation cannot be estimated correctly.

It is very difficult to support global transaction management, specially to support updates in spite of the autonomy of the component DBMSs. Due to the existence of local as well as global transactions, it is very difficult to recognise when the execution order differs from the serialisation order at any site. In the proposed architecture there is a delineation between the global updates and the local updates. Local updates will deal with only those local data items, which are private to the local database and do not appear in the export schema and no way constrained by any item on the export schema, whereas all data items that appear on the export schema will be controlled by the controlling object in the integrating application. We have seen that some work has already been done to support a global concurrency control[124] scheme where the heterogeneity of local concurrency control scheme exists.

The integrating object-based application has been reviewed, in the Appendix-XVIII, in terms of the object interaction dimensions of a reference architecture for distributed systems.

---

[122] Sheth, A.P. and Larson, J.A. (1990), Federated Database Systems for Managing Distributed, Heterogeneous, and Autonomous Databases, *ACM Computing Surveys*, Vol. 22, No. 3, pp 183-236, September 1990.
[123] A multidatabase language provides functions that may not be present in the data manipulation language of a DBMS. The capability needed is to define federated schemas as views over multiple database schemas and to formulate queries against such views.
[124] Cho H., Kim Y.S., Moon S. (1996), *Design and Implementation of an Autonomous Heterogeneous Distributed Database System: DIME*, Document Supply Service, Yonset University, Seol, Korea

----

Co-operations In Distributed Transaction Processing

Though the proposed architecture is designed primarily to solve schema conflicts by asserting correspondence between schema objects of more than one applications, we may extend the solution to solve data conflicts and assert correspondence between the instances of objects, say to assert equivalence between an instance of one application object and an instance of an object of another application. In such cases, it is necessary to ensure that when transactions are processed in these distributed applications, the correspondence or equivalence of these instances is not affected

Distributed transaction processing in an integrated application system need to ensure atomicity, serializability and durability of transactions. The actions of a transaction may be executed differently in different systems. For example, one system may use locks to guarantee the serializability property, while another may employ time-stamps, still another may use optimistic concurrency control strategy. Integrating application need develop strategies for meshing together these different transaction processing mechanisms. An object-oriented application can co-ordinate the strategies of individual applications without any modifications. Each local system receives transactions either locally or from the integrating O-O application, it treats all transactions in the same fashion; the integrating O-O application ensures, by operational mapping, that the transaction properties are guaranteed for all non-local transactions.

www.ingramcontent.com/pod-product-compliance
Lightning Source LLC
Chambersburg PA
CBHW070933050326
40689CB00014B/3187